3rd Workshop on the Use of Computational Methods in the Study of Endangered Languages 2019 (ComputEL-3)

Honolulu, Hawaii, USA
26-27 February 2019

ISBN: 978-1-5108-9141-8

Printed from e-media with permission by:

Curran Associates, Inc.
57 Morehouse Lane
Red Hook, NY 12571

Some format issues inherent in the e-media version may also appear in this print version.

Copyright© (2019) by the Association for Computational Linguistics
All rights reserved.

Printed by Curran Associates, Inc. (2019)

For permission requests, please contact the Association for Computational Linguistics
at the address below.

Association for Computational Linguistics
209 N. Eighth Street
Stroudsburg, Pennsylvania 18360

Phone: 1-570-476-8006
Fax: 1-570-476-0860

acl@aclweb.org

Additional copies of this publication are available from:

Curran Associates, Inc.
57 Morehouse Lane
Red Hook, NY 12571 USA
Phone: 845-758-0400
Fax: 845-758-2633
Email: curran@proceedings.com
Web: www.proceedings.com

ComputEL-3

Proceedings of the

3rd
Workshop on the
Use of Computational Methods in
the Study of Endangered
Languages

Volume 1 (Papers)

February 26–27, 2019
Honolulu, Hawai'i, USA

Support:

©2019 The Association for Computational Linguistics

Preface

These proceedings contain the papers presented at the 3rd Workshop on the Use of Computational Methods in the Study of Endangered languages held in Hawai'i at Mānoa, February 26–27, 2019. As the name implies, this is the third workshop held on the topic—the first meeting was co-located with the ACL main conference in Baltimore, Maryland in 2014 and the second one in 2017 was co-located with the 5th International Conference on Language Documentation and Conservation (ICLDC) at the University of Hawai'i at Mānoa.

The workshop covers a wide range of topics relevant to the study and documentation of endangered languages, ranging from technical papers on working systems and applications, to reports on community activities with supporting computational components.

The purpose of the workshop is to bring together computational researchers, documentary linguists, and people involved with community efforts of language documentation and revitalization to take part in both formal and informal exchanges on how to integrate rapidly evolving language processing methods and tools into efforts of language description, documentation, and revitalization. The organizers are pleased with the range of papers, many of which highlight the importance of interdisciplinary work and interaction between the various communities that the workshop is aimed towards.

We received 34 submissions as papers or extended abstracts. After a thorough review process, 12 of the submissions were selected for this volume as papers (35%) and an additional 7 were accepted as extended abstracts which appear in Volume 2 of the workshop proceedings. The organizing committee would like to thank the program committee for their thoughtful input on the submissions. We are also grateful to the NSF for funding part of the workshop (award #1550905), and the Social Sciences and Humanities Research Council (SSHRC) of Canada for supporting the workshop through their Connections Outreach Grant #611-2016-0207. We would moreover want to acknowledge the support of the organizers of ICLDC6, in particular Gary Holton, Brad McDonnell and Jim Yoshioka.

ANTTI ARPPE
JEFF GOOD
MANS HULDEN
JORDAN LACHLER
ALEXIS PALMER
LANE SCHWARTZ
MIIKKA SILFVERBERG

Organizing Committee:

Antti Arppe (University of Alberta)
Jeff Good (University at Buffalo)
Mans Hulden (University of Colorado)
Jordan Lachler (University of Alberta)
Alexis Palmer (University of North Texas)
Lane Schwartz (University of Illinois at Urbana-Champaign)
Miikka Silfverberg (University of Helsinki)

Program Committee:

Oliver Adams (Johns Hopkins University)
Antti Arppe (University of Alberta)
Dorothee Beermann (Norwegian University of Science and Technology)
Emily M. Bender (University of Washington)
Martin Benjamin (Kamusi Project International)
Steven Bird (University of Melbourne)
Emily Chen (University of Illinois at Urbana-Champaign)
Andrew Cowell (University of Colorado Boulder)
Christopher Cox (Carleton University)
Robert Forkel (Max Planck Institute for the Science of Human History)
Jeff Good (University at Buffalo)
Michael Wayne Goodman (University of Washington)
Harald Hammarström (Max Planck Institute for Psycholinguistics, Nijmegen)
Mans Hulden (University of Colorado Boulder)
Anna Kazantseva (National Research Council of Canada)
František Kratochvíl (Palacký University)
Jordan Lachler (University of Alberta)
Terry Langendoen (National Science Foundation)
Krister Lindén (University of Helsinki)
Worthy N Martin (University of Virginia)
Michael Maxwell (University of Maryland, CASL)
Steven Moran (University of Zurich)
Graham Neubig (Carnegie Mellon University)
Alexis Palmer (University of North Texas)
Taraka Rama (University of Oslo)
Kevin Scannell (Saint Louis University)
Lane Schwartz (University of Illinois at Urbana-Champaign)
Miikka Silfverberg (University of Helsinki)
Richard Sproat (Google)
Nick Thieberger (University of Melbourne / ARC Centre of Excellence for the Dynamics of
Language)

Laura Welcher (The Long Now Foundation)
Menzo Windhouwer (KNAW Humanities Cluster — Digital Infrastructure)

Table of Contents

Conference Program

Tuesday, February 26th, 2019

08:30–09:00 *Imin Conference Center, Asia Room/Arrival, coffee and chat*

09:00–09:15 *Opening remarks*

First morning: Tools and processes for language documentation and description, Corpus creation

09:15–09:45 *An Online Platform for Community-Based Language Description and Documentation*
Rebecca Everson, Wolf Honoré and Scott Grimm

09:45–10:15 *Developing without developers: choosing labor-saving tools for language documentation apps*
Luke Gessler

10:15–10:45 *Future Directions in Technological Support for Language Documentation*
Daan van Esch, Ben Foley and Nay San

10:45–11:15 *Break*

11:15–11:45 **Towards a General-Purpose Linguistic Annotation Backend. Graham Neubig, Patrick Littell, Chian-Yu Chen, Jean Lee, Zirui Li, Yu-Hsiang Lin and Yuyan Zhang**

11:45–12:15 *OCR evaluation tools for the 21st century*
Eddie Antonio Santos

12:15–12:45   **Building a Common Voice Corpus for Laiholh (Hakha Chin). Kelly Berkson, Samson Lotven, Peng Hlei Thang, Thomas Thawngza, Zai Sung, James Wamsley, Francis M. Tyers, Kenneth Van Bik, Sandra Kübler, Donald Williamson and Matthew Anderson**

12:45–14:15   *Lunch*

First afternoon: Language technologies – lexical and syntactic

14:15–14:45   **Digital Dictionary Development for Torwali, a less-studied language: Process and Challenges. Inam Ullah**

14:45–15:15   *Handling cross-cutting properties in automatic inference of lexical classes: A case study of Chintang*
Olga Zamaraeva, Kristen Howell and Emily M. Bender

15:15–15:45   **Applying Support Vector Machines to POS tagging of the Ainu Language. Karol Nowakowski, Michal Ptaszynski, Fumito Masui and Yoshio Momouchi**

15:45–16:15   *Break*

16:15–16:45   *Finding Sami Cognates with a Character-Based NMT Approach*
Mika Hämäläinen and Jack Rueter

16:45–17:15   *Seeing more than whitespace — Tokenisation and disambiguation in a North Sámi grammar checker*
Linda Wiechetek, Sjur Nørstebø Moshagen and Kevin Brubeck Unhammer

17:15–20:00   *Dinner*

Wednesday, February 27th, 2019

09:00–09:30   *Arrival, coffee and chat*

Second morning: Use (and reuse) of corpora and collections, Language technologies – speech and morphology

09:30–10:00   **Using computational approaches to integrate endangered language legacy data into documentation corpora: Past experiences and challenges ahead. Rogier Blokland, Niko Partanen, Michael Rießler and Joshua Wilbur**

10:00–10:30   **A software-driven workflow for the reuse of language documentation data in linguistic studies. Stephan Druskat and Kilu von Prince**

10:30–11:00   *Break*

11:00–11:30   *Corpus of usage examples: What is it good for?*
Timofey Arkhangelskiy

11:30–12:00   *A Preliminary Plains Cree Speech Synthesizer*
Atticus Harrigan, Antti Arppe and Timothy Mills

12:00-12:30   *A biscriptual morphological transducer for Crimean Tatar*
Francis M. Tyers, Jonathan Washington, Darya Kavitskaya, Memduh Gökırmak, Nick Howell and Remziye Berberova

12:30–14:00   *Lunch*

Second afternoon: Language technologies – speech and morphology

14:00-14:30 *Improving Low-Resource Morphological Learning with Intermediate Forms from Finite State Transducers*
Sarah Moeller, Ghazaleh Kazeminejad, Andrew Cowell and Mans Hulden

14:30–15:00 Bootstrapping a Neural Morphological Generator from Morphological Analyzer Output for Inuktitut. Jeffrey Micher

15:00–15:30 *Bootstrapping a Neural Morphological Analyzer for St. Lawrence Island Yupik from a Finite-State Transducer*
Lane Schwartz, Emily Chen, Benjamin Hunt and Sylvia L.R. Schreiner

15:30–16:00 *Break*

16:00–17:00 *Discussions, Looking ahead: CEL-4 and new ACL Special Interest Group*

An Online Platform for Community-Based Language Description and Documentation

Rebecca Everson
Independent
reverson94@gmail.com

Wolf Honoré
Yale University
wolf.honore@yale.edu

Scott Grimm
University of Rochester
scott.grimm@rochester.edu

Abstract

We present two pieces of interlocking technology in development to facilitate community-based, collaborative language description and documentation: (i) a mobile app where speakers submit text, voice recordings and/or videos, and (ii) a community language portal that organizes submitted data and provides question/answer boards whereby community members can evaluate/supplement submissions.

1 Introduction

While engagement of language communities, and diverse members thereof, is crucial for adequate language documentation and description, this is often a challenging task given the finite resources of field linguists. We present a technological platform designed to accelerate and make more inclusive the process of documenting and describing languages with the goal of enabling language communities to become researchers of their own languages and curators of language-based facets of their culture.

We are currently developing two pieces of interlocking technology: (i) a mobile app whose functionality and simplicity is reminiscent of WhatsApp (which is widespread in, for instance, West Africa) through which speakers submit text, voice recordings and/or videos, and (ii) an community language portal that, for each language, organizes and displays submitted data and provides discussion and question/answer boards (in the style of Quora or Stack Exchange) where community members can evaluate, refine, or supplement submissions. Together, these permit field linguists, community educators and other stakeholders to serve in the capacity as "language community coordinator", assigning tasks that are collaboratively achieved with the community. This technology shares similarities with recent efforts such as Aikuma (Bird et al., 2014) or Kamusi (Benjamin and Radetzky, 2014); however, the focus is on developing a limited range of functionalities with an emphasis on simplicity to engage the highest numbers of community members. This in turn will accelerate the most common tasks facing a language description and/or documentation project and do so at a technological level in which all community members who are capable of using a mobile phone app may participate.

In this paper, we first exemplify the mobile app with the process of developing language resources with developing a lexicon. Section 2 contains an overview of the application, Section 3 is a discussion of the different user interfaces, and Section 4 gives the implementation details. Finally, we address extensions currently under development in Section 5.

2 Language Resource Development

Lexica and other resources are developed through the interaction between coordinators and contributors. The coordinator, who could be a linguist and/or community member, puts out queries for information and accepts submissions through a web console written in TypeScript using the React framework. Contributors use the mobile interface, built with React Native, a popular JavaScript framework for mobile development, to add words in both spoken and written form, along with pictures. The accepted submissions are used to automatically generate and update interactive online resources, such as a lexicon.

For lexicon development, the platform is able to accommodate a wide variety of scenarios: monolingual or bilingual, textual and/or audio along with possible contribution of pictures or video files. Thus, in one scenario a coordinator working on a language for which textual submissions

Proceedings of the 3rd Workshop on the Use of Computational Methods in the Study of Endangered Languages: Vol. 1 Papers, pages 1–5,
Honolulu, Hawai'i, USA, February 26–27, 2019.

are infeasible could send requests in the form of recorded words soliciting "folk definitions" of those words (Casagrande and Hale, 1967; Laughren and Nash, 1983), that is, the speakers themselves supply the definition of a word, typically producing more words that can be requested by the coordinator. Alternately, semantic domains may serve as the basis of elicitation in the style of Albright and Hatton (2008) or in relation to resources such as List et al. (2016). Built into our approach is the ability to record language variation: For lexicon entries, multiple definitions and forms can be provided by different speakers, which can then be commented and/or voted on, until a definition (or definitions) is generally accepted and variation is properly recorded.

Analogous processes allow speakers to contribute varieties of language-based cultural content: folktales, oral histories, proverbs, songs, videos explaining cultural practices and daily tasks (cooking, sewing, building houses, etc.). Accordingly, this method may be used to develop (i) data repositories and resources for researchers in linguistics and allied fields, especially those touching on studies in language and culture, and (ii) educational materials and other materials that may benefit the community.

3   User Interface

For the purposes of this section, we focus on the task of developing a lexicon on the basis of a predetermined wordlist, such as the SIL Comparative African Word List (Snider and Roberts, 2004), a common scenario for a fieldworker working on an under-described language for which the speakers also speaks an administrative language such as English or French.

Users of the application fall into three categories: coordinators, contributors, and consumers. A coordinator can be a member of the language community, such as an elder or group of elders, or she might be a field linguist working within the community. Coordinators handle adding new words to translate, assigning words to contributors, and accepting or rejecting submitted translations. Coordinators also have the ability to assign contributors and words to subgroups. This is useful if there are specialized vocabularies specific to only a portion of the community, for example, hunters who use a different vocabulary while hunting. A contributor is a community member who has been chosen by the coordinators to complete the translation work. Finally, a consumer is anyone who has access to the community language portal that is created from the submissions accepted by the coordinators.

We see the development of the community language portal and the presentation of speakers sharing their language as key for motivating continued contributions. We expect that the varieties of language-based cultural content speakers contribute as part of the documentation activities, e.g., folk tales or oral histories, will be a key motivator for community members to use and contribute to the platform. We provide functionality for consumers to also become contributors. For instance, next to contributed videos, a button allows consumers to contribute their own video. Content so contributed will not be directly accepted to the database, but will require approval from the coordinator, so as to provide a check on inappropriate content.

The following subsections give sample user stories for each type of user. As will be detailed in Section 4, users will sign in with a Google account, which provides a straightforward solution for user authentication. In the following user stories we use English and Konni [kma] as our example languages, though the application can work for any pairing.

3.1   Contributor

A new contributor joins the language description and documentation effort. They belong to a Ghanaian community that speaks English and Konni, which is the language they want to describe and document. They open the mobile application and sign in with their Google account credentials. Upon the initial sign in, the contributor must provide responses to secure consent in accordance with an IRB protocol. Then the contributor is presented with a demographic survey. Once successfully logged in, they see the home screen, which displays their assignments, e.g., a list of semantic prompts or words in English (see Figure 1). They select a word from the list by tapping it. They are then taken to a form with fields for the translation of the word in Konni, a sample sentence using the word in English, and a translation of the sentence in Konni. There are also two fields for audio recordings of the word and sentence in Konni. When the user selects these fields they see a screen

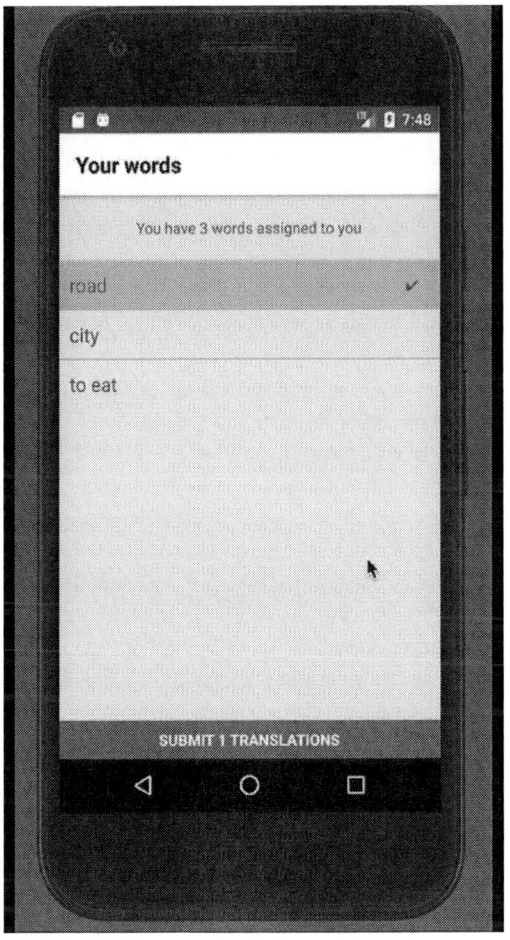

Figure 1: Application home page.

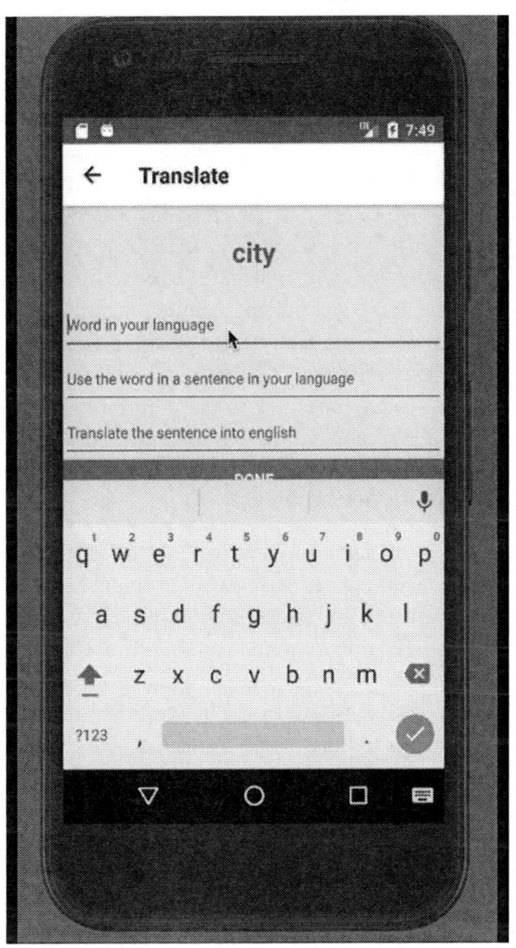

Figure 2: Word translation page.

3.2 Coordinator

with *Start* and *Stop* buttons. Pressing *Start* begins recording using the phone's microphone and *Stop* ends the recording and saves the audio as a WAV file. When they have filled in all of the fields, they press the *Submit* button at the bottom of the screen and are taken back to the home screen. Now the word that they just translated is green and has a check-mark next to it (see Figure 2). They now also see a button at the bottom of the home screen that reads *Submit 1 translation(s).* When they are ready to submit their completed translations, they press that button. If their phone is currently connected to the Internet, the translated words will be removed from the list and new words will appear. If not, they can continue translating or wait to enter an area with WiFi.

A coordinator wants to review some translations and assign more words to contributors. He starts by opening a web browser and navigating to his documentation project's web page. After logging in with his Google account credentials he sees that a contributor has just submitted three new translations that need to be reviewed. The coordinator reviews all of the translations and decides that two of them are ready for publishing, but one of them needs a better example sentence. He rejects the translation with a note explaining why it was rejected, and the word is put back into circulation automatically by the system. The two accepted words will no longer be added to users' word lists unless manually added back into the database.

3.3 Consumer

A consumer who visits the Community Language
Portal navigates to a part of the website providing
a picture gallery of everyday and cultural artifacts.
As she looks through the pictures and their captions, she notices that the word for *water pitcher*
has a different form than is used in her village.
She clicks on the 'Contribute' button, and is able
to either leave a comment about the caption or go
through the sign-up process to become a contributor. The coordinator reviews her submission, and,
if appropriate, adds her to the contributors, later
sending out more invitations to contribute.

4 Implementation Details

Users of the application only see information relevant to their current task, but all user and language
data is stored and managed in a remote database.
The application communicates with a CherryPy
web server, which acts as the glue between these
two components. For example, consider the Konni
contributor trying to submit some translations. Before doing anything, the user must first sign in.
To avoid having to manage passwords we require
users to connect to the application using a Google
account. Then the application communicates with
Google's Authentication Server using the OAuth
2.0 protocol to retrieve an authentication token
that uniquely identifies the user. When the contributor presses *Submit*, the phone will first store
the translation information locally and wait until
it enters an area with a strong Internet connection. Once connected, it then sends an HTTP request to the web server containing the translations
to be submitted (multiple translations are batched
together for efficiency), as well as the authentication token. Upon receiving the request, the server
uses the token to verify that the user exists and has
the proper permissions. It then adds the translations to the database and queries it for a new set of
untranslated words. Finally the server responds to
the application indicating that the submission was
successful and containing the new words.

At the lowest level of the application stack is
a MySQL database that is responsible for storing
user information and translations. It consists of
three tables: `words` for the words that are to be
translated, `users` for all the application users,
and `translations` for all submitted translations, both reviewed and unreviewed. An entry in
`words` contains the word itself, as well as other
grammatical information, such as part-of-speech.
The `users` table contains users' names, their
Google authentication tokens, their roles (contributor or coordinator), and the maximum number of
words that can be assigned to them. Each row in
`translations` consists of the word translated
to the target language, a sentence containing the
word in the source language, the same sentence
translated, paths to audio files containing recordings of the word and sentence, and a flag indicating whether the translation has been accepted.

This is a natural division of the data that allows the tables to grow independently of one another (e.g. adding a new user only affects the
`users` table). However, we often want to make
queries that depend on information from multiple tables, such as searching for words with no
accepted translations that are assigned to fewer
than three users. To facilitate these searches we
also introduce links between the tables. A word
can have multiple translations, but each translation
corresponds to exactly one word, so `words` and
`translations` have a 1-many relation. Similarly, because a user may have many submitted
translations, and each translation was submitted by
one user, `users` and `translations` also have
a 1-many relation. On the other hand, a word can
be assigned to several users, and a user may have
multiple assigned words, so `words` and `users`
have a many-many relation.

5 Current Developments

With this groundwork laid on the application, we
are expanding other aspects of the project. Since
one of our primary goals is to engage community
members, we are pursuing more ways for them to
engage with the software and data. To that end, we
are designing a discussion board for raising questions about accepted materials, asking for clarifi-
cation on words, debates, polls, and so forth. Anyone from the community will be able to use this
software. In short, we aim to leverage successful
examples of online community building to further
language description and documentation.

It is possible that contributors use slightly different lexica within the community. For example, in a community that has a designated group of
hunters, the hunters might use different words in
the field that community members who stay in the
village most of the time don't know. In this example, a coordinator might want to gather lexical data

from both groups, so they should be able to mark
which users belong to which sub-communities in
the database. At the moment, we have back-end
functionality for this sub-grouping of words and
users, but no way for a coordinator to interact with
this feature from the application. In the meantime,
words are assigned to users automatically.

Having a way for a coordinator to assign words
to specific users will also be an important feature.
It is very likely that contributors will sometimes
be working in areas with a lot of background noise,
and not everyone will have a phone that can record
high-quality audio. Giving coordinators the ability to reassign words to users who they know can
record with better sound quality will ensure high-
quality data, which can then be used later in linguistic analysis.

References

Eric Albright and John Hatton. 2008. Wesay: A tool
for engaging native speakers in dictionary building. *Documenting and revitalizing Austronesian
languages*, (1):189.

Martin Benjamin and Paula Radetzky. 2014. Small languages, big data: Multilingual computational tools
and techniques for the lexicography of endangered
languages. In *Proceedings of the 2014 Workshop on
the Use of Computational Methods in the Study of
Endangered Languages*, pages 15–23.

Steven Bird, Florian R Hanke, Oliver Adams, and Hae-
joong Lee. 2014. Aikuma: A mobile app for collaborative language documentation. In *Proceedings
of the 2014 Workshop on the Use of Computational
Methods in the Study of Endangered Languages*,
pages 1–5.

J.B. Casagrande and K.L. Hale. 1967. Semantic Relationships in Papago Folk-Definitions. In *Studies
in Southwestern Ethnolinguistics*, pages 165–193.
Mouton, The Hague.

M. Laughren and D. Nash. 1983. Warlpiri dictionary project: Aims, method, organization and problems of definition. *Papers in Australian Linguistics*,
15(1):109–133.

Johann-Mattis List, Michael Cysouw, and Robert
Forkel. 2016. Concepticon: A resource for the link-
ing of concept lists. In *Proceedings of the Tenth International Conference on Language Resources and
Evaluation, May 23-28, 2016, Portorož, Slovenia*,
pages 2393–2400.

Keith Snider and James Roberts. 2004. Sil comparative
african wordlist (silcawl). *JWAL*, 31(2):73–122.

Developing without developers: choosing labor-saving tools for language documentation apps

Luke D. Gessler
Department of Linguistics
Georgetown University
`lg876@georgetown.edu`

Abstract

Application software has the potential to greatly reduce the amount of human labor needed in common language documentation tasks. But despite great advances in the maturity of tools available for apps, language documentation apps have not attained their full potential, and language documentation projects are forgoing apps in favor of less specialized tools like paper and spreadsheets. We argue that this is due to the scarcity of software development labor in language documentation, and that a careful choice of software development tools could make up for this labor shortage by increasing developer productivity. We demonstrate the benefits of strategic tool choice by reimplementing a subset of the popular linguistic annotation app ELAN using tools carefully selected for their potential to minimize developer labor.

1 Introduction

In many domains like medicine and finance, application software has dramatically increased productivity, allowing fewer people to get more done. This kind of labor reduction is sorely needed in language documentation, where there is not nearly enough labor to meet all the demand in the world for language documentation.

There is every reason to think that application software ("apps") could also help language documentation (LD) practitioners get their work done more quickly. But despite the availability of several LD apps, many practitioners still choose to use paper, spreadsheets, or other generic tools (Thieberger, 2016). Why aren't practitioners using apps?

1.1 Perennial problems in LD apps

The simplest explanation is that the apps are not helpful enough to justify the cost of learning and adjusting to them. While it is clear by now from progress in natural language processing that it is technically possible to make laborious tasks such as glossing and lexicon management less time-consuming by orders of magnitude, flashy features like these turn out to be only one part of the practitioner's decision to adopt an app. It seems that other factors, often more mundane but no less important, can and often do nullify or outweigh these benefits in today's apps. Three kinds of problems can be distinguished which are especially important for LD apps.

First, there is the unavoidable fact that the user will need to make unwanted changes to their workflow to work within an app. By virtue of its structure, an app will always make some tasks prerequisites for others, or at least make some sequences of tasks less easy to perform than others. Ideally, an app designer will be successful in identifying the task-sequences that are most likely to be preferred by their user and ensure that these workflows are supported and usable within the app. But no matter how clever they are, their app will always push some users away from their preferred workflow. For app adoption, this presents both a barrier to entry and a continuous cost (if a user is never able to fully adapt themselves to the app's structure).

Second, app developers often make simplifying assumptions which sacrifice generality for development speed. For instance, an app's morphological parser might not be capable of recognizing diacritics as lexically meaningful, which would limit the app's usability, e.g. for the many languages which represent lexical tone with diacritics.

Third, an app might lack a feature altogether. An app might only work on a particular operating system like Windows, or might not work without an internet connection, both of which might single-handedly make an app unusable. In another vein, it might be critical for a project to have texts

Proceedings of the 3rd Workshop on the Use of Computational Methods in the Study of Endangered Languages: Vol. 1 Papers, pages 6–13,
Honolulu, Hawai'i, USA, February 26–27, 2019.

be annotated with a syntactic parse, or for all texts to be exportable into a particular format, like as an ELAN (Wittenburg et al., 2006) or FLEx (Moe, 2008) project. If a user cannot perform a crucial kind of linguistic annotation, or move their data into another app which is critically important for them, they are likely to not use the app at all, no matter how good it might be at segmenting text into tokens, morphologically parsing words, or managing a lexical inventory. Indeed, the features which might be absolutely necessary for any given practitioner are in principle at least as numerous as the number of formalisms and levels of analysis used by all linguists, and it is to be expected that an app will be inadequate for a great number of potential users.

1.2 The need for more developer labor

Whatever the exact proportions of these problems in explaining the under-adoption of apps, it seems clear that they all could be solved relatively straightforwardly with more software engineering labor. Much of the hard work of inventing the linguistic theories and algorithms that would enable an advanced, labor-saving LD app has already been done. What remains is the comparatively mundane task of laying a solid foundation of everyday software on which we might establish these powerful devices, and the problem is that in LD, software engineering labor is—as in most places in science and the academy—markedly scarce.

With a few notable exceptions[1], LD apps have largely been made by people (often graduate students) who have undertaken the project on top of the demands of their full time occupation. Considering how in industry entire teams of highly-skilled full-time software engineers with ample funding regularly fail to create successful apps, it is impressive that LD apps have attained as much success as they have. Nevertheless, most LD software will continue to be produced only in such arid conditions, and so the question becomes one of whether and how it might be possible to create and maintain a successful app even when the only developers will likely be people like graduate students, who must balance the development work with their other duties.

While pessimism here would be understandable, we believe it is possible to create an app that

is good enough to be worth using for most practitioners even under these circumstances. While there is still not much that is known with certainty about productivity factors in software engineering (Wagner and Ruhe, 2018), many prominent software engineers believe that development time can be affected dramatically by the tools that are used in the creation of an app (Graham, 2004).

Apps depend on existing software libraries, and these libraries differ in dramatic ways: some databases are designed for speed, and others are designed for tolerating being offline; some user interface frameworks are designed for freedom and extensibility, and others double down on opinionated defaults that are good enough most of the time; some programming languages are always running towards the cutting edge of programming language research, and others aim to be eminently practical and stable for years to come. It is obvious that these trade-offs might have great consequences for their users: a given task might take a month with one set of tools, and only a few days with another.

We should expect, then, that the right combination of tools could allow LD app developers to be much more productive. If this is true, then if only we could choose the right set of tools to work with, we might be able to overcome the inherent lack of development labor available for LD apps.

2 Cloning ELAN

To put this hypothesis to the test, we recreated the rudiments of an app commonly used for LD, ELAN (Wittenburg et al., 2006). Choosing an existing app obviated the design process, saving time and eliminating a potential confound. ELAN was chosen in particular because of its widespread use in many areas of linguistics, including LD, and because its user interface and underlying data structures are complicated. We reasoned that if our approach were to succeed in this relatively hard case, we could be fairly certain it could succeed in easier ones, as well.

With an eye to economic problems of LD app development outlined in section 1.2, we first determined what features we thought an advanced LD app would need to prioritize in order to make development go quickly without compromising on quality. Then, we chose software libraries in accord with these requirements.

---

[1] FLEx, ELAN, and Miromaa all have at least one full-time software engineer involved in their development.

2.1 Requirements and tool choices

There were four requirements that seemed most important to prioritize for an LD app. These were: (1) that the app be built for web browsers, (2) that the app work just as well without an internet connection, (3) that expected "maintenance" costs be as low as possible, and (4) that graphical user interface development be minimized and avoided at all costs.

2.1.1 Choice of platform: the browser

15 years ago, the only platform that would have made sense for an LD app was the desktop. These days, there are three: the desktop, the web browser, and the mobile phone. While the mobile phone is ubiquitous and portable, it is constrained by its form factor, making it unergonomic for some kinds of transcription and annotation. The desktop platform has the advantage of not expecting an internet connection, and indeed the most widely used LD apps such as FLEx and ELAN have been on the desktop, but it is somewhat difficult to ensure that a desktop app will be usable on all operating systems, and the requirement that the user install something on their machine can be prohibitively difficult.

The web browser resolves both of these difficulties: no installation is necessary, since using an app is as easy as navigating to a URL, and the problem of operating system support is taken care of by web browser developers rather than app developers.

2.1.2 Offline support: PouchDB

The notable disadvantage of web browsers compared to these other platforms, however, is that the platform more or less assumes that you will have an internet connection. The simple problem is that language documentation practitioners will often not have a stable internet connection, and if an app is unusable without one, they will never use the app at all.

Fortunately, there are libraries that can enable a browser app to be fully functional even without an internet connection. The main reason why a typical browser app needs an internet connection is that the data that needs to be retrieved and changed is stored in a database somewhere on the other end of a network connection. But there are databases that can be installed locally, removing the need for an uninterrupted internet connection.

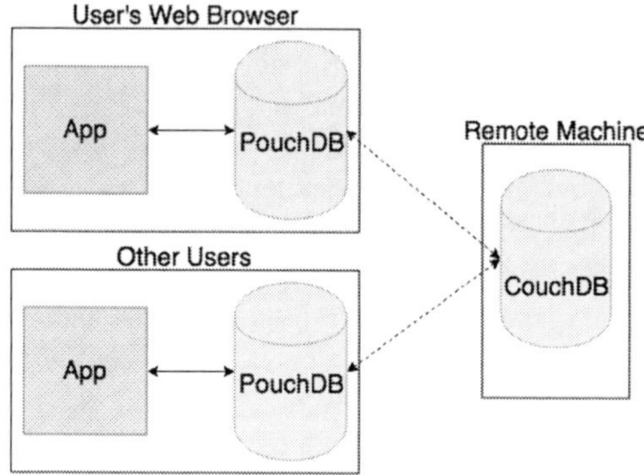

Figure 1: PouchDB imitates a traditional database, but it exists alongside the app in a user's local machine rather than on a remote server. When an internet connection becomes available, PouchDB can sync with the remote server and other clients, meaning that sharing and securely backing up data is still possible.

The most advanced database for this purpose is PouchDB. PouchDB is a browser-based implementation of the database system CouchDB. This means that PouchDB acts just like a normal database would, except it is available locally instead of over a network connection. And when an internet connection does become available, PouchDB is able to share changes with a remote instance of CouchDB, which then makes them available to other collaborators, as seen in figure 1. PouchDB and CouchDB were specially designed to make this kind of operation easy, and retrofitting the same behavior with a more traditional choice of tools would be extremely time consuming.

An added benefit of adopting this database strategy is that it dramatically reduces the need for client-server communication code. Normally, an entire layer of code is necessary to package, transmit, and unpackage data between the client and the server, which most of the time amounts to nothing more than boilerplate. With this approach, all of that is taken care of by the replication protocol which allows PouchDB instances to sync with CouchDB instances, and the server code that is required by a small set of cases (e.g. triggering a notification email) can still exist alongside this architecture.

We are not the first to realize PouchDB's potential for writing an LD app: FieldDB (aka LingSync) (Dunham et al., 2015) uses PouchDB.

2.1.3 Minimizing maintenance: ClojureScript

Software requires some degree of modification as time goes on. Almost all software relies on other software, and when breaking changes occur in a dependency, an app must also have its code modified to ensure that it can continue operating with the latest version of its dependency. For instance, much of the Python community is still migrating their code from Python 2 to Python 3, an error-prone process that has consumed many thousands of developer-hours worldwide.

This kind of maintenance is, at present, quite common for browser apps: web browsers, JavaScript, and JavaScript frameworks are evolving at a quick pace that often requires teams to constantly modify their code and compilers, and sometimes to even abandon a core library altogether in favor of a better one, which incurs a massive cost as the team excises the old library and stitches in the new one. These maintenance costs are best avoided if possible, as they contribute nothing valuable to the user: in the best case, after maintenance, no change is discernible; and if the best case is not achieved, the app breaks.

We surveyed programming languages that can be used for developing browser applications and were impressed by the programming language called ClojureScript. ClojureScript is a Lisp-family functional programming language that compiles to JavaScript. The language is remarkably stable: ClojureScript written in 2009 still looks essentially the same as ClojureScript written in 2018. The same cannot often be said for JavaScript code.

A full discussion of the pros and cons of ClojureScript is beyond the scope of this paper, but it might suffice to say that ClojureScript offers very low maintenance costs and powerful language features at the cost of a strenuous learning process. Unlike Python, Java, or JavaScript, ClojureScript is not object-oriented and does not have ALGOL-style syntax, making it syntactically and semantically unfamiliar. This is a serious penalty, as it may reduce the number of number of people who could contribute to the app's development. However, this may turn out to be a price worth paying, and as we will see in section 2.3.2, this disadvantage can be mitigated somewhat by allowing users and developers to extend the app using more familiar programming languages.

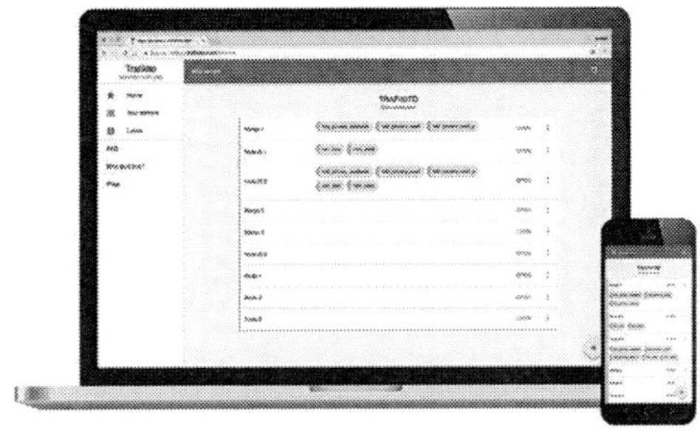

Figure 2: Trafikito, an app that uses Material-UI to support for mobile and desktop clients.

2.1.4 Minimizing GUI development: Material-UI

Creating user interface components for the browser from scratch is extremely time consuming. In the past several years, however, numerous comprehensive and high-quality open source component libraries for the browser have been released. Most parts of an LD app can be served well by these off-the-shelf components, making it an obvious choice to outsource as much UI development as possible to them.

The only concern would be that these libraries might be abandoned by their maintainers. While this is always a possibility, the communities that maintain the most prominent among these libraries are very active, and in the event that their current maintainers abandoned them, it seems likely that the community would step up to take over maintenance.

We chose to work with Material-UI, a library of components for Facebook's React UI framework that adheres to Google's Material Design guidelines. Beyond providing a set of high-quality components, with the v1.0 release of Material-UI, all components have been designed to work well on mobile clients, which has the potential to make an app developed with Material-UI usable on mobile phones at no extra development cost for the app developer, an incredible timesaving benefit. (See figure 2.)

2.2 Results

Using these tools, we were able to create a browser app that implements a subset of ELAN in about 3

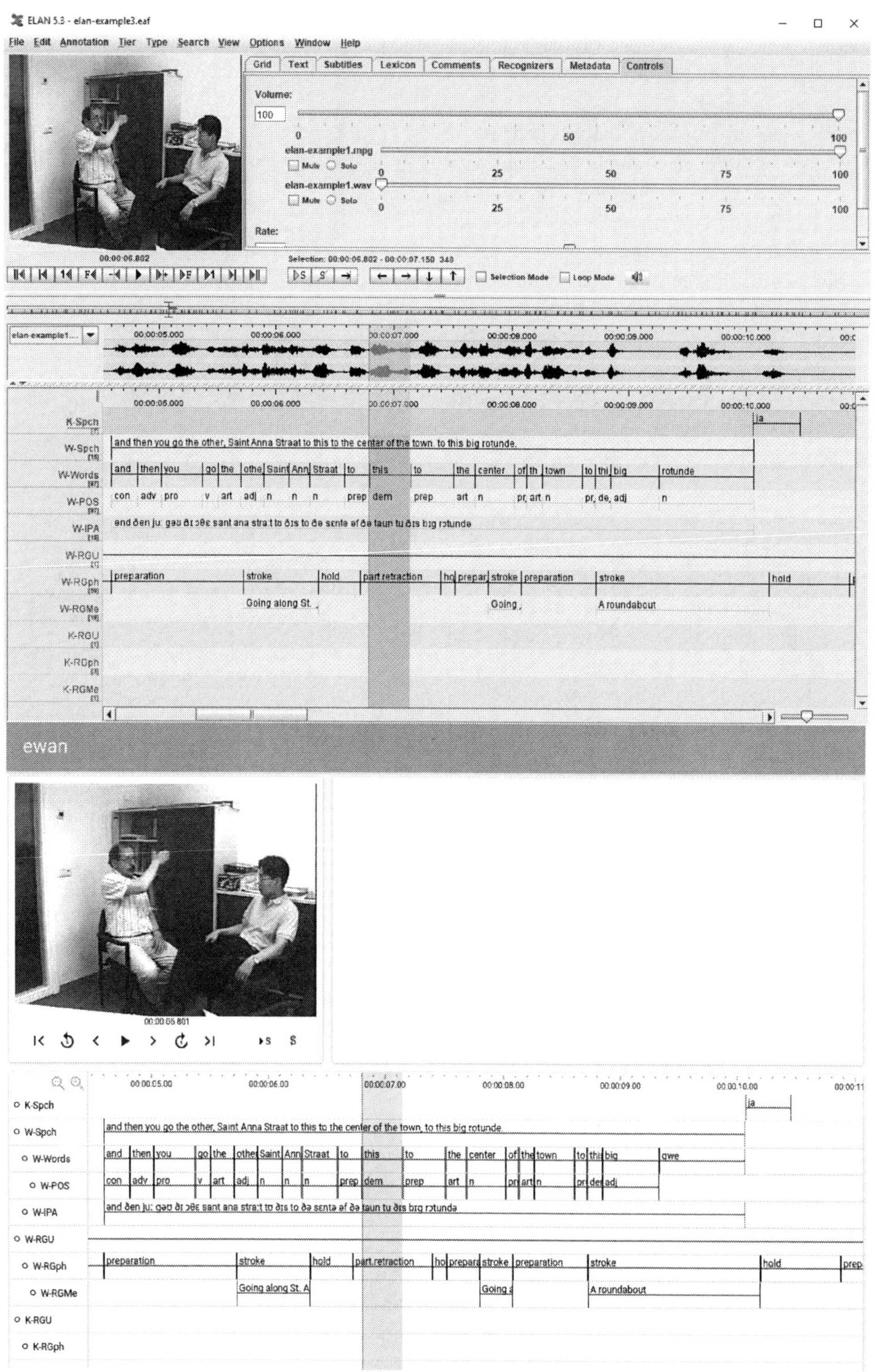

Figure 3: A screenshot of ELAN, above, and EWAN, below, for a given sample project.

weeks of development time[2]. Our implementation process basically confirmed our hypothesis: that our careful choice of tools made developers more productive, and vastly simplified the implementation of certain features that are critical to LD apps.

ELAN is an app that allows users to annotate a piece of audio or video along multiple aligned "tiers", each of which represents a single level of analysis for a single kind of linguistic or non-linguistic modality. For instance, in the example project in figure 3 (shown in both ELAN and our reimplementation, EWAN), for one of the speakers, there is a tier each for the speaker's sentence-level utterance, the speaker's utterance tokenized into words, IPA representations of those words, and the parts of speech for those words; and there is another tier for describing the speaker's gesticulations. Users are able to configure tiers so that e.g. a child tier containing parts of speech may not have an annotation that does not correspond to a word in the parent tier, and the app coordinates the UI so that the annotation area always stays in sync with the current time of the media player.

We implemented ELAN's behavior to a point where we felt we had been able to evaluate our hypothesis with reasonable confidence. In the end, this amounted to implementing the following features: (1) a basic recreation of the ELAN interface, (2) importing and exporting ELAN files, (3) read-only display and playback of projects, (4) editing of existing annotations, and (5) completely offline operation with sync capabilities. Most notably missing from this list is the ability to create new tiers and annotations, but we did not feel that implementing these features would have significantly changed our findings.

The creation of the interface with Material-UI was straightforward. The only UI components that involved significant custom development were the tier table and the code that kept the table and the video in sync: everything else, including the forms that allowed users to create new projects and import existing projects, was simply made with the expected Material-UI components.

ClojureScript's XML parsing library made importing and exporting ELAN project files a straightforward matter. Internally, EWAN uses the ELAN project file format as its data model, so there was no additional overhead associated with translating between EWAN and ELAN formats. To ensure the validity of the data under any changes that might be made in EWAN, we used ClojureScript's cljs.spec library to enforce invariants[3]. cljs.spec is one language feature among many that we felt made ClojureScript a good choice for enhancing developer productivity: cljs.spec allows developers to declaratively enforce data model invariants, whereas in most other languages more verbose imperative code would have to be written to enforce these invariants.

Projects were stored in PouchDB, and all the expected benefits were realized: an internet connection is no longer needed. Indeed, on the demo deployment of the app, there is not even a remote server to accompany it: once the app has been downloaded, users may use the app in its entirety without an internet connection. With ease, we were able to set up an instance of CouchDB on a remote server and sync our EWAN projects with it, even in poor network conditions.

2.3 Extensions

At the point in development where we stopped, there were features which we were close enough to see with clarity, even though we did not implement them. These are features we expect would be easily within reach if a similar approach were taken to creating a LD app.

2.3.1 Real-time collaboration

Google Docs-style real-time collaboration, where multiple clients collaborate in parallel on a single document, is well supported by our choice of PouchDB. Implementation is not entirely trivial, but the hard part—real-time synchronization without race conditions or data loss—is handled by CouchDB's replication protocol. It is debatable how useful this feature might be in an LD app, but if it were needed, it would be easily within reach.

2.3.2 User scripts with JavaScript

Power users delight in the opportunity to use a scripting language to tackle tedious or challenging tasks. Because this app was built in the web browser, we already have a language with excellent support at our disposal that was designed to

---

[2]Our app can be seen at `https://lgessler.com/ewan/` and our source code can be accessed at `https://github.com/lgessler/ewan`.

[3]An invariant in this context is some statement about the data that must always be true. For example, one might want to require that an XML element referenced by an attribute in another element actually exists.

```javascript
// a collection of functions
const s = window.ewan.script;

// imagined feature 1: a programmatic interface for making arbitrary
// substitutions for regular expressions
s.replaceAll("tierId", /colour/g, "color");

// imagined feature 2: a more complicated interface that lets you apply a
// function to all annotation values on a tier. Suppose we made a transcription
// error in our words and forgot to lengthen [u] in front of voiced consonants
// in English. We could use this function to correct the issue:
s.updateAnns("phoneticTierId", function(ann) {
  const text = ann.value;
  const uIndex = text.indexOf("u");

  // check if we have u followed by a voiced consonant (just consider [b] and [d]
  // here for simplicity) and replace with u: if it is
  if (uIndex > -1
      && uIndex < text.length - 1
      && ['b', 'd'].indexOf(uIndex.charAt(uIndex + 1)) > -1) {
    ann.value = text.substring(0, uIndex) + "u:" + text.substring(uIndex + 1);
  }
});
```

Figure 4: Examples of what a JavaScript scripting interface for EWAN might look like. An API implemented in ClojureScript with functions intended for use in JavaScript that can modify EWAN's data structures is made available in a global namespace, and power users can use the scripting functions to perform bulk actions and customize their experience.

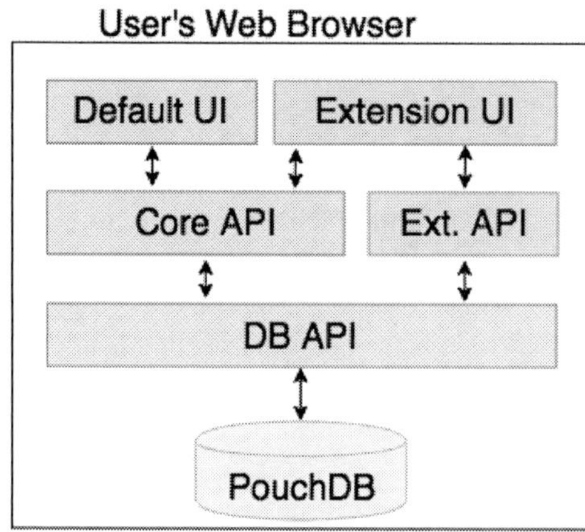

Figure 5: A high-level representation of EWAN's API layers and how UI and business logic layers could be extended if extension functions at the DB and business logic layers were made.

be easy for users to pick up and write small snippets with: JavaScript.

Since ClojureScript compiles to JavaScript and is designed for interoperation, it is very easy to make such a system available. As shown in figure 4, a special module containing user-facing functions that are meant to be used from a JavaScript console could be created. This could be used for anything from bulk actions to allowing users to hook into remote NLP services (e.g. for morphological parsing, tokenization, etc.).

The possibilities are endless with a user-facing API, and a thoughtfully constructed scripting API could do much to inspire and attract users. It's worth noting that this feature was made possible by our choice of platform: had we not been using the browser, we would have had either implement an entire scripting language or embed an existing one (like Lua) into the app.

2.3.3 Extensions

As noted in section 1.1, there will always be formalisms or levels of analysis that will not have robust support in an app. Normally, this pushes users who really need such support to either use another app or revert to a more generic medium.

To try to tackle this issue, an app structured like EWAN could be enriched with API's to allow users to customize deeper parts of the app, as shown in figure 5. Suppose that a user is a semanticist who has designed a new semantic parsing formalism, and wants to be able to annotate texts with it. This would require the creation of at least a new UI. If the user is comfortable with writing JavaScript, the user could use these extension API's to implement support for their own formalism, provided these extension API's are powerful and approachable enough for use by novice programmers. The user could then not only benefit themselves, but also share the extension with the community.

If this were done well, a major problem driving the continued fragmentation of the LD app landscape would be solved, and the LD community could perhaps begin to converge on a common foundation for common tasks in LD.

3 Conclusion

Because of the economic conditions that are endemic to software development in language documentation, app developers cannot reasonably hope to succeed by taking software development approaches unmodified from industry, where developer labor is much more abundant. We have argued these economic conditions are the major reason why LD apps have not realized their full potential, and that the way to solve this problem is to be selective in the tools that are used in making LD apps. We have shown that choice of tools does indeed affect how productive developers can be, as demonstrated by our experience recreating a portion of the app ELAN.

It is as yet unclear whether our choices were right—both our choices in which requirements to prioritize, and in which tools to use to address those requirements. Offline support seems secure as a principal concern for LD apps, but perhaps it might actually be the case that it is better to choose a programming language that is easy to learn rather than easy to maintain. What we hope is clear, however, is that choice of tools can affect developer productivity by orders of magnitude, and that the success of language documentation software will be decided by how foresighted and creative its developers are in choosing tools that will minimize their labor.

Acknowledgments

Thanks to Mans Hulden, Sarah Moeller, Anish Tondwalkar, and Marina Bolotnikova for helpful comments on an earlier version of this paper.

References

J. Dunham, A. Bale, and J. Coon. 2015. LingSync: web-based software for language documentation. In *Proceedings of the 4th International Conference on Language Documentation Conservation.*

P. Graham. 2004. *Hackers and Painters: Essays on the Art of Programming.* O'Reilly & Associates, Inc., Sebastopol, CA, USA.

R. Moe. 2008. FieldWorks Language Explorer 1.0. *SIL Forum for Language Fieldwork.*

N. Thieberger. 2016. Language documentation tools and methods summit report http://bit.ly/LDTAMSReport.

S. Wagner and M. Ruhe. 2018. A systematic review of productivity factors in software development. *Computing Research Repository*, abs/1801.06475.

P. Wittenburg, H. Brugman, A. Russel, A. Klassmann, and H. Sloetjes. 2006. ELAN: a professional framework for multimodality research. In *Proceedings of LREC 2006, Fifth International Conference on Language Resources and Evaluation.*

Future Directions in Technological Support for Language Documentation

Daan van Esch
Google
dvanesch@google.com

Ben Foley
The University of Queensland,
ARC Centre of Excellence for
the Dynamics of Language
b.foley@uq.edu.au

Nay San
Stanford University,
Australian National University,
ARC Centre of Excellence for
the Dynamics of Language
nay.san@stanford.edu

Abstract

To reduce the annotation burden placed on linguistic fieldworkers, freeing up time for deeper linguistic analysis and descriptive work, the language documentation community has been working with machine learning researchers to investigate what assistive role technology can play, with promising early results. This paper describes a number of potential follow-up technical projects that we believe would be worthwhile and straightforward to do. We provide examples of the annotation tasks for computer scientists; descriptions of the technological challenges involved and the estimated level of complexity; and pointers to relevant literature. We hope providing a clear overview of what the needs are and what annotation challenges exist will help facilitate the dialogue and collaboration between computer scientists and fieldwork linguists.

1 The Transcription and Annotation Challenge

Language documentation projects typically yield more data than can be reasonably annotated and analyzed by the linguistic fieldworkers that collect the data. For example, transcribing one hour of audio recordings can take 40 hours or more (Durantin et al., 2017), and potentially even longer where the language is severely under-studied or under-described. To reduce the annotation burden placed on linguistic fieldworkers, freeing up time for deeper linguistic analysis and descriptive work, the language documentation community has been working with machine learning (ML) researchers to investigate what role technology can play. As a result, today enterprising fieldwork linguists can use a number of toolkits to help accelerate the annotation process by automatically proposing candidate transcriptions. Such toolkits include CoEDL Elpis (Foley et al., 2018), Persephone (Adams et al., 2018; Michaud et al., 2018), and SPPAS (Bigi, 2015).

2 A Technological Development Roadmap

These toolkits are already showing promising results across a number of languages. Arguably, however, their current incarnation only scratches the surface of what is technically possible, even today. In this paper, we aim to describe a number of potential extensions to these systems, which we believe would be reasonably straightforward to implement, yet which should significantly improve the quality and usefulness of the output. Specifically, we look at the annotation steps in the language documentation process beyond just phonemic or orthographic transcription, and describe what assistive role technology can play for many other steps in the language documentation process, such as automatically proposing glossing and translation candidates.

To be clear, this paper does not actually describe complete systems that have been implemented. Rather, our goal is to describe technical projects that we believe would be worthwhile and straightforward to do. We provide examples of the annotation tasks for computer scientists; descriptions of the technological challenges involved and the estimated level of complexity; and pointers to relevant literature on both the computational and the linguistic side. Our hope is that this overview of what the needs are and what annotation challenges exist will help facilitate the dialogue and collaboration between computer scientists and fieldwork linguists.

Our higher-level vision is for a toolkit that lets fieldwork linguists process data at scale, with limited technical knowledge needed on the side of the user. This toolkit should make it as easy as possible to apply the most relevant well-known techniques in natural language processing and machine learning to any language. This will likely involve providing a simple, pre-configured graph-

Proceedings of the 3rd Workshop on the Use of Computational Methods in the Study of Endangered Languages: Vol. 1 Papers, pages 14–22,
Honolulu, Hawai'i, USA, February 26–27, 2019.

ical user interface; for the purposes of this paper, however, we focus on the underlying technology.

For our purposes, we assume there is an audio corpus where orthographic transcriptions are available for at least some subset of the recordings. If no orthographic transcriptions exist at all, then there are a number of techniques around audio-only corpus analysis that can be applied, such as those explored in the Zero-Resource Speech Challenges (Dunbar et al., 2017), but those approaches are outside of the scope of this paper.

We also assume that the corpus at hand was created in a relatively ubiquitous tool for language documentation — e.g. ELAN (Max Planck Institute for Psycholinguistics; Brugman and Russel, 2004), Praat (Boersma and Weenink, 2001), or Transcriber (DGA, 2014) — for which there would be a ready-to-use conversion tool to convert the corpus into a common format that can be understood by the toolkit. Finally, we assume that the linguist has access to a tool to create keyboards for use on a desktop/laptop system, such as Keyman (SIL), so an appropriate orthography can be used, and that the linguist has access to an entry input method for the International Phonetic Alphabet (IPA).

Broadly, we see two areas where automation toolkits for language documentation can make significant headway still: automatic analysis of existing data in the corpus, and automatic processing of unannotated data. To facilitate the discussion below, Table 1 briefly walks through a reasonably comprehensive set of annotations for an audio recording. Specifically, for each word in our Nafsan example utterance, Table 1 includes:

- a speaker label to indicate which of the speakers in the recording spoke this word

- the orthographic form, or simply spelling, of this word

- an interlinear gloss, which we will describe in further detail below for readers who are unfamiliar with this practice

- a part-of-speech tag, e.g. using the conventions from (Petrov et al., 2012)

- a phonemic transcription, e.g. in the International Phonetic Alphabet

In addition, our example annotation shows a translation of the entire utterance into a single language.[1]

3 Analysis of Existing Data

3.1 Text Analytics

In terms of automatic analysis of existing data, there appears to be a significant amount of low-hanging fruit around text-based analytics. Once a language worker has put the effort into preparing a corpus for use in a toolkit, by normalizing and consolidating files, the data becomes suitable for automatic analysis to obtain corpus-wide metrics. For example, a toolkit could easily emit the following metrics on the orthographic transcriptions in the corpus:

- the total number of words observed[2]

- the number of unique words observed

- a frequency-ranked wordlist, with word counts

- the average number of words in each utterance, and a histogram of words per utterance

These metrics can also be broken down by speaker, if multiple speakers are present in the corpus and speaker annotations are available in the metadata. In that case, a toolkit could also automatically compute statistics such as pointwise mutual information score for the usage of each word by each speaker, or by speaker group, for example if multiple varieties are represented in the corpus. This may point to interesting inter-speaker or inter-variety lexical frequency differences that merit further investigation. Per-speaker lexical analyses could also be used to inform field-work elicitation adjustments, e.g. when some words were not elicited from a particular speaker in the data set. For a literature review describing a large number of automatic analysis options in this space, see (Wieling and Nerbonne, 2015).

Frequency-ranked wordlists in particular can also be helpful for quality assurance purposes:

---

[1] Fieldwork linguists can, naturally, choose to create this translation in any language. In our example, for expository purposes, we used English.

[2] We use "words" here to mean specifically orthographic units separated by whitespace in the target-language orthography; if such separation is not part of the orthography, then more complex approaches are needed, as is the case when users wish to run these analyses based on lexical roots (after morphological analysis).

Speaker	Spelling	Gloss	Part-of-Speech	Phonemes
SPEAKER1	waak	pig	NOUN	wak
SPEAKER1	nen	that	DET	nan
SPEAKER1	i=	3SGREALISSUBJECT	PRON	i
SPEAKER1	p̃as	chase	VERB	p̃as
SPEAKER1	=ir	3PLOBJECT	PRON	ir

Table 1: Annotations for an example recording in Nafsan (ISO 639 erk), DOI 10.4225/72/575C6E9CC9B6A. Here, the English translation would be "That pig chased them."

words at the bottom of the list may occur only as one-off *hapax legomena*, but they may also be misspelled versions of more frequent words. Reviewing a frequency-ranked list may help find orthographic inconsistencies in the data set. In fact, an automatic toolkit could also emit additional information around annotation quality, such as:

- a frequency-ranked character list, with pointers to utterances that contain rarely used characters (on the assumption that they may be data entry mistakes)

- words that seem to be misspellings of another word, based on edit distance and/or context

For datasets in languages where comprehensive, clean wordlists are available, a transcription tool with built-in spell-checking or word-completion features would benefit users. If no clean wordlist exists yet, a frequency-based wordlist is a good start and can be human-curated. Going beyond just orthographic words, finite-state technologies may also be needed, especially for morphologically complex languages where stems may have more variations than could ever be covered by a simple wordlist, as is frequently described in the literature; two relevant recent surveys are (Mager et al., 2018; Littell et al., 2018).

If interlinear glosses are available in the corpus, the toolkit could also easily emit a list of all words and their glosses, highlighting words with multiple glosses, as these may (but do not necessarily) represent data entry inconsistencies; the same is true for part-of-speech tags.

Where phoneme annotations are present, a forced-alignment with the orthographic transcription may be carried out to surface any outliers, as these may represent either orthographic or phonemic transcription errors (Jansche, 2014). Of course, a phoneme frequency analysis could also be produced and may yield interesting insights.

It should also be straightforward, though the linguistic value of this would remain to be deter-

mined, to apply an unsupervised automatic morphemic analyzer like Morfessor (Virpioja et al., 2013).

3.2 Visualization

Language documentation toolkits will benefit from integration with information visualization tools. Visual data analysis can give a linguist a general overview of the nature of a corpus, and narrow in on data to support new, detailed insights. For example, a broad view of a language collection can be given by visualizing metadata from the corpus, representing the activity of the documentation process as a heatmap of the recording dates/times/participants. Date and time visualizations could show patterns within recording locations and events, indicating how long it took to create the corpus, and how old the data is.

Visualizations showing which time spans within a corpus have been annotated on particular annotation tiers would allow a linguist to quickly obtain a sense of the state of transcription. A representation of transcription state showing what has been transcribed, the types of existing transcriptions, with summaries of metadata, will assist the language worker to understand the shape of their parallel layered data, and develop well-constructed corpora. This information could help prevent unexpected data loss when moving from complex multi-tier transcription to other modes of representation (Thieberger, 2016).

Detailed visualizations can also represent linguistic features of the data, giving the linguist on-demand access to explore a variety of phenomena — e.g. using ANNIS (Krause and Zeldes, 2016) — such as compositional structure of linguistic units (hierarchical data), associations between words (relational data) and alternative word choices (Culy and Lyding, 2010).

Finally, a toolkit could output a high-level overview of statistics and visualizations for a given corpus as a landing page: a description of the collection for online publishing, or to facilitate discovery of the data within an archive (Thieberger, 2016).

4 Extending Automatic Processing of Unannotated Data

4.1 Audio Analysis

Generally, part of the data set at hand will be missing at least some of the annotation layers in our example above. At the most basic level, it may not be known what parts of an audio collection contain human speech, what parts contain other types of sound (e.g. only nature or car noise), or are even just quiet. A speech vs. non-speech classifier, known as a voice activity detector or VAD (Ramirez et al., 2007), should be built into the toolkit. One open-source VAD is the WebRTC Voice Activity Detector, with an easy-to-use Python wrapper in (Wiseman, 2016). Beyond voice activity detection, speaker identification or diarization may also be necessary. In this regard, the work recently done as part of the First DIHARD Speech Diarization Challenge (Church et al., 2018) is particularly relevant for fieldwork recordings, which are challenging corpora for these technologies.

Practically, entirely unannotated data sets are rare: usually at least the language of the data set is known. Where it isn't, or where multiple languages exist within a given recording, it will also be helpful to be able to identify the language spoken in each part of the audio, based on the recording alone, though this is a hard technical challenge (Gonzalez-Dominguez et al., 2014). As a first step, multiple existing recognizers could be executed, and their output could be analyzed to determine which one produces the most likely transcript, using an approach like that by (Demšar, 2006).

4.2 Automatic Phonemic and Orthographic Transcription

Once the location(s) and the language(s) of speech within the target audio recordings are known, the relevant audio fragments can be processed by speech recognition systems such as Elpis (Foley et al., 2018) or Persephone (Adams et al., 2018) in order to produce automatic machine hypotheses for phonemic and orthographic transcriptions. Today's Elpis and Persephone pipelines are maturing, and are relatively complete packages, but they could be made easier to use for people without backgrounds in speech science.

4.2.1 Pronunciations

For example, Elpis currently requires the linguist to provide a machine-readable grapheme-to-phoneme mapping. However, these may already be available from current libraries (Deri and Knight, 2016), derivable from existing databases like Ausphon-Lexicon (Round, 2017), or present in regional language collections such as the Australian Pronunciation Lexicon (Estival et al., 2014) and Sydney Speaks (CoEDL, 2018). These resources could be integrated directly into the toolkit. Elpis currently also offers no support for handling not-a-word tokens like numbers (van Esch and Sproat, 2017), but this could be supported using a relatively accessible grammar framework where the number grammar can be induced using a small number of examples (Gorman and Sproat, 2016).

4.2.2 Text Corpora

Toolkits should also facilitate easy ingestion of additional text corpora, which is particularly useful for training large-vocabulary speech recognition systems. For some endangered languages, text corpora such as Bible translations or Wikipedia datasets may be available to augment low-volume data sets coming in from language documentation work. Of course, the content of these sources may not be ideal for use in training conversational systems, but when faced with low-data situations, even out-of-domain data tends to help. As more text data becomes available, it would also be good to sweep language model parameters (such as the n-gram order) automatically on a development set to achieve the best possible result.

4.2.3 Audio Quality Enhancement

In terms of audio quality, it's worth pointing out that audio recorded during fieldwork is often made in noisy conditions, with intrusive animal and bird noises, environmental sounds, or air-conditioners whirring. Noisy corpora may become easier to process if automatic denoising and speech enhancement techniques are integrated into the pipeline. Loizou (2013) provides a recent overview of this particular area.

4.2.4 Multilingual Models

To further improve the quality of the output produced by the automatic speech recognition

(ASR) systems within toolkits such as Elpis and Persephone, multilingual acoustic models can be trained on data sets from multiple languages (Besacier et al., 2014; Toshniwal et al., 2018). This could allow so-called zero-shot model usage, meaning the application of these acoustic models to new languages, without any training data at all in the target language. Of course, the accuracy of such an approach would depend on how similar the target language is to the languages that were included in the training data for the multilingual model. Another approach is simply to reuse a monolingual acoustic model from a similar language. Either way, these models can be tailored towards the target language as training data becomes available through annotation.

4.2.5 Automatic Creation of Part-of-Speech Tags and Interlinear Glosses

Beyond automatically generating hypotheses for phonemic and orthographic transcriptions, it would technically also be relatively straightforward to produce candidate part-of-speech tags or interlinear glosses automatically. Both types of tags tend to use a limited set of labels, as described by e.g. the Universal Part-of-Speech Tagset documentation (Petrov et al., 2012) and the Leipzig Glossing Rules (Comrie et al., 2008). Where words occur without a part-of-speech tag or an interlinear gloss in the corpus (for example, because a linguist provided an orthographic transcription but no tag, or because the orthographic transcription is an automatically generated candidate), a tag could be proposed automatically.

Most straightforwardly, this could be done by re-using an existing tag for that word, if the word was already tagged in another context. Where multiple pre-existing interlinear glosses occur for the same surface form, it would be possible to contextually resolve these homographs (Mazovetskiy et al., 2018). For part-of-speech tagging, many mature libraries exist, such as the Stanford Part-of-Speech Tagger (Toutanova et al., 2003). However, in both cases, given the limited amount of training data available within small data sets, accuracy is likely to be low, and it may be preferable to simply highlight the existing set of tags for a given word for a linguist to resolve. Surfacing these cases to a linguist may even bring up an annotation quality problem that can be fixed (if, in fact, there should have been only one tag for this form).

Deriving interlinear glosses or part-of-speech tags for new surface forms that have not previously been observed could be significantly harder, depending on the target language. Achieving reasonable accuracy levels will require the use of morphological analyzers in many languages, e.g. as in (Arkhangeskiy et al., 2012). In polysynthetic languages in particular, development of such analyzers would be a challenging task (Mager et al., 2018; Littell et al., 2018), though see (Haspelmath, 2018) for a cautionary note on the term *polysynthetic*.

4.2.6 Automatic Machine Translation (MT)

Many language documentation workflows involve the translation of sentences from the target-language corpus into some other language, such as English, to make the content more broadly accessible. In effect, this creates a parallel corpus which can be used for training automatic machine translation (MT) systems. These MT systems could then, in turn, be used to propose translation candidates for parts of the corpus that are still lacking these translations: this may be because the linguist did not yet have time to translate their transcriptions, or because only machine-generated hypotheses are available for the transcriptions (in which case the cascading-error effect typically causes accuracy of translations to be lower). Such candidate translations would still require human post-editing, but for limited-domain applications, machine translations may be sufficiently accurate to accelerate the annotation process. Of course, where other parallel corpora exist (e.g. bilingual story books, or religious material like the Bible), these can also be used as training data. In addition, any existing bilingual word lexicons (like dictionaries) can also help in building machine translation systems, as in (Klementiev et al., 2012).

Many high-quality open-source machine translation toolkits already exist, e.g. SockEye (Hieber et al., 2017), TensorFlow (Luong et al., 2017), and Moses (Koehn et al., 2007). Phrase-based machine translation still tends to yield better results than neural machine translation (NMT) for small data sets (Östling and Tiedemann, 2017), but multilingual NMT models seem promising for cases where similar languages exist that do have large amounts of training data (Johnson et al., 2017; Gu et al., 2018). Recent advances even allow the creation of speech-to-translated-text models (Bansal et al., 2018) and enable the use of existing translations to enhance ASR quality (Anastasopoulos and Chiang, 2018).

5 Putting structured data and models to work more broadly

A toolkit designed to facilitate transcription and annotation efforts can benefit language workers and language communities beyond just the annotation output. Structured data sets used in these toolkits are ripe for conversion into formats needed for various other tasks, such as dictionary creation, e.g. Electronic Text Encoding and Interchange (TEI, 2018), or for dictionary publishing pipelines, as in Yinarlingi (San and Luk, 2018). Exported data could be formatted for import into a range of dictionary/publishing applications such as lexicon apps for mobile devices or ePub format (Gavrilis et al., 2013) for publishing on a wide range of devices such as smartphones, tablets, computers, or e-readers. Automatically generated pronunciations, word definitions, part-of-speech information and example sentences could easily be included. For difficult work such as automatic lemmatization, the output could be presented in a simple interface for human verification/correction before publication (Liang et al., 2014).

For languages to thrive in the digital domain, some technologies are considered essential: a standardized encoding; a standardized orthography; and some basic digital language resources, such as a corpus and a spell checker (Soria, 2018). If toolkits make it easy to create structured data sets and models for these languages, then these resources can also be applied outside the fields of language documentation, lexicography, and other linguistic research fields.

For example, Australia has a vibrant community-owned Indigenous media broadcasting sector. For these users, there is potential to re-use the ASR models to generate closed captions (subtitles) for the broadcast material. ASR transcription and translation technologies could be used to enrich the output of these Indigenous community media broadcasters, which would yield a significant improvement in the accessibility of broadcast content. Another option would be to facilitate the creation of smartphone keyboards with predictive text in the target languages, using toolkits like Keyman (SIL).

Language archives like PARADISEC could also benefit by applying these models, once created, on existing content for the same language that may have been contributed by other linguists, or that may have come in through other avenues. It may even be possible for these archives to offer web-based services to language communities, e.g. to allow them to use machine translation models for a given language in a web-based interface. Linguists could archive their models alongside their corpus; for some collections, the published models may inherit the same access permissions as the training data used in their creation, while some models may be able to be published under less restrictive conditions.

5.1 Data Set Availability

In general, to support the development of language technologies like the ones we described earlier, it is critical that software engineers are aware of, and have access to data sets reflecting the diversity of endangered languages. Already, data sets are available for a range of languages, and in formats suitable for ASR, text-to-speech synthesis (TTS) and other tasks on the Open Speech and Language Resources website (Povey, 2018). The addition of ML-ready data sets for more endangered languages would enable software engineers, whose primary concern may not be the language documentation process, to be involved in developing and refining speech tools and algorithms. However, access protocols and licenses in place for existing data sets can prohibit experimental development. Recording corpora specifically for the purposes of enabling ML experiments would avoid potentially lengthy negotiations of access rights.

6 Reaching more languages

Extending the reach of a toolkit beyond the (typically) few languages which are used when building and testing is critical. Applying technology to more diverse use cases encourages a tool to become more robust. With more use cases, a community of support can grow. A community of users, contributors and developers around a toolkit is important to encourage potential participants (Foley, 2015), and to reduce the burden of support on individual developers.

Being proactive in community discussions to publicize the abilities of tools, providing in-person access to training workshops, publishing online support material and tutorials, and ensuring tools have high-quality documentation for different levels of users, are all important (albeit labor-intensive) methods of promoting and encouraging language technology to reach more languages.

7 Conclusion

Speech and language technology toolkits, designed specially for users without backgrounds in speech science, have the potential for significant impact for linguists and language communities globally. Existing toolkits can be enhanced with richer feature sets, and connection with workflow processes, helping language documentation workers. These toolkits enable language documentation workers to focus on deeper linguistic research questions, by presenting the results of automated systems in ways that let language experts easily verify and correct the hypotheses, yielding annotation speed-ups. At the same time, making these technologies and the structured data they help produce more widely available would benefit language communities in many ways.

Most of the technologies described here are readily available and easily implemented, while others are still highly experimental in their application and potential benefits for Indigenous languages. With language technology as a whole making rapid progress, and with an increasing amount of dialogue between fieldwork linguists and computer scientists, it is an exciting time to be working on computational methods for language documentation, with many advances that look to be within reach for the near future.

Acknowledgments

We would like to thank all the participants in the Transcription Acceleration Project (TAP), run by the Centre of Excellence for the Dynamics of Language, for many fruitful discussions on how technology could be applied in the language documentation context to assist fieldwork linguists. We would like to add a special word of thanks to Nick Thieberger, who provided the Nafsan example, and who offered valuable input on a draft version of this paper. We would also like to thank Zara Maxwell-Smith and Nicholas Lambourne for all of their insightful suggestions and contributions.

References

Oliver Adams, Trevor Cohn, Graham Neubig, Hilaria Cruz, Steven Bird, and Alexis Michaud. 2018. Evaluating phonemic transcription of low-resource tonal languages for language documentation. In *Proceedings of LREC 2018*.

Antonis Anastasopoulos and David Chiang. 2018. Leveraging translations for speech transcription in low-resource settings. *CoRR*, abs/1803.08991.

Timofey Arkhangeskiy, Oleg Belyaev, and Arseniy Vydrin. 2012. The creation of large-scale annotated corpora of minority languages using uniparser and the eanc platform. In *Proceedings of COLING 2012: Posters*, pages 83–92. The COLING 2012 Organizing Committee.

Sameer Bansal, Herman Kamper, Karen Livescu, Adam Lopez, and Sharon Goldwater. 2018. Low-resource speech-to-text translation. *CoRR*, abs/1803.09164.

Laurent Besacier, Etienne Barnard, Alexey Karpov, and Tanja Schultz. 2014. Automatic speech recognition for under-resourced languages: A survey. *Speech Commun.*, 56:85–100.

Brigitte Bigi. 2015. SPPAS: Multi-lingual approaches to the automatic annotation of speech. *The Phonetician*, 111-112(ISSN:0741-6164):54–69.

Paul Boersma and David Weenink. 2001. Praat, a system for doing phonetics by computer. 5:341–345.

Hennie Brugman and Albert Russel. 2004. Annotating multi-media/multi-modal resources with ELAN. In *Proceedings of LREC 2004*.

Kenneth Church, Christopher Cieri, Alejandrina Cristia, Jun Du, Sriram Ganapathy, Mark Liberman, and Neville Ryant. 2018. The First DIHARD Speech Diarization Challenge. https://coml.lscp.ens.fr/dihard/index.html.

CoEDL. 2018. Sydney Speaks Project. http://www.dynamicsoflanguage.edu.au/sydney-speaks.

Bernard Comrie, Martin Haspelmath, and Balthasar Bickel. 2008. The Leipzig glossing rules: Conventions for interlinear morpheme-by-morpheme glosses.

Chris Culy and Verena Lyding. 2010. Visualizations for exploratory corpus and text analysis. In *Proceedings of the 2nd International Conference on Corpus Linguistics CILC-10*, pages 257–268.

Janez Demšar. 2006. Statistical comparisons of classifiers over multiple data sets. *J. Mach. Learn. Res.*, 7:1–30.

Aliya Deri and Kevin Knight. 2016. Grapheme-to-phoneme models for (almost) any language. In *Proceedings of the 54th Annual Meeting of the Association for Computational Linguistics (Volume 1: Long Papers)*, volume 1, pages 399–408.

DGA. 2014. TranscriberAG: a tool for segmenting, labeling and transcribing speech. http://transag.sourceforge.net.

Ewan Dunbar, Xuan-Nga Cao, Juan Benjumea, Julien Karadayi, Mathieu Bernard, Laurent Besacier, Xavier Anguera, and Emmanuel Dupoux. 2017. The zero resource speech challenge 2017. *CoRR*, abs/1712.04313.

Gautier Durantin, Ben Foley, Nicholas Evans, and Janet Wiles. 2017. Transcription survey.

Daan van Esch and Richard Sproat. 2017. An expanded taxonomy of semiotic classes for text normalization. In *Proceedings of Interspeech 2017*.

Dominique Estival, Steve Cassidy, Felicity Cox, and Denis Burnham. 2014. Austalk: an audio-visual corpus of australian english. In *Proceedings of LREC 2014*.

Ben Foley. 2015. Angkety map digital resource report. Technical report.

Ben Foley, Josh Arnold, Rolando Coto-Solano, Gautier Durantin, T. Mark Ellison, Daan van Esch, Scott Heath, František Kratochvíl, Zara Maxwell-Smith, David Nash, Ola Olsson, Mark Richards, Nay San, Hywel Stoakes, Nick Thieberger, and Janet Wiles. 2018. Building Speech Recognition Systems for Language Documentation: The CoEDL Endangered Language Pipeline and Inference System. In *Proceedings of the 6th International Workshop on Spoken Language Technologies for Under-resourced Languages (SLTU 2018)*.

Dimitris Gavrilis, Stavros Angelis, and Ioannis Tsoulos. 2013. Building interactive books using EPUB and HTML5. In *Ambient Media and Systems*, pages 31–40, Cham. Springer International Publishing.

Javier Gonzalez-Dominguez, Ignacio Lopez-Moreno, and Hasim Sak. 2014. Automatic language identification using long short-term memory recurrent neural networks. In *Proceedings of Interspeech 2014*.

Kyle Gorman and Richard Sproat. 2016. Minimally supervised number normalization. *Transactions of the Association for Computational Linguistics*, 4:507–519.

Jiatao Gu, Hany Hassan, Jacob Devlin, and Victor O.K. Li. 2018. Universal neural machine translation for extremely low resource languages. In *Proceedings of the 2018 Conference of the North American Chapter of the Association for Computational Linguistics: Human Language Technologies, Volume 1 (Long Papers)*, pages 344–354. Association for Computational Linguistics.

Martin Haspelmath. 2018. The last word on polysynthesis: A review article. 22:307–326.

Felix Hieber, Tobias Domhan, Michael Denkowski, David Vilar, Artem Sokolov, Ann Clifton, and Matt Post. 2017. Sockeye: A toolkit for neural machine translation. *CoRR*, abs/1712.05690.

Martin Jansche. 2014. Computer-aided quality assurance of an icelandic pronunciation dictionary. In *Proceedings of the Ninth International Conference on Language Resources and Evaluation (LREC'14)*, Reykjavik, Iceland. European Language Resources Association (ELRA).

Melvin Johnson, Mike Schuster, Quoc V. Le, Maxim Krikun, Yonghui Wu, Zhifeng Chen, Nikhil Thorat, Fernanda Viégas, Martin Wattenberg, Greg Corrado, Macduff Hughes, and Jeffrey Dean. 2017. Google's multilingual neural machine translation system: Enabling zero-shot translation. *Transactions of the Association for Computational Linguistics*, 5:339–351.

Alexandre Klementiev, Ann Irvine, Chris Callison-Burch, and David Yarowsky. 2012. Toward statistical machine translation without parallel corpora. In *Proceedings of the 13th Conference of the European Chapter of the Association for Computational Linguistics*, EACL '12, pages 130–140, Stroudsburg, PA, USA. Association for Computational Linguistics.

Philipp Koehn, Hieu Hoang, Alexandra Birch, Chris Callison-Burch, Marcello Federico, Nicola Bertoldi, Brooke Cowan, Wade Shen, Christine Moran, Richard Zens, Chris Dyer, Ondrej Bojar, Alexandra Constantin, and Evan Herbst. 2007. Moses: Open source toolkit for statistical machine translation. In *The Annual Conference of the Association for Computational Linguistics*.

Thomas Krause and Amir Zeldes. 2016. Annis3: A new architecture for generic corpus query and visualization. *Digital Scholarship in the Humanities*, 31(1):118–139.

Y Liang, K Iwano, and Koichi Shinoda. 2014. Simple gesture-based error correction interface for smartphone speech recognition. pages 1194–1198.

Patrick Littell, Anna Kazantseva, Roland Kuhn, Aidan Pine, Antti Arppe, Christopher Cox, and Marie-Odile Junker. 2018. Indigenous language technologies in canada: Assessment, challenges, and successes. In *Proceedings of the 27th International Conference on Computational Linguistics*, pages 2620–2632. Association for Computational Linguistics.

Philipos C. Loizou. 2013. *Speech Enhancement: Theory and Practice*, 2nd edition. CRC Press, Inc., Boca Raton, FL, USA.

Minh-Thang Luong, Eugene Brevdo, and Rui Zhao. 2017. Neural machine translation (seq2seq) tutorial. *https://github.com/tensorflow/nmt*.

Manuel Mager, Ximena Gutierrez-Vasques, Gerardo Sierra, and Ivan Meza. 2018. Challenges of language technologies for the indigenous languages of the Americas.

Gleb Mazovetskiy, Kyle Gorman, and Vitaly Nikolaev. 2018. Improving homograph disambiguation with supervised machine learning. In *LREC*.

Alexis Michaud, Oliver Adams, Trevor Anthony Cohn, Graham Neubig, and Séverine Guillaume. 2018. Integrating automatic transcription into the language documentation workflow: Experiments with Na data and the Persephone toolkit.

Robert Östling and Jörg Tiedemann. 2017. Neural machine translation for low-resource languages. *CoRR*, abs/1708.05729.

Slav Petrov, Dipanjan Das, and Ryan McDonald. 2012. A universal part-of-speech tagset. In *Proceedings of the Eight International Conference on Language Resources and Evaluation (LREC'12)*, Istanbul, Turkey. European Language Resources Association (ELRA).

Dan Povey. 2018. Open speech and language resources. http://www.openslr.org.

The Language Archive Max Planck Institute for Psycholinguistics. ELAN. https://tla.mpi.nl/tools/tla-tools/elan/.

J. Ramirez, J. M., and J. C. 2007. Voice activity detection. fundamentals and speech recognition system robustness. In *Robust Speech Recognition and Understanding*. I-Tech Education and Publishing.

Erich R. Round. 2017. The AusPhon-Lexicon project: Two million normalized segments across 300 Australian languages.

Nay San and Ellison Luk. 2018. Yinarlingi: An R package for testing Warlpiri lexicon data. https://github.com/CoEDL/yinarlingi.

SIL. Keyman: Type to the world in your language. https://keyman.com/.

Claudia Soria. 2018. Digital Language Survival Kit. http://www.dldp.eu/en/content/digital-language-survival-kit.

TEI. 2018. Guidelines for electronic text encoding and interchange. http://www.tei-c.org/P5/.

Nick Thieberger. 2016. Language documentation tools and methods summit report. https://docs.google.com/document/d/1p2EZufVIm2fOQy4aIZ100jnZjfcuG-Bb9YKiXMggDRQ.

Shubham Toshniwal, Tara N. Sainath, Ron J. Weiss, Bo Li, Pedro J. Moreno, Eugene Weinstein, and Kanishka Rao. 2018. Multilingual speech recognition with a single end-to-end model. *2018 IEEE International Conference on Acoustics, Speech and Signal Processing (ICASSP)*, pages 4904–4908.

Kristina Toutanova, Dan Klein, Christopher D. Manning, and Yoram Singer. 2003. Feature-rich part-of-speech tagging with a cyclic dependency network. In *Proceedings of the 2003 Conference of the North American Chapter of the Association for Computational Linguistics on Human Language Technology - Volume 1*, NAACL '03, pages 173–180, Stroudsburg, PA, USA. Association for Computational Linguistics.

Sami Virpioja, Peter Smit, Stig-Arne Grönroos, and Mikko Kurimo. 2013. Morfessor 2.0: Python Implementation and Extensions for Morfessor Baseline. Technical report.

Martijn Wieling and John Nerbonne. 2015. Advances in dialectometry. *Annual Review of Linguistics*, 1(1):243–264.

John Wiseman. 2016. Python interface to the WebRTC Voice Activity Detector. https://github.com/wiseman/py-webrtcvad.

OCR evaluation tools for the 21st century

Eddie Antonio Santos

Canadian Indigenous languages technology project, National Research Council Canada
Alberta Language Technology Lab, University of Alberta, Edmonton, Canada
`Eddie.Santos@nrc-cnrc.gc.ca`

Abstract

We introduce `ocreval`, a port of the ISRI OCR Evaluation Tools, now with Unicode support. We describe how we upgraded the ISRI OCR Evaluation Tools to support modern text processing tasks. `ocreval` supports producing character-level and word-level accuracy reports, supporting all characters representable in the UTF-8 character encoding scheme. In addition, we have implemented the Unicode default word boundary specification in order to support word-level accuracy reports for a broad range of writing systems. We argue that character-level and word-level accuracy reports produce confusion matrices that are useful for tasks beyond OCR evaluation—including tasks supporting the study and computational modeling of endangered languages.

1 Introduction

Optical Character Recognition (OCR) is the process of detecting text in a image, such as a scan of a page, and converting the written language into a computer-friendly text format. While OCR is well-established for majority languages (Tesseract Langdata), the same cannot be said for endangered languages (Hubert et al., 2016). When developers create OCR models for low-resources languages, they must have a tool for evaluating the accuracy of their models. This will aid in making decisions on how to model the language, and how to tweak parameters in order to accurately recognize text in that language, especially when labelled materials are scarce.

A further complication encountered when developing OCR models for endangered languages is that of orthography—a language may have *many* orthographies, or may not have a standardized orthography at all. And if any orthographies exist, they likely contain characters beyond the non-accented Latin alphabet. IPA-influenced glottal stop (ʔ) and schwa (ə) characters have a tendency to sneak into new orthographies. Historically, computer software provides poor support for characters outside the range of those characters commonly found in Western European majority language orthographies.

The ISRI OCR Evaluation Tools were last released in 1996 by the University of Nevada, Las Vegas's Information Science Research Institute (Rice and Nartker, 1996). Despite their age, the tools continue to be useful to this day for the task of evaluating new OCR models (Hubert et al., 2016). Its `accuracy` and `wordacc` tools are of particular utility. However, being somewhat dated, it has limited and awkward support for non-European orthographies. Since the tools' 1996 release, the Unicode standard has gradually improved support for non-European characters, introducing many new scripts and characters. However, the ISRI OCR Evaluation Tools have not been upgraded since.

In this paper, we present an updated version of the ISRI OCR Evaluation Tools, which we named `ocreval`. Our contributions include

- Port the ISRI OCR Evaluation Tools onto modern macOS and Ubuntu Linux systems;

- Add support for UTF-8, enabling the analysis of 1,112,064 unique characters;

- Implement the default Unicode word boundary specification to evaluate word accuracy.

We describe in more depth what we have changed and why; and we postulate how `ocreval` can be used to support **tasks unrelated to OCR** that may benefit people working in endangered language study and tool development.

Before continuing, we would be remiss not to mention OCRevalUAtion (Carrasco, 2014), an alternative to the toolkit presented in this paper.

Proceedings of the 3rd Workshop on the Use of Computational Methods in the Study of Endangered Languages: Vol. 1 Papers, pages 23–27,
Honolulu, Hawai'i, USA, February 26–27, 2019.

2 How does `ocreval` extend the ISRI OCR Evaluation Tools?

`ocreval` is a port of the ISRI OCR Evaluation Tools to modern systems. This means that much of the codebase and functionality is the same as the codebase written in 1996; however, the original code presents many incompatibilities with current systems (usage of older programming language features and reliance on out-of-date source code libraries). When we downloaded the ISRI OCR Evaluation Tools for the first time, its C programming language source code would not compile (translate source code into a usable application). After a few modifications to the source code, we were able to compile and run the ISRI OCR Evaluation Tools on our systems.

The second problem is how text was represented in the system. The ISRI OCR Evaluation Tools were written in the early days of Unicode, when Unicode was strictly a 16-bit character set. As such, the ISRI OCR Evaluation Tools can handle the first 65,536 characters defined in the Unicode standard; however, as of Unicode 11.0 (Unicode Consortium, 2018), there are 1,112,064 possible characters total.[1] Only 137,374 (12.33%) characters are defined in the Unicode standard, with the rest of the code space reserved for future use. This means that the ISRI OCR Evaluation Tools can only represent half of the characters defined in the modern day Unicode standard. Among the characters that are not representable in the ISRI OCR Evaluation Tools are characters in recently created writing systems, such as the Osage alphabet (Everson et al., 2014), as well as historical writing systems (Cuneiform, Linear B, Old Italic). Thus, `ocreval` extends the ISRI OCR Evaluation Tools by internally representing characters using the UTF-32 character encoding form, allowing for the analysis of characters from writing systems both new and old.

2.1 UTF-8 support

The most significant hurdle remaining is how Unicode characters are input and output into `ocreval`. As of October 2018, UTF-8 is the most common character encoding scheme on the web, used for 92.4% of websites (W3Techs). This is not surprising, as UTF-8 represents *all* 1,112,064 characters possible in the Unicode standard in a way that is backwards-compatible with 7-bit ASCII. The ISRI OCR Evaluation Tools predate the widespread adoption of UTF-8; as such, it assumes that any text input is encoded in ISO-8859-1 or "Latin-1" encoding. Latin-1, intended for use with Western European languages, only encodes about 192 printable characters, most of which are Latin alphabetic characters; as such, Latin-1 is usually inadequate for encoding endangered and minority languages. The ISRI OCR Evaluation Tools *does* support 16-bit Unicode (65,536 characters), however, it uses an *ad hoc* format called "Extended ASCII". The ISRI OCR Evaluation Tools bundled the `uni2asc` and `asc2uni` tools to convert to and from the Extended ASCII format and the (now outdated) 16-bit UCS-2 character encoding. Anybody wishing to use characters outside the range of Latin-1 would have to first use `uni2asc` before using their documents with any of the available tools. If their original documents were encoded in UTF-8, they would have to do two conversions: first, convert from UTF-8 to UCS-2 using a tool such as `iconv`; then, convert the UCS-2 file into Extended ASCII using `uni2asc`.

In a time when UTF-8 exists and is readily available, we find that Extended ASCII is too much of a hassle. As such, we modified the file reading and writing routines used in all utilities provided in `ocreval` to open files in the UTF-8 character encoding scheme exclusively, obviating the need to convert into an *ad hoc* format such as Extended ASCII. Since all input and output is done in UTF-8, we removed the now-redundant `asc2uni` and `uni2asc` utility programs from `ocreval`.

2.2 Unicode word segmentation

One of the ISRI OCR Evaluation Tools's most useful utilities is `wordacc`. As its name implies, `wordacc` computes the recognition accuracy for entire words, rather than for single characters alone. However, what constituted as a "word" was rather narrowly defined in the previous version. Originally, a "word" was a series of one or more consecutive characters in the range of lowercase ASCII characters (U+0061–U007A), or lowercase Latin-1 characters (U+00DF–U+00F6, U+00F8–U+00FF). Input would have to be converted to lowercase before calculating word accuracy. Any other characters were *not* considered to be part of a word, and hence, would not appear in word accu-

---

[1] There are 1,114,112 values defined in the Unicode 11.0 code space, however 2048 of these are *surrogate characters* which cannot encode a character by themselves; hence, we removed these characters from the total.

racy summaries or confusion matrices. This narrow definition of a "word" limits the usefulness of `wordacc`, even for Latin-derived scripts.

To broaden its usefulness, we changed how `ocreval` finds words in text by adopting Unicode's default word boundary specification (Unicode Standard Annex #29). This specifies a reasonable default for finding the *boundaries* between words and other words, and between words and non-word characters. Then, to find words proper, we extract character sequences between boundaries that start with a "word-like" character, such as letters, syllables, digits, and symbols that frequently appear as parts of words. We also considered *private-use characters* to be "word-like" characters so that if a language's orthography is not yet encoded or is poorly-supported in Unicode, its characters can be represented using private-use characters—which are set aside by the Unicode standard as allocated code points to represent any character the user requires.

A caveat is that this algorithm will *not* work for all writing systems. Scripts like Thai, Lao, and Khmer, which do not typically have any spaces separating words, will not be handled properly. As such, this is not a "one-size-fits-all" solution, and may need to be tailored depending on the language.

2.3 Installing `ocreval`

In all cases, the user must have a basic understanding of the command line interface of their computer. However, we have tried to document and streamline the process when possible.

`ocreval` can be installed on a modern macOS system using the Homebrew package manager:

```
$ brew tap eddieantonio/eddieantonio
$ brew install ocreval
```

On Ubuntu Linux, the tools can be installed from its source code. After downloading the zip archive,[2] install all system dependencies and extract the contents of the source code archive. Within the newly created directory, issue the `make` command from the command line:

```
$ sudo apt update
$ sudo apt install build-essential \
    libutf8proc-dev unzip
$ unzip ocreval-master.zip
$ cd ocreval-master/
$ make
$ sudo make install
```

____

[2] `https://github.com/eddieantonio/ocreval/archive/master.zip`

`ocreval` can also be installed on Windows 10 within the Ubuntu app, obtainable in the Microsoft app store. Copy the downloaded zip archive into the Ubuntu subsystem, then follow the same steps as the Ubuntu Linux install.

2.4 The importance of open source

Software is **open source** when its source code is publicly-accessible, under a license that permits anyone to make modifications and share the modifications with others. We have released `ocreval` as open source for many reasons: it maximizes the amount of people that can benefit from the tool by making it freely-accessible; hosting the software on the collaborative coding platform GitHub allows for people around the world to share enhancements to `ocreval` for everybody's benefit; and the ISRI OCR Evaluation Tools were originally released as open source.

`ocreval` is maintained on GitHub at `https://github.com/eddieantonio/ocreval`. On GitHub, changes to the source code are transparent and publicly-visible. Contributions are welcome in the form of **issue reports** and **pull requests**. Issue reports alert us to any bugs or inadequacies found in the currently published version of the software; pull requests allow volunteers to write suggested source code enhancements to share with the rest of the community. Creating an issue report or a pull request both require a GitHub account. We welcome anyone who wants to contribute to join in; no contribution is too small!

The ISRI OCR Evaluation Tools were released under an open source licence. The significance of this cannot be overstated. If the original source code was not available on (the now defunct) Google Code repository, this paper would not have been possible. As such, our contributions are also released under an open source license, in the hopes that it may also be useful in 20 years time.

3 How can `ocreval` help endangered languages?

Hubert et al. (2016) have already used `ocreval` to evaluate the accuracy of OCR models for Northern Haida, a critically-endangered language spoken in Western Canada. Unicode support was integral to representing and evaluating the idiosyncratic orthography specific to the corpus in question (which differs from modern-day Haida orthographies).

Previously, we mentioned that among the ISRI

OCR Evaluation Tools' most useful utilities are `accuracy` and `wordacc`. We see these utilities in `ocreval` to be much more general-purpose tools, not only limited to the evaluation of OCR output. Fundamentally, these tools compare two text files, producing a report of which character sequences are misclassified or "confused" for other character sequences. This concept is useful beyond the evaluation of OCR models.

One possible non-OCR application could be to study language change. Parallel texts—whether it be prose, or a word list—could be fed into `accuracy`. One part of the input pair would be representative of language spoken or written in the modern day, and the other part of the input would be a historical example, reconstructed text, or text from a distinct dialect. `accuracy` will then produce minimal "confusions", or sequences of commonly misclassified sequences. Since `accuracy` prints statistics for how often a confusion is found, `accuracy` inadvertently becomes a tool for reporting systematic changes, along with how often the effect is attested. Preliminary work by Arppe et al. (2018) used `ocreval` to compare Proto-Algonquian to contemporary Plains Cree. Using an extensive database with over ten thousand pairings of morphologically simple and complex word stems—mapping each modern Cree word form with the corresponding reconstructed Proto-Algonquian form—they found that the contents of the confusion matrix matched quite closely with the posited historical sound change rules. In addition, the confusion matrix can be used to quantify how often a particular rule applies in the overall Cree vocabulary. The benefit of `ocreval`'s added Unicode support facilitates this use case, as sound change rules are hardly ever representable in only Latin-1 characters.

Lastly, throughout this paper we have made the assumption that corpora are encoded in UTF-8—thus, using `ocreval` should be straightforward. However, this is not always the case for minority language resources, even if they are encoded digitally. One way minority language texts may have been encoded is by "font-encoding" or "font-hacking". This is a specially-designed font *overrides* the display of existing code points, as opposed to using existing Unicode code points assigned for that particular orthography. This may be because the font was defined for pre-Unicode systems, or because Unicode lacked appropriate char-

acter assignments at the development of said font. For example, in place of the ordinary character for "©", the font will render "ğ", and in place of "¬", the font will render "í". For these cases, `ocreval` alone is insufficient; an external tool must be used such as `convertextract` (Pine and Turin, 2018).

4   Conclusion

We presented `ocreval`, an updated version of the ISRI OCR Evaluation Tools. `ocreval` provides a suite of tools for evaluating the accuracy of optical character recognition (OCR) models—however, we postulate that the evaluation tools can be generalized to support other tasks. Our contributions include porting the old codebase such that it works on modern systems; adding support for the ubiquitous UTF-8 character encoding scheme, as well internally representing characters using the full Unicode code space; and the implementation of the default Unicode word boundary specification, which facilitates finding words in a variety of non-Latin texts. We released `ocreval` online as open-source software, with the intent to make our work freely-accessible, as well as to encourage contributions from the language technology community at large.

Acknowledgments

The author wishes to thank Isabell Hubert for involving us in this project; the author is grateful to Antti Arppe, Anna Kazantseva, and Jessica Santos for reviewing early drafts of this paper.

References

Antti Arppe, Katherine Schmirler, Eddie Antonio Santos, and Arok Wolvengrey. 2018.   Towards a systematic and quantitative identification of historical sound change rules — Algonquian historical linguistics meets optical character recognition evaluation.   Working paper presented in Alberta Language Technology Lab seminar, November 19, 2018. `http://altlab.artsrn.ualberta.ca/wp-content/uploads/2019/01/OCR_and_proto-Algonquian_nonanon.pdf`.

Rafael C Carrasco. 2014. An open-source OCR evaluation tool. In *Proceedings of the First International Conference on Digital Access to Textual Cultural Heritage*, pages 179–184. ACM. `https://github.com/impactcentre/ocrevalUAtion`.

Michael Everson, Herman Mongrain Lookout, and Cameron Pratt. 2014. Final proposal to encode the

Osage script in the UCS. Technical report, ISO/IEC JTC1/SC2/WG2. Document N4619.

Homebrew. 2009. Homebrew: The missing package manager for macOS. `https://brew.sh/`. (Accessed on 10/22/2018).

Isabell Hubert, Antti Arppe, Jordan Lachler, and Eddie Antonio Santos. 2016. Training & quality assessment of an optical character recognition model for Northern Haida. In *LREC*.

Aidan Pine and Mark Turin. 2018. Seeing the Heiltsuk orthography from font encoding through to Unicode: A case study using convertextract. *Sustaining Knowledge Diversity in the Digital Age*, page 27.

Stephen V Rice and Thomas A Nartker. 1996. The ISRI analytic tools for OCR evaluation. *UNLV/Information Science Research Institute, TR-96-02*.

Tesseract Langdata. 2018. tesseract-ocr/langdata: Source training data for Tesseract for lots of languages. `https://github.com/tesseract-ocr/langdata`. (Accessed on 10/22/2018).

The Unicode Consortium, editor. 2018. *The Unicode Standard, Version 11.0.0*. The Unicode Consortium, Mountain View, CA.

Unicode Standard Annex #29. 2018. Unicode text segmentation. Edited by Mark Davis. An integral part of The Unicode Standard. `http://unicode.org/reports/tr29/`. (Accessed on 10/22/2018).

W3Techs. 2018. Usage statistics of character encodings for websites, october 2018. `https://w3techs.com/technologies/overview/character_encoding/all`. (Accessed on 10/22/2018).

Handling cross-cutting properties in automatic inference of lexical classes: A case study of Chintang

Olga Zamaraeva[*]
University of Washington
Department of Linguistics
olzama@uw.edu

Kristen Howell[*]
University of Washington
Department of Linguistics
kphowell@uw.edu

Emily M. Bender
University of Washington
Department of Linguistics
ebender@uw.edu

Abstract

In the context of the ongoing AGGREGA-TION project concerned with inferring grammars from interlinear glossed text, we explore the integration of morphological patterns extracted from IGT data with inferred syntactic properties in the context of creating implemented linguistic grammars. We present a case study of Chintang, in which we put emphasis on evaluating the accuracy of these predictions by using them to generate a grammar and parse running text. Our coverage over the corpus is low because the lexicon produced by our system only includes intransitive and transitive verbs and nouns, but it outperforms an expert-built, oracle grammar of similar scope.

1 Introduction

Machine-readable grammars are useful for linguistic hypothesis testing via parsing and treebanking (selecting the best parse for each sentence) because they represent internally coherent models and can be explored automatically (Bender et al., 2011, 2012a; Fokkens, 2014; Müller, 1999, 2016). Multilingual grammar engineering frameworks such as CoreGram (Müller, 2015) and the LinGO Grammar Matrix (Bender et al., 2002, 2010) facilitate the development of machine-readable grammars by providing shared analyses, but still require significant human effort to select the appropriate analyses for a given language. To partially automate this process, the AGGREGA-TION project takes advantage of the stored analyses in the Grammar Matrix and the linguistic information encoded in Interlinear Glossed Text (IGT). While at this stage the project efforts are mostly experimental in nature and focus on evaluating grammars obtained in this way, there already have been successful collaborations with documentary linguists which in at least one case led

to insights into the language's morphological patterns (Zamaraeva et al., 2017).

The IGT data format, widely used by linguists, is well suited to inference tasks because it features detailed morpheme-by-morpheme annotation and translations to high-resource languages (Xia and Lewis, 2007; Bender et al., 2013). However, the inference processes required are heterogeneous. On the morphological side, an inference system identifies position and inflectional classes. On the syntactic side, an inference system uses syntactic generalizations to identify broad characteristics and defines lexical classes according to syntactic properties. The challenge we address here is in integrating the two. In this paper, we integrate a system that identifies morphological patterns in IGT data with one that predicts syntactic properties to define lexical classes that encode both morphological and syntactic features. We evaluate by replicating the case study of Bender et al. (2014), in which they automatically produced separate grammar fragments based on morphotactic and syntactic information and evaluated their system on a corpus of Chintang. We compare their results to our integrated system which includes both morphotactic and syntactic properties.[1]

2 Chintang

Chintang (ISO639-3: ctn) is a Sino-Tibetan language spoken by ∼5000 people in Nepal (Bickel et al., 2010; Schikowski et al., 2015). Here we summarize the characteristics of the language that are directly relevant to this case study.

The relative order of the verb and its core arguments (hereafter 'word order') in Chintang is described as free by Schikowski et al. (2015), in that all verb and argument permutations are valid

---

[*]The first two authors made equal contribution.

[1]Our code and sample data are available here: https://git.ling.washington.edu/agg/repro/compute13-ctn.

Proceedings of the 3rd Workshop on the Use of Computational Methods in the Study of Endangered Languages: Vol. 1 Papers, pages 28–38,
Honolulu, Hawai'i, USA, February 26–27, 2019.

Tool	Task
SIL Toolbox	Export original IGT data to plain text
Xigt	Convert data into a robust data model with associated processing package
INTENT	Enrich the data: add phrase structure, POS tags to translation line and project to source language line
Inference code	**Create grammar specification: Case system, case frames of verbs**
MOM	**Create grammar specification: Inflection and position classes**
Grammar Matrix	Create grammar on the basis of specifications
LKB	Run the grammar on held-out sentences
[incr tsdb()]	Treebank: Inspect the parses for correctness

Table 1: AGGREGATION pipeline, **bold** indicates this paper's contribution

in the language, with the felicity of these combinations being governed primarily by information structure. Although Schikowski et al. (2015) note that no detailed analysis has been carried out regarding what other factors condition word order, they say that SV, APV and AGTV are the most frequent orders that they observe.[2] Dropping of core arguments is also common in the language (Schikowski et al., 2015).

The case system follows an ergative-absolutive pattern, with some exceptions (Stoll and Bickel, 2012; Schikowski et al., 2015). In ergative-absolutive languages, the subject of an intransitive verb has the same case marking as the most patient-like argument of a transitive verb, typically referred to as absolutive. The most agent-like argument of a transitive verb has a distinct case marking, usually called ergative. In Chintang, ergative case is marked with an overt marker while absolutive is zero-marked. A number of exceptions to the ergative-absolutive pattern arise due to valence changing operations (such as reflexive and benefactive). Other exceptions include variable ergative marking on first and second person pronouns and an overt absolutive marker on the pronoun *sa-* 'who'.[3]

Chintang's flexible word order, scarcity of overt case marking, and frequent argument dropping introduce challenges to grammar inference. First, the variety of phrase structure rules required to accommodate free word order in addition to argument optionally introduces potential for ambiguity to any implemented grammar. In some cases, this ambiguity is legitimate (in that multiple parses map to multiple semantic readings), but in other cases it may be an indication of under-

constrained rules. Second, the lack of overt absolutive case marking in Chintang, together with common pronoun dropping, results in relatively few overt case morphemes in the corpus for a syntactic inference script to use.

3 AGGREGATION

The AGGREGATION project[4] is dedicated to automating the creation of grammars from IGT.[5] Table 1 presents all the tools involved in the pipeline, with information on which task each performs. We elaborate on the pieces of the pipeline below and encourage the reader to refer back to this table as needed to track what each component is.

As part of the AGGREGATION project, Bender et al. (2014) present the first end-to-end study of grammar inference from IGT by extracting broad syntactic properties (namely, word order, case system and case frame) and morphological patterns and testing the coverage of the resulting grammars on held out data. They used the methodology of Bender et al. (2013) for syntactic inference and Wax (2014) for morphological inference. However, they left integrating the two and creating grammars which benefit from both types of information to future work.

Like Bender et al. (2014), we take advantage of the Grammar Matrix customization system (Bender et al., 2002, 2010), which creates precision grammars that emphasize syntactically accurate coverage and attempt to minimize ambiguity. It uses stored analysis for particular phenomena to

---

[2]S = subject, P = patient, G = goal, T = theme, A = agent

[3]For a much more detailed account of the case frame for various verb types, see Schikowski et al. 2015.

[4]http://depts.washington.edu/uwcl/aggregation/

[5]We are aware of one project with similar goals: Type-Gram (see e.g. Hellan and Beermann, 2014), couched in HPSG as well. Our pipeline places fewer expectations on the IGT annotation, inferring phrase structure, part of speech, and valence automatically.

create a grammar based on a user's specification of linguistic properties. These specifications are recorded in a 'choices file'. We follow the methodology of Bender et al. (2014) of formatting the output of our inference systems as a choices file, so that it can be directly input to the Grammar Matrix for grammar customization.

Unlike Bender et al. (2014), we take advantage of the Xigt data model (Goodman et al., 2015). This extensible and flexible format encodes the information in IGT data in such a way that relations between bits of information, such as the connection between a morpheme and its gloss, can be easily identified. Data encoded with Xigt is compatible with the INTENT system for enriching IGT by parsing the English translation and projecting that information onto the source language text (Georgi, 2016). Where Bender et al. (2014) use the methodology of Xia and Lewis (2007), in this work we use INTENT. We also use updated, Xigt-compatible versions of morphological and lexical class inference (Zamaraeva, 2016; Zamaraeva et al., 2017) and case system inference (Howell et al., 2017).

4 Methodology

Our goal is to maximize the information that we can learn about a language both morphologically and syntactically in order to produce grammars that parse strings with minimal ambiguity. We present a methodology that analyzes morphological and syntactic information independently and then creates lexical classes that share the information from both analyses.

4.1 Morphotactic inference with MOM

MOM is a system which infers morphotactic graphs from IGT. Developed originally by Wax (2014) to infer position classes, it was updated to work with the Xigt data model by Zamaraeva (2016) and to infer inflectional classes by Zamaraeva et al. (2017). Below we summarize the main inference algorithm shared across these different versions. As with most work using MOM and the Grammar Matrix, we target the morpheme-segmented line, and assume that the grammars produced will eventually need to be paired with a morphophonological analyzer to map to surface spelling or pronunciation.

MOM starts by reading in IGT that has been enriched with information about each morpheme,

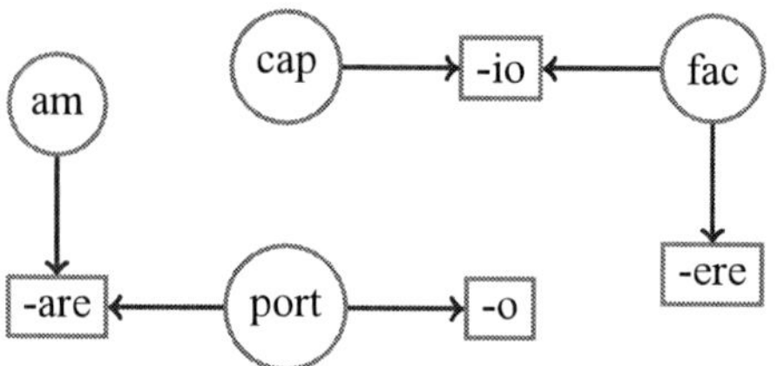

Figure 1: Sample graph MOM will initially build on the example training data consisting of Latin verbs *am-are* ('to love'), *port-are* ('to carry'), *port-o* ('I carry'), *cap-io* ('I take'), *fac-io* ('I do'), and *fac-ere* ('to do').

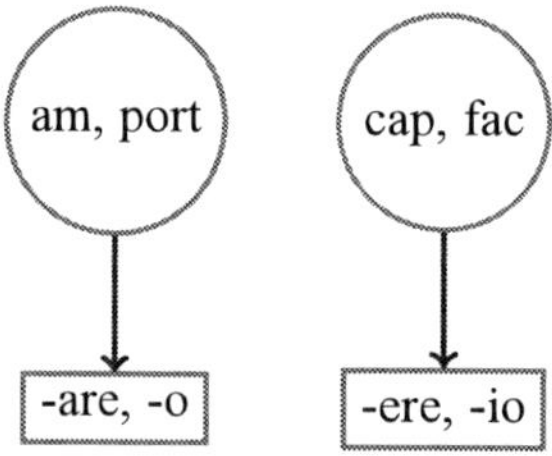

Figure 2: Sample MOM output, after compressing the graph in Figure 1 with a 50% overlap value.

including a part of speech (POS) tag of the word it belongs to as well as whether it is an affix or a stem. Then MOM iterates over the items with the relevant POS tag and builds a graph where nodes are stems and affixes while edges are input relationships. For example, if MOM sees the Latin verbs *am-are* ('to love'), *port-are* ('to carry'), *port-o* ('I carry'), *cap-io* ('I take'), *fac-io* ('I do'), and *fac-ere* ('to do') in the training data, it will create nodes and edges as depicted in Figure 1. Finally, after the original graph has been constructed, MOM will recursively merge nodes which have edge overlap above the threshold provided by the user (e.g. 50%, see Figure 2), in order to discover position classes for affixes and inflectional classes for stems.

4.2 Case and Valence Inference

Whereas MOM creates lexical classes based on morphotactics, the inference system described in this section creates lexical classes for verbs based on their valence in two steps: We first infer the overall case system of the language and second infer whether each verb in the training data is transitive or intransitive. We then create lexical classes that specify the argument structure and case requirements on those arguments.

We begin by predicting the overall case system, using the methodology developed by Bender et al. (2013) and updated by Howell et al. (2017). We reimplement Bender et al.'s GRAM method, which counts the case grams in the corpus and uses a heuristic to assign nominative-accusative, ergative-absolute, split-ergative or none to the language based on the relative frequencies of the case grams. We apply one change to this system: because the split-ergative prediction does not give any information regarding the nature of the split (e.g. whether it is split according to features of nouns or verbs), we map the split-ergative (which it predicts for Chintang) to ergative-absolutive.

To determine the transitivity of verbs in the corpus, we take advantage of the English translation in the IGT. The dataset, which has been partially enriched by INTENT (Georgi, 2016),[6] includes parse trees and POS tags for the English translation. Furthermore, the Chintang words in the dataset are annotated for part of speech by the authors of the corpus. To infer transitivity using this information, we first do a string comparison between the gloss of the Chintang verb and each word in the language line to identify the English verb that it corresponds to. If no match is found, for example the verb is glossed with *have*, but the English translation contains *get* instead, the verb is skipped. However, if a match is found, we traverse the English parse tree to check if the V is sister to an NP. If so, it is classified as transitive, otherwise it is classified as intransitive. We exclude passive sentences from consideration; however, under this algorithm, verbs that take a verbal complement are classified as intransitive. We leave further fine-tuning in this respect to future work. Finally, once we have the case system and the transitivity for each verb, we assign the verb's case frame according to a heuristic specific to the case system. In the case of ergative-absolutive, we specify ergative case on the subject of transitive verbs and absolutive on the subject of intransitive verbs and object of transitive verbs.

4.3 Extensions to Morphological Analysis

We modified the MOM system by extending the data structure that it expects as input with fields for transitivity and case frame and by making it check these fields every time it considers which lexical class to assign to an item (we describe this process in more detail in §4.4).

We added functionality so that MOM infers case lexical rules for nouns. Next, we added functions to collapse all homonym stems in each class into one stem with a disjunctive predication (e.g. stem *bekti*, predication *_youngest.son-or-youngest.male.sibling_n_rel*).[7] Furthermore, we improved the way MOM is dealing with stems that occur bare in the data. Previously, MOM put all bare stems into a lexical class which could not merge with inflecting classes later, even if the same stem occurred with affixes in other portions of the data. Our fixing this problem led to fewer lexical classes in the grammar, which means better coverage potential. Finally, we made necessary additions to MOM's output format so that all relevant information for each lexical class, including case features and transitivity values, would be encoded into a valid choices file that can be customized by the Grammar Matrix.

4.4 Integrating Inference Systems

We integrated the systems described in §4.2 and §4.3 such that lexical types are defined according to the output of both systems. We expect our grammars produced in this fashion to outperform either of the kinds of grammars produced by Bender et al. (2014), because our integrated verb classes contain both morphological and valence constraints, rather than leaving one of these categories underspecified.

We run the syntactic inference system before MOM, so that transitivity and case frame are included in MOM's input. While MOM builds lexical classes based on morphology, it also checks transitivity and case frame for compatibility before adding an item to a lexical class. Verbs for which there is no case frame prediction are classified in a 'dummy' category, rather than being thrown out in order to maximize the morphological patterns that can be detected by MOM. That is, we want to include these verbs in the graph during the morphological inference process.[8] However, without constraints on their valence, their inclusion in the final grammar would result in spurious ambiguity. Therefore, we allow these verbs in the grammar, but change their orthography to contain

---

[6]For this particular dataset, INTENT was not able to produce bilingual alignments. This means that we were not able to take advantage of word to word mappings.

[7]This follows the conventions of Minimal Recursion Semantics, see Copestake et al. 2005 and Flickinger et al. 2014.

[8]As will be mentioned in §5.2.4, we also allow MOM to merge together verbs with no valence information into lexical classes with valence constraints, based on morphological patterns.

Grammar spec	Origin	description
ORACLE	Bender et al. 2012b	Expert-constructed
BASELINE	Bender et al. 2014	Full-form lexicon, free word order (WO), no case
MOM-DEFAULT-NONE	Bender et al. 2014	MOM-inferred lexicon, free WO, no case
FF-AUTO-GRAM	Bender et al. 2014	Full-form lexicon, V-final WO, erg-abs case system
INTEGRATED	This paper	MOM-inferred lexicon, case frames, free WO, erg-abs

Table 2: Grammars used in evaluation

a non-Chintang string, so that they are effectively excluded from the working grammar unless they were merged into a verb class with valid valence constraints.

5 Case Study

So far we have described a methodology that extracts both syntactic and morphological information from IGT data, and outputs this information in a format compatible with the Grammar Matrix customization system. Now we present a case study of this system on a Chintang dataset, described in §5.1. We describe our comparison grammars as well as the output of our system (§5.2) and grammar development and parsing process (§5.3) before presenting the results in §6 and the discussion in §7.

5.1 Dataset

For our experiment, we use the same subset of the Chintang Language Resource Program (CLRP)[9] corpus as Bender et al. (2014), which contains 10862 instances of Interlinnear Glossed Text. These IGT comprise narratives and other recorded speech that were transcribed, translated and glossed by the CLRP. Example (1) illustrates the thorough glossing of IGT in this corpus. However, it is noteworthy, especially for the purposes of inference, that syntactic characteristics that do not correspond with an overt morpheme (such as SG and ABS) are not glossed in this data. We use the same train (8863 IGT), dev (1069 IGT) and test (930 IGT) splits as Bender et al. (2014).

(1) unisaŋa   khatte
    u-nisa-ŋa   khatt-e
    3sPOSS-younger.brother-ERG.A take-IND.PST
    mo   kosiʔ   moba
    mo   kosi-iʔ   mo-pe
    DEM.DOWN river-LOC DEM.DOWN-LOC

    'The younger brother took it to the river.' [ctn]
    (Bickel et al., 2013)

---

[9]https://www.uzh.ch/clrp/

```
section=word-order
word-order=free
has-dets=no
...
section=case
case-marking=erg-abs
erg-abs-erg-case-name=erg
erg-abs-abs-case-name=abs
  case1_name=loc
  case2_name=dat...
...
verb1029_valence=intrans
verb1029_stem2_pred=_cry_v_rel
verb1029_stem2_orth=ratt
...
verb-pc6_inputs=verb-pc1, verb1029
verb-pc6_lrt1_lri1_orth=-a
verb-pc6_lrt1_lri1_inflecting=yes
```

Figure 3: Excerpts from a choices file

We use a version of the training portion of the data that has been converted to the Xigt data model. The converter skipped 169 IGT, resulting in a slightly smaller training set than that used by Bender et al. (2014). This dataset was enriched with English parses and part of speech tags using INTENT (Georgi, 2016).

5.2 Grammar Specification

The output of the morphotactic and syntactic inference scripts described earlier in this section is encoded in a 'choices file', illustrated in Figure 3, which is the suitable input to the Grammar Matrix customization system (Bender et al., 2010). In this subsection, we describe the choices files we developed for the baseline, oracle and our inference system, as well as the comparison choices from the 2014 experiment.[10]

5.2.1 Oracle Choices File

Our first point of comparison is a manually constructed 'oracle' choices file, from Bender et al.

---

[10]For this comparison, we regenerated the BASELINE and the ORACLE grammars from their choices files. For MOM-DEFAULT-NONE and FF-AUTO-GRAM we worked from the same parsing results analyzed in Bender et al. 2014.

2012b. This choices file was developed by importing CLRP's Toolbox lexicon and defining the rest of the specifications by hand, based on linguistic analysis. As a result, the grammar produced by this choices file is expected to have very high precision, with moderate recall. It specifies the word order as verb-final (corresponding to the most frequent word orders observed by Schikowski et al. (2015)) and the case system as ergative-absolutive, and it defines both subject and object dropping as possible for all verbs. It also includes hand-specified lexical rules based on the analysis in Schikowski 2012.

Because the Grammar Matrix only included simple transitive and intransitive verbs at the time this choices file was developed, only those two classes were defined. Their case frames were specified by hand such that the intransitive verb class has an absolutive subject and the transitive verb class has an ergative subject and an absolutive object. Finally, because the Grammar Matrix did not support adjectives, adverbs, and many other lexical categories, the resulting grammar is not expected to parse any sentence containing those lexical categories. Conveniently, the limitations of the grammar defined by Bender et al. (2012b) make it a good comparison to the grammar we are able to produce using only the inference described in this paper.[11]

5.2.2 Baseline Choices File

As a second point of comparison, we use a choices file that is designed to create a working grammar with a sufficient lexicon that is otherwise naïve with respect to the particular grammatical characteristics of Chintang. We take this choices file from Bender et al. (2014), but make some modifications. The lexicon was extracted according to the methodology of Xia and Lewis (2007), defining bare bones classes for nouns, verbs and determiners. Because the inference system we use in the this paper does not consider determiners, we removed them from the baseline choices file. Finally, the baseline predicts free word order, no case system and argument dropping for subjects and objects of all verbs because these choices are expected to result in the highest coverage (though low precision) for any language.[12]

5.2.3 Bender et al. (2014) choices files

Our final comparison is to the results for the choices files created by Bender et al. (2014) that are most comparable to our present work. We look at their MOM-DEFAULT-NONE and FF-AUTO-GRAM grammars which represent the two types of inference that we have integrated.

The MOM-DEFAULT-NONE choices file uses a lexicon produced by MOM and the default choices for word order (free), case system (none), and argument optionality (all arguments are optional). The FF-AUTO-GRAM uses a lexicon of full word forms, as in the baseline but with case frames for each verb as observed in the data. The word order (V-final) and case system (ergative-absolutive) were inferred using syntactic inference.

5.2.4 Integrated Inference Output

We produced the inferred choices file by extracting the lexicon, case system and morphological rules, as described in §4.1, §4.2 and §4.3. We ran the inference system on training data, debugging and selecting an overlap value by parsing the dev data with the resulting grammars. Our system predicted ergative-absolutive case and a robust lexicon and set of morphological rules. We used the default word order (free) and default argument optionality choices (any verb can drop subject or object) from Bender et al. 2014. We also added the necessary choices for the 'dummy verb' category described in §4.3.

Choosing the overlap value We ran MOM with 10 overlap values from 0.1 to 1.0. Then we parsed sentences from the development set to identify the grammar that optimizes both coverage and ambiguity. For these data, that showed the optimum overlap value to be 0.2.[13] We inspected the differences in coverage and verified that they fall into three categories. First, some lexical entries which originally lacked a valence frame (the inference script was not able to assign one) successfully merged into lexical classes which did have a valid valence frame.[14] Second, some entries happened to merge into only an intransitive class in one grammar but only into a transitive class in another. Finally, upon merging into lexical classes,

---

[11]We do still have to add some default choices to our inferred grammar, as described in §5.2.4.

[12]It is incidental that these word order and argument dropping predictions are arguably valid analyses for this language.

[13]The 0.1 grammar had marginally lower ambiguity (2.76 fewer parses on average), but it parsed two fewer sentences.

[14]We assume that if a verb without a known valence frame has similar morphotactic possibilities as a verb with a known valence frame, it has the same valence frame.

lexical entries gained access to morphological patterns which were unseen in the training data. This happens with both noun and verb lexical entries. For example, not all grammars that we produced were able to successfully produce a parse tree for (2), because they did not merge the stem *sil* with a class that is compatible with the prefix *u-*.

(2) u-   sil   -u -set   -kV
     3SA- bite.and.pull.out -3P -DESTR.TR -3P
     -ce
     -IND.NPST -3NSP
     'They snatch and kill them' [ctn] (Bickel et al., 2013)

5.3   Grammar customization and parsing

After producing the choices files, we used the Grammar Matrix customization system[15] to produce customized grammars. We loaded these into the LKB parsing software (Copestake, 2002) and used [incr tsdb()] (Flickinger and Oepen, 1998) to create stored profiles of syntactic and semantic parses. We treebanked these parses using [incr tsdb()] to identify correct parses, or parses that produce the desired semantic representation for the sentence. In particular, we checked to make sure that the predicate-argument structure matched what was indicated in the gloss, but did not require information such as negation, person and number or tense and aspect (all morphologically marked in Chintang), as our system doesn't yet attempt to extract these.

6   Results

To put the results of parsing the strings from Chintang in context, we first describe the produced grammars in terms of their size. Table 3 reports the size of the lexicons and the number of affixes of each grammar. The ORACLE grammar's lexicon includes the imported Toolbox lexicon from CLRP, so it includes many more stems than the others. The BASELINE and FF-AUTO-GRAM lexicons include full form lexical entries,[16] while the grammar produced by our INTEGRATED system has lexicons that include stems extracted from the training data. MOM-DEFAULT-NONE only did morphological analysis on verbs; for nouns it includes full-form entries. The ORACLE grammar has a number of morphological rules for nouns and verbs that were hand-crafted, while MOM-DEFAULT-NONE and INTEGRATED's lexical rules were extracted from the training data.

The results are reported in Table 4. 'Lexical coverage' is the number of sentences for which the grammar could produce an analysis (via full form lexical entry or morphological rules) for every word form. These numbers are quite small because there are no lexical entries for categories other than nouns and verbs. 'Parsed' shows the number of sentences in test data that received some spanning syntactic analysis, and 'correct' the number of items for which there was a correct parse, according to manual inspection and treebanking. Finally we report the number of readings, which shows the degree of ambiguity in the grammar. Our INTEGRATED system had the highest coverage as well as the highest correct coverage, but also had the most ambiguity.

7   Discussion

We expect INTEGRATED to have broader coverage than FF-AUTO-GRAM and BASELINE because it includes morphological rules allowing it to generalize to unseen entries. We also expect INTEGRATED to have higher precision (a higher proportion of correct parses) than MOM-DEFAULT-NONE because unlike MOM-DEFAULT-NONE, it integrates case frames which can rule out spurious analyses. We also expect it to have higher coverage than MOM-DEFAULT-NONE because it includes inferred morphological rules for nouns (in addition to verbs). Though the absolute numbers are small, these predictions are borne out by the data in Table 4.

To get a better sense of the differences between the systems, we performed an error analysis. We looked at all the parsed items (not just the treebanked ones) to get a broader view into the behavior of the grammars. This section provides the results of our analysis as well as some exploration into the higher ambiguity found by INTEGRATED.

7.1   Error Analysis

As expected (and as with the other grammars), the parsing errors for INTEGRATED are due to either lexical or syntactic failures. For 825 items, the parser did not succeed in **lexical analysis**. In principle, this includes both lack of stem or affix forms and failures due to the grammar's inability to construct the morphological pattern, even though all morphemes are found in the grammar. We examined a

---

[15] svn://lemur.ling.washington.edu/shared/matrix/trunk at revision 41969

[16] Note that the FF-AUTO-GRAM grammar only included verbs for which a case frame could be predicted.

Choices file	# verb entries	# noun entries	# verb affixes	# noun affixes
ORACLE	899	4750	233	36
BASELINE	3005	1719	0	0
FF-AUTO-GRAM	739	1724	0	0
MOM-DEFAULT-NONE	1177	1719	262	0
INTEGRATED	911	1755	220	76

Table 3: Amount of lexical information in each choices file

choices file	lexical coverage (%)	parsed (%)	correct (%)	readings
ORACLE	116 (12.5)	20 (2.2)	10 (1.1)	1.35
BASELINE [*]	38 (0.4)	15 (1.6)	8 (0.9)	27.67
FF-AUTO-GRAM	18 (1.9)	4 (0.4)	2 (0.2)	5.00
MOM-DEFAULT-NONE	39 (4.2)	16 (1.7)	3 (0.3)	10.81
INTEGRATED	105 (11.3)	32 (3.4)	15 (1.6)	91.56

[*] We report slightly different results for lexical coverage and average readings for the baseline than Bender et al. (2014) because we removed determiners from the choices file.

Table 4: Results on 930 held-out sentences

sample of 50 such items and only found instances of missing stems and affixes, and no failed combinatorics. The remaining 73 errors are accounted for on the **syntactic level**. These break into three categories: (1) both a V/VP and an NP could be formed, but the NP had a case marker incompatible with the verb's case frame (e.g. locative; 6 items of this kind total);[17] (2) a sentence did not contain a word which could be analyzed as a verb by the grammar (only as a noun, e.g. a sentence fragment; 23 total); (3) finally, the sentence was complex, i.e., contained more than one verb. This third category was the most common (44 total), as the grammar does not include subordination or coordination rules.

We also compared our results on the held-out data to the baseline and the oracle grammars. While INTEGRATED outperforms both BASELINE and ORACLE, BASELINE and ORACLE parse some sentences that INTEGRATED does not.

Integrated vs. oracle   Comparison between ORACLE and INTEGRATED yields 130 different results. Of these, most are due to differences in lexical analysis. In particular, there are 55 items which fail due to lexical analysis in INTEGRATED but fail due to syntactic analysis in ORACLE. In all of these cases, our grammar lacked a lexical entry that the oracle grammar had; this is expected as the oracle lexicon is based on a different source. There are 38 items for which ORACLE cannot provide lexical

analysis and INTEGRATED can but fails at the syntactic stage. Of these, most are missing stems and affixes in the oracle grammar but for one item, ORACLE is actually lacking the required affix ordering that INTEGRATED picks up from the training data. In addition, there are 11 cases where ORACLE fails at lexical analysis and INTEGRATED succeeds at both lexical and syntactic analysis. In two of those eleven cases, INTEGRATED outperforms ORACLE due to the robustness of the morphological rules, not the lexicon. In contrast, there are 3 items at which INTEGRATED fails lexically and ORACLE gives a parse, all due to lexicon differences. In 6 cases, ORACLE fails at the syntactic stage where INTEGRATED succeeds. Of these, 1 was rejected in treebanking,[18] two items are true wins due to morphotactic inference for nouns; two are because ORACLE only has a noun entry for something which INTEGRATED picked up as a verb, and finally one is parsed by INTEGRATED because it admits head-initial word orders while ORACLE insists on V-final. In contrast, ORACLE can parse one item for which INTEGRATED can perform lexical analysis but fails to parse. The sentence is *cor cor* and ORACLE has both a verb and a noun entry for the word *cor* while INTEGRATED does not.

Integrated vs. Baseline   The difference between INTEGRATED and BASELINE is mainly due to lexical coverage. The BASELINE grammar featuring

---

[17]What is missing here is a grammar rule that handles e.g. locative NPs functioning as modifiers.

[18]If none of the parses have a structure and a semantic representation that are meaningful with respect to the translation, all parses for the item are rejected.

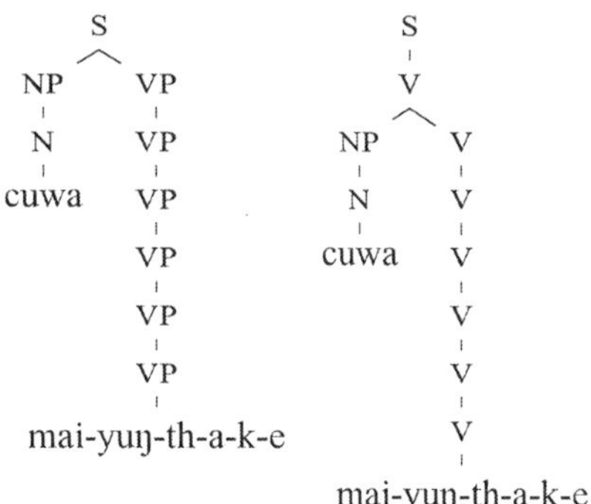

Figure 4: Analyses like the one above (for (3)) use homonymous intransitive (left) and transitive verb entry with a dropped argument (right). Together with the homonymous verb position classes, this produces ambiguity.

full-form lexical entries can lexically analyze 6 items that INTEGRATED cannot, while INTEGRATED analyzes 22 items that BASELINE cannot. Neither wins at syntactic analysis.[19]

7.2 Ambiguity

INTEGRATED produces noticeably more trees per sentence than either the oracle grammar or the baseline grammar, on average (see 'readings' column in Table 4). The baseline's low ambiguity is not striking, because it only parses a few syntactically and morphologically simple sentences. Still, on some items the baseline grammar produces hundreds of trees. The oracle grammar clearly has less ambiguity. The main reason for more ambiguity in INTEGRATED is simple combinatorics. We infer noun and verb inflectional and position classes, and often end up with homophonous affixes as well as homophonous transitive and intransitive entries for verbs. For example, the verb *yuŋ*, meaning 'sit', 'be' or 'squat', is associated with both a transitive and an intransitive entry in INTEGRATED. Figure 4 illustrates two of the trees that this grammar finds for (3).

(3) cuwa mai-yuŋ-th-a-k-e
     water NEG-be.there-NEG-PST-IPFV-IND.PST
     'Was there water?'

These homophonous lexical resources combine with the argument optionality rules, word order

flexibility and the actual complexity of Chintang morphotactics to create a large search space for the parser.

7.3 Future work

The default setting in MOM is to produce morphological rules which are optional. Furthermore, MOM does not yet infer non-inflecting lexical rules. This means that uninflected forms are passed through to the syntax without being associated with the morphosyntactic or morphosemantic information that the zero in the paradigm actually reflects. In future work, we will explore how to automatically posit such zero-marked rules, including how to make sure that their position classes are required, so that the grammar can properly differentiate 'zero' and 'uninflected'.

We plan to extend our syntactic inference algorithm to account for verbs with alternate or 'quirky' case frames. Another avenue that our error analysis shows as particularly promising is to handle complex clauses, as there are tools to model coordination (Drellishak and Bender, 2005) and subordination (Howell and Zamaraeva, 2018; Zamaraeva et al., 2019) in the Grammar Matrix framework.

8 Conclusion

We have demonstrated the value of integrating morphological and syntactic inference for automatic grammar development. Although inferring these properties is most easily handled separately, we show that combining information about morphotactic and inflectional patterns with syntactic properties such as transitivity improves coverage. While this study looked at case and transitivity, the benefits of creating lexical classes that encode syntactic information alongside morphological information should generalize. This methodology can be extended to other linguistic phenomena on the morphosyntactic interface, such as agreement, and the coverage of grammars can be further extended by expanding the lexical classes and clause types that can be inferred from the syntax. In the future, we would like to perform further, in-depth studies in collaboration with documentary linguists, for example to see if our system can help refine the analysis of morphological classes in the lexicon of the language in question and whether a grammar fragment automatically produced this way can be easily extended to broader coverage.

---

[19]A few of these differences are due to the fact that BASE-LINE includes pronouns and other word categories (such as interjections) as 'nouns' in the lexicon. We built INTEGRATED assuming only things marked as nouns go in. In future work, we will include pronouns (but not interjections).

Acknowledgments

This material is based upon work supported by the National Science Foundation under Grant No. BCS-1561833. Any opinions, findings, and conclusions or recommendations expressed in this material are those of the author(s) and do not necessarily reflect the views of the National Science Foundation.

We would like to thank Alex Burrell for providing code from a previous project that we built on in order to infer transitivity.

We thank previous AGGREGATION research assistants for converting the corpus into Xigt and enriching it with INTENT.

References

Emily M Bender, Dan Flickinger, and Stephan Oepen. 2002. The Grammar Matrix: An open-source starter-kit for the rapid development of cross-linguistically consistent broad-coverage precision grammars. In John Carroll, Nelleke Oostdijk, and Richard Sutcliffe, editors, *Proceedings of the Workshop on Grammar Engineering and Evaluation at the 19th International Conference on Computational Linguistics*, pages 8–14, Taipei, Taiwan, 2002.

Emily M Bender, Scott Drellishak, Antske Fokkens, Laurie Poulson, and Safiyyah Saleem. 2010. Grammar customization. *Research on Language & Computation*, 8:1–50. ISSN 1570-7075.

Emily M. Bender, Dan Flickinger, and Stephan Oepen. 2011. Grammar engineering and linguistic hypothesis testing: Computational support for complexity in syntactic analysis. In Emily M. Bender and Jennifer E. Arnold, editors, *Language from a Cognitive Perspective: Grammar, Usage and Processing*, pages 5–29. CSLI Publications, Stanford, CA.

Emily M. Bender, Sumukh Ghodke, Timothy Baldwin, and Rebecca Dridan. 2012a. From database to treebank: Enhancing hypertext grammars with grammar engineering and treebank search. In Sebastian Nordhoff and Karl-Ludwig G. Poggeman, editors, *Electronic Grammaticography*, pages 179–206. University of Hawaii Press, Honolulu.

Emily M Bender, Robert Schikowski, and Balthasar Bickel. 2012b. Deriving a lexicon for a precision grammar from language documentation resources: A case study of Chintang. *Proceedings of COLING 2012*, pages 247–262.

Emily M Bender, Michael Wayne Goodman, Joshua Crowgey, and Fei Xia. August 2013. Towards creating precision grammars from interlinear glossed text: Inferring large-scale typological properties. In *Proceedings of the 7th Workshop on Language Technology for Cultural Heritage, Social Sciences, and Humanities*, pages 74–83, Sofia, Bulgaria, August 2013. Association for Computational Linguistics. URL `http://www.aclweb.org/anthology/W13-2710`.

Emily M Bender, Joshua Crowgey, Michael Wayne Goodman, and Fei Xia. June 2014. Learning grammar specifications from IGT: A case study of Chintang. In *Proceedings of the 2014 Workshop on the Use of Computational Methods in the Study of Endangered Languages*, pages 43–53, Baltimore, Maryland, USA, June 2014. Association for Computational Linguistics. URL `http://www.aclweb.org/anthology/W14-2206`.

Balthasar Bickel, Manoj Rai, Netra Paudyal, Goma Banjade, Toya Nath Bhatta, Martin Gaenszle, Elena Lieven, Iccha Purna Rai, Novel K Rai, and Sabine Stoll. 2010. The syntax of three-argument verbs in Chintang and Belhare (Southeastern Kiranti). *Studies in ditransitive constructions: a comparative handbook*, pages 382–408.

Balthasar Bickel, Martin Gaenszle, Novel Kishore Rai, Vishnu Singh Rai, Elena Lieven, Sabine Stoll, G. Banjade, T. N. Bhatta, N Paudyal, J Pettigrew, and M Rai, I. P.and Rai. 2013. Tale of a poor guy. URL `https://corpus1.mpi.nl/qfs1/media-archive/dobes_data/ChintangPuma/Chintang/Narratives/Annotations/phengniba_tale.tbt`. Accessed: 22 October 2018.

Ann Copestake. 2002. *Implementing typed feature structure grammars*. CSLI publications, Stanford.

Ann Copestake, Dan Flickinger, Carl Pollard, and Ivan A Sag. 2005. Minimal recursion semantics: An introduction. *Research on Language and Computation*, 3(2-3):281–332.

Scott Drellishak and Emily Bender. 2005. A coordination module for a crosslinguistic grammar resource. In *International Conference on Head-Driven Phrase Structure Grammar*, volume 12, pages 108–128. URL `http://web.stanford.edu/group/cslipublications/cslipublications/HPSG/2005/drellishak-bender.pdf`.

Dan Flickinger, Emily M Bender, and Stephan Oepen. 2014. ERG semantic documentation. URL `http://www.delph-in.net/esd`. Accessed on 2018-10-22.

Daniel P. Flickinger and Stephan Oepen. 1998. Towards systematic grammar profiling. Test suite technology ten years after. In *Beiträge zur 6. Fachtagung der Sektion Computerlinguistik der DGfS*, Heidelberg, 1998.

Antske Sibelle Fokkens. 2014. *Enhancing Empirical Research for Linguistically Motivated Precision Grammars*. PhD thesis, Department of Computational Linguistics, Universität des Saarlandes.

Ryan Georgi. 2016. *From Aari to Zulu: Massively Multilingual Creation of Language Tools Using Interlinear Glossed Text*. PhD thesis, University of Washington.

Michael Wayne Goodman, Joshua Crowgey, Fei Xia, and Emily M Bender. 2015. Xigt: Extensible interlinear gloss text for natural language processing. *Language Resources and Evaluation*, 49 (2): 455–485.

Lars Hellan and Dorothee Beermann. 2014. Inducing grammars from IGT. In Mariani J. Vetulani Z., editor, *Human Language Technology Challenges for Computer Science and Linguistics.*, volume 8287 of *LTC 2011. Lecture Notes in Computer Science.* Springer.

Kristen Howell and Olga Zamaraeva. 2018. Clausal modifiers in the Grammar Matrix. In *Proceedings of the 27th International Conference on Computational Linguistics*, pages 2939–2952.

Kristen Howell, Emily M Bender, Michael Lockwood, Fei Xia, and Olga Zamaraeva. 2017. Inferring case systems from IGT: Impacts and detection of variable glossing practices. *ComputEL-2*, pages 67–75.

Stefan Müller. 1999. *Deutsche Syntax deklarativ: Head-Driven Phrase Structure Grammar für das Deutsche*. Number 394 in Linguistische Arbeiten. Max Niemeyer Verlag, Tübingen.

Stefan Müller. 2015. The CoreGram project: Theoretical linguistics, theory development and verification. *Journal of Language Modelling*, 3(1): 21–86. URL `https://hpsg.hu-berlin.de/~stefan/Pub/coregram.html`.

Stefan Müller. 2016. *Grammatical theory: From transformational grammar to constraint-based approaches*. Language Science Press.

Robert Schikowski. Chintang morphology. Unpublished ms, University of Zürich, 2012.

Robert Schikowski, NP Paudyal, and Balthasar Bickel. 2015. Flexible valency in Chintang. *Valency Classes: a Comparative Handbook*.

Sabine Stoll and Balthasar Bickel. 2012. How to measure frequency? Different ways of counting ergatives in Chintang (Tibeto-Burman, Nepal) and their implications. In Frank Seifart, Geoffrey Haig, Nikolaus P. Himmelmann, Dagmar Jung, Anna Margetts, and Paul Trilsbeek, editors, *Potentials of Language Documentation: Methods, Analyses, and Utilization*, pages 83–89. University of Hawai'i Press.

David Wax. 2014. Automated grammar engineering for verbal morphology. Master's thesis, University of Washington.

Fei Xia and William D. Lewis. 2007. Multilingual structural projection across interlinear text. In *Proc. of the Conference on Human Language Technologies (HLT/NAACL 2007)*, pages 452–459, Rochester, New York, 2007.

Olga Zamaraeva. 2016. Inferring morphotactics from interlinear glossed text: combining clustering and precision grammars. In *Proceedings of the 14th SIGMORPHON Workshop on Computational Research in Phonetics, Phonology, and Morphology*, pages 141–150.

Olga Zamaraeva, František Kratochvíl, Emily M Bender, Fei Xia, and Kristen Howell. 2017. Computational support for finding word classes: A case study of Abui. In *Proceedings of the 2nd Workshop on the Use of Computational Methods in the Study of Endangered Languages*, pages 130–140.

Olga Zamaraeva, Kristen Howell, and Emily M. Bender. 2019. Modeling clausal complementation for a grammar engineering resource. In *Proceedings of the Society for Computation in Linguistics*, volume 2, page Article 6. URL `https://scholarworks.umass.edu/scil/vol2/iss1/6/`.

Finding Sami Cognates with a Character-Based NMT Approach

Mika Hämäläinen
Department of Digital Humanities
University of Helsinki
`mika.hamalainen@helsinki.fi`

Jack Rueter
Department of Digital Humanities
University of Helsinki
`jack.rueter@helsinki.fi`

Abstract

We approach the problem of expanding the set of cognate relations with a sequence-to-sequence NMT model. The language pair of interest, Skolt Sami and North Sami, has too limited a set of parallel data for an NMT model as such. We solve this problem on the one hand, by training the model with North Sami cognates with other Uralic languages and, on the other, by generating more synthetic training data with an SMT model. The cognates found using our method are made publicly available in the Online Dictionary of Uralic Languages.

1 Introduction

Sami languages have received a fair share of interest in purely linguistic study of cognate relations. Although various schools of Finno-Ugric studies have postulated contrastive interpretations of where the Sami languages should be located within the language family, there is strong evidence demonstrating regular sound correspondence between Samic and Balto-Finnic, on the one hand, and Samic and Mordvin, on the other. The importance of this correspondence is accentuated by the fact that the Samic might provide insight for second syllable vowel quality, as not all Samic-Mordvin vocabulary is attested in Balto-Finnic (cf. Korhonen, 1981). The Sami languages themselves (there are seven written languages) also exhibit regular sound correspondence, even though cognates, at times, may be opaque to the layman. One token of cognate relation studies is the Álgu database (Kotus, 2006), which contains a set of inter-Sami cognates. Cognates have applicability in NLP research for low-resource languages as they can, for instance, be used to induce the predicate-argument structures from bilingual vector spaces (Peirsman and Padó, 2010).

The main motivation for this work is to extend the known cognate information available in the Online Dictionary of Uralic Languages (Hämäläinen and Rueter, 2018). This dictionary, at its current stage, only has cognate relations recorded in the Álgu database.

Dealing with true cognates in a non-attested hypothetical proto-language presupposes adherence to a set of sound correlations posited by a given school of thought. Since Proto-Samic is one such language, we have taken liberties to interpret the term cognate in the context of this paper more broadly, i.e. not only words that share the same hypothesized origin in Proto-Samic are considered cognates (hence forth: true cognates), but also items that might be deemed loan words acquired from another language at separate points in the temporal-spatial dimensions. This more permissive definition makes it possible to tackle the problem computationally easier given the limitation imposed by the scarcity of linguistic resources.

Our approach does not presuppose a semantic similarity of the meaning of the cognate candidates, but rather explores cognate possibilities based on grapheme changes. The key idea is that the system can learn what kinds of changes are possible and typical for North Sami cognates with other Uralic languages in general. Taking leverage from this more general level knowledge, the model can learn the cognate features between North Sami and Skolt Sami more specifically.

We assimilate this problem with that of normalization of historical spelling variants. On a higher level, historical variation within one language can be seen as discovering cognates of different temporal forms of the language. Therefore, we want to take the work done in that vein for the first time in the context of cognate detection. Using NMT (neural machine translation) on a character level has been shown to be the single most accurate

Proceedings of the 3rd Workshop on the Use of Computational Methods in the Study of Endangered Languages: Vol. 1 Papers, pages 39–45,
Honolulu, Hawai'i, USA, February 26–27, 2019.

method in normalization by a recent study with historical English (Hämäläinen et al., 2018).

In this paper, we use NMT in a similar character level fashion for finding cognates. Furthermore, due to the limited availability of training data, we present an SMT (statistical machine translation) method for generating more data to boost the performance of the NMT model.

2 Related Work

Automatic identification of cognates has received a fair share of interest in the past from different methodological stand points. In this section, we will go through some of these approaches.

Ciobanu and Dinu (2014) propose a method based on orthographic alignment. This means a character level alignment of cognate pairs. After the alignment, the mismatches around the aligned pairs are used as features for the machine learning algorithm.

Another take on cognate detection is that of Rama (2016). This approach employs Siamese convolutional networks to learn phoneme level representation and language relatedness of words. They based the study on Swadesh lists and used hand-written phonetic features and 1-hot encoding for the phonetic representation.

Cognate detection has also been done by looking at features such as semantics, phonetics and regular sound correspondences (St. Arnaud et al., 2017). Their approach implements a general model and language specific models using support vector machine (SVM).

Rama et al. (2017) present an unsupervised method for cognate identification. The method consists of extracting suitable cognate pairs with normalized Levenshtein distance, aligning the pairs and counting a point-wise mutual information score for the aligned segments. New sets of alignments are generated and the process of aligning and scoring is repeated until there are no changes in the average similarity score.

3 Finding Cognates

In this section, we describe our proposed approach in finding cognates between North Sami and Skolt Sami. We present the dataset used for the training and an SMT approach in generating more training data.

3.1 The Data

Our training data consists of Álgu (Kotus, 2006), which is an etymological database of the Sami languages. From this database, we use all the cognate relations recorded for North Sami to all the other Finno-Ugric languages in the database. This produces a parallel dataset of North Sami words and their cognates in other languages.

The North Sami to other languages parallel dataset consists of 32905 parallel words, of which 2633 items represent the correlations between North Sami and Skolt Sami.

We find cognates for nouns, adjectives, verbs and adverbs recorded in the Giellatekno dictionaries (Moshagen et al., 2013) for North Sami and Skolt Sami. These dictionaries serve as an input for the trained NMT model and for filtering the output produced by the model.

3.2 The NMT Model

For the purpose of our research we use OpenNMT (Klein et al., 2017) to train a character based NMT model that will take a Skolt Sami word as its input and produce a potential North Sami cognate as its output. We use the default settings for OpenNMT[1].

We train a sequence to sequence model with the list of known cognates in other languages as the source data and their North Sami counterparts as the target data. In this way, the system learns a good representation of the target language, North Sami, and can learn what kind of changes are possible between cognates in general. Thus, the model can learn additional information about cognates that would not be present in the North Sami-Skolt Sami parallel data.

In order to make the model adapt more to the North Sami-Skolt Sami pair in particular, we continue training the model with only the North Sami-Skolt Sami parallel data for an additional 10 epochs. The idea behind this is to bring the model closer to the language pair of interest in this research, while still maintaining the additional knowledge it has learned about cognates in general from the larger dataset.

3.3 Using SMT to Generate More Data

Research in machine translation has shown that generating more synthetic parallel data that can be

---

[1] Version from the project's master branch on the 13 April of 2018

noisy in the source language end but is not noisy in the target end, can improve the overall translations of an NMT model (Sennrich et al., 2015). In light of this finding, we will try a similar idea in our cognate detection task as well.

Due to the limited amount of North Sami-Skolt Sami training data available, we use SMT instead of NMT to train a model that will produce plausible but slightly irregular Skolt Sami cognates for the word list of North Sami words obtained from the Giellatekno dictionaries.

We use Moses (Koehn et al., 2007) baseline[2] to train a translation model to the opposite direction of the NMT model with the same parallel data. This means translating from North Sami to Skolt Sami. We use the same parallel data as for the NMT model, meaning that on the source side, we have North Sami and on the target side we have all the possible cognates in other languages. The parallel data is aligned with GIZA++ (Och and Ney, 2003).

Since we are training an SMT model, there are two ways we can make the noisy target of all the other languages resemble more Skolt Sami. One is by using a language model. For this, we build a 10-gram language model with KenLM (Heafield et al., 2013) from Skolt Sami words recorded in the Giellatekno dictionaries.

The other way of making the model more aware of Skolt Sami in particular is to tune the SMT model after the initial training. For the tuning, we use the Skolt Sami-North Sami parallel data exclusively so that the SMT model will go more towards Skolt Sami when producing cognates.

We use the SMT model to translate all of the words extracted from the North Sami dictionary into Skolt Sami. This results in a parallel dataset of real, existing North Sami words and words that resemble Skolt Sami. We then use this data to continue the training of the previously explained NMT model for 10 additional epochs.

3.4 Using the NMT Models

We use both of the NMT models, i.e. the one without SMT generated additional data and the one with the data separately to assess the difference in their performance. We feed in the extracted Skolt Sami words from the dictionary and translate each word to a North Sami word as it would look like if

there were a cognate for that word in North Sami.

The approach produces many non-words which we filter out with the North Sami dictionary. The resulting list of translated words that are actually found in the North Sami dictionary are considered to be potential cognates found by the method.

4   Results and Evaluation

In this section, we present the results of both of the NMT models, the one without SMT generated data and the one with generated data. The results shown in Table 1 indicate that the model with the additional SMT generated data outperformed the other model. The evaluation is based on a 200 randomly selected cognate pairs output by the models. These pairs have then been checked by an expert linguist according to principles outlined in (4.1).

	NMT	NMT + SMT
accuracy	67.5%	83%

Table 1: Percentage of correctly found cognates

Table 2 gives more insight on the number of cognates found and how they are represented in the original Álgu database. The results show that while the models have poor performance in finding the cognates in the training data, they work well in extending the cognates outside of the known cognate list.

	NMT	NMT + SMT
Same as in Álgu	75	61
North Sami word in Álgu but no cognates with Skolt Sami	211	226
North Sami word in Álgu with other Skolt Sami cognates	646	577
North Sami word not in Álgu	848	936
Cognates found in total	*1780*	*1800*

Table 2: Distribution of cognates in relation to Álgu

As one of the purposes of our work is to help evaluate and develop etymological research, we will conduct a more qualitative analysis of the correctly and incorrectly identified cognates for the better working model, i.e. the one with SMT generated data. This means that the developers should

---

[2]As described in
http://www.statmt.org/moses/?n=moses.baseline

be aware not only of the comparative-linguistic rules etymologists use when assessing the regularity of cognate candidates but semantics as well.

In an introduction to Samic language history (Korhonen, 1981: 110–114), the proto-language is divided into 4 separate phases. The first phase involves vowel changes in the first and second syllables (*ä–e » e–ẹ, u–e » ọ–ẹ, e–ä » e–à, i–e » ẹ–ẹ*, etc.) followed by vowel rotation in the first syllable dependent on the quality of the second-syllable vowel (*e–e » e–ẹ* but *e–ä » ε–à*). The second phase entails the loss of quantitative distinction for first-syllable vowels such that high vowels are normalized as short, and non-high first-syllable vowels are normally long (*e–ẹ » ē–ẹ, ε–à » ε̄–ē*, etc.). The third phase involves a slight vowel shift in the first syllable and vowel split in the second. And finally, the fourth phase introduces diphthongization of non-high vowels in the first syllable (*ē–ẹ » ie–ẹ, ε̄–ē » eä–ē*, etc.).

In Table 3, below, we provide an approximation of a few hypothesized sound changes for three words that are attested in Balto-Finnic and Mordvin, alike. **käte* 'hand; arm' has true cognates in Finnish *käsi*, Northern Sami *giehta*, Skolt Sami *ǩiõtt*, Erzya *ked'* and Moksha *käd'*, **tule* 'fire' is represented by Finnish *tuli*, Northern Sami *dolla*, Skolt Sami *toll*, and Mordvin *tol*, while **pesä* 'nest' is attested in Finnish *pesä*, Northern Sami *beassi*, Skolt Sami *pie'ss*, Erzya *pize*, and Moksha *piza*. The Roman numerals in the table correspond to four separate phases in Proto-Samic.

	I	II	III	IV
'hand; arm'	*käte*	*ketẹ*	*kētẹ*	*kietẹ*
'fire'	*tule*	*tolẹ*	*tolẹ*	*tolẹ*
'nest'	*pesä*	*pεsà*	*pε̄sē*	*peäsē*

Table 3: Illustration of some vowel correlations in 4 phases of Proto-Samic

In the evaluation, our attention was drawn to the adherence of (143) items to accepted sound correlations while there were (57) candidates that failed in this respect (cf. Korhonen, 1981; Lehtiranta, 2001; Aikio, 2009). Irregular sound correlation can be exemplified in the North Sami word *bierdna* 'bear' and its counterpart the Skolt Sami word *peä'rnn* (the *'* prime indicates palatalization in Skolt Sami orthography) 'bear cub'. The former appears to represent the word type found in 'hand' North Sami *giehta* and Skolt Sami *ǩiõtt*,

whereas the latter represents the word type found in 'nest' North Sami *beassi* and Skolt Sami *pie'ss* and 'swamp' North Sami *jeaggi* and Skolt Sami *jeä'ǧǧ*. Hence, on the basis of the North Sami word *bierdna* 'bear', one would posit a Skolt Sami form **piõrnn*, whereas the Skolt Sami word *peä'rnn* 'bear cub' would presuppose a North Sami form **beardni*. Both types have firm representation in both languages, so it would seem that these borrowings have entered the languages at separate points in the spatio-temporal dimensions.

4.1 Analysis of the Correct Cognates

Correct cognates were selected according to two simples principles of similarity. On the one hand, there was the principle of conceptual similarity in their referential denotations (i.e., this refers to future work in semantic relations). On the other hand, a feasible cognate pair candidate should demonstrate adherence or near adherence to accepted sound law theory. The question of adherence versus near adherence indicated here can be directed to concepts of sound law theory, where conceivable irregularities may further be attributed to points in spatio-temporal dimensions (i.e., when and where a particular word was introduced into the lexica of the two languages involved in the investigation).

In the investigation of 200 random cognate pair candidates, 166 cognate pair candidates exhibited conceptual similarity which in some instances surpassed what might have been discovered using a bilingual dictionary. Of the 166 acceptable cognate pairs 131 candidate pairs demonstrated regular correlation to received sound law theory.

Adherence to concepts of sound law theory can be observed in the alignment of the North Sami words *čuoika* 'mosquito' and *ađa* 'marrow' with their Skolt Sami counterparts *čuõškk* and *õõđ*, respectively. Although these words may appear opaque to the layman, and thus this alignment might be deemed dubious at first, awareness of cognate candidates in the Erzya Mordvin *śeśke* 'mosquito' and *ud'em* 'marrow' helps to alleviate initial misgivings.

As may be observed above, North Sami frequently has two-syllable words where Skolt Sami attests to single-syllable words. This relative length correlation between North Sami and Skolt Sami is described through measurement in prosodic feet (cf. Koponen and Rueter, 2016). While North Sami exhibits retention of the theoretical stem-final vowel in two-syllable words, Skolt Sami appears to have lost it. In fact, stem-final vowels in Skolt Sami are symptomatic of proper nouns and participles (derivations). In contrast, two-syllable words with consonant-final stems appear in both North Sami and Skolt Sami, which means we can expect a number of basic verbs attesting to two-syllable infinitives (North Sami *bidjat* 'put' and Skolt Sami *piijjâd*) and contract-stem nouns (North Sami *guoppar* and Skolt Sami *kuõbbâr* 'mushroom'). Upon inspection of longer words, it will appear that Skolt Sami words are at least one syllable shorter than their cognates in North Sami, which can be attributed to variation in foot development.

Cognate word correlations between North Sami and Skolt Sami can be approached by counting syllables in the lemmas (dictionary forms). Through this approach, we can attribute some word lengths automatically to parts-of-speech, i.e. there is only one single-syllable verb in Skolt Sami *lee'd* 'be', and it correlates to a single-syllable verb in North Sami *leat*. Other verbs are therefore two or more syllables in length in both languages. While two-syllable verbs in North Sami correlate with two-syllable verbs in Skolt Sami, multiple-syllable verbs in North Sami usually correlate to Skolt Sami counterparts in an X<=>X-1 relationship (number of syllables in the language forms, repectively), where North Sami is one orthographical syllable longer.

Short word pairs demonstrate a clear correlation between two-syllable base words in North Sami and single-syllable base words in Skolt Sami, which with the exception of 4 words were all nouns (54 all told). The high concentration of noun attestation for single-syllable cognate nouns in the two languages of investigation is counterbalanced by the representation of verbs in other word-length correlation groups.

Cognate pairs where both North Sami and Skolt Sami attested to two-syllable lemmas were overrepresented by verbs. There were 47 verbs, 22 nouns, 10 adjectives and 1 adverb. This result is symptomatic of lemma-based research. Surprisingly enough, however, the three-to-two syllable correlation between North Sami and Skolt Sami also showed a similar representation: verbs (13), nouns (2) and adverbs (1).

There was one attested correlation for a 5-syllable word *eŋgelasgiella* 'English language' in North Sami and its 3-syllable counterpart in Skolt Sami *eŋgglõskiõll*. Since we are looking at a compound word with 3-to-2 and 2-to-1 correlations, we can assume that our model is recognizing individual adjacent segments within a larger unit.

Correct cognates do not necessarily require etymologically identical source forms or structure. The recognized cognate pairs represent both recent loan words or possible irregularities in sound law theory (35) and presumably older mutual lexicon (131) (see 4.2, below). They also attest to differed structure and length (i.e., this may also include derivation and compounding). While a majority of the cognate candidate pairs linked words sharing the same derivational level, 11 represented instances of additional derivation in either the North Sami or Skolt Sami word, and 3 recognized instances where one of the languages was represented by a compound word.

4.2 Analysis of the Incorrect Cognates

Incorrect cognates often offer vital input for cognate detection development. There are, of course, words pairs that diverge in regard to both accepted sound law theory and semantic cohesion. These pairs have not yet been applied to development. In contrast, word pairs that appear to adhere to sound law theory yet are not matched semantically might be regarded as false friends. These pairs can be potentially useful in further development.

Of 34 semantically non-feasible candidates, 12 stood out as false friends. One such example pair is observed in the North Sami *álgu* 'beginning' and the Skolt Sami *älgg* 'piece of firewood'. These two words, it should be noted, can be associated with the Finnish cognates *alku* 'beginning' and *halko* 'piece of split firewood [NB! there is a loss of the word initial *h*]', respectively. Since the theoretically expected vowel equivalent of the first syllable *a* in Finnish is *uo* and *ue* in North Sami and Skolt Sami, respectively, we might assume that neither word comes from a mutual Samic-Finnic proto-language.

We do not know to what extent random selection has affected our results. Had the first North Sami noun *álgu* been replaced with its paradigmatic verb *álgit* 'begin', the Skolt Sami *ä'lǧǧed*, also translated as 'begin', would have shown direct correlation for *á* and *ä* in North Sami and

Skolt Sami, respectively. The second noun, meaning 'piece of split firewood', is actually *hálgu* in North Sami, which simply demonstrates *h* retention and the possible recognition problems faced in the absence of semantic knowledge.

4.3 Summary of the Analyses

The cognate candidates were evaluated according to two criteria: One query checked for conceptual similarity (correct vs incorrect), and the other checked for regularity according to received sound law theory. While the majority (65%) of the word pairs evaluated were both conceptually similar and correlated to received sound law theory, an additional 17% of the candidates represented irregular sound correlation, as indicated by the figures *131* and *35* below, respectively.

	Similar	Dissimilar
Regular	131	12
Irregular	35	22

Table 4: Cognate candidate evaluation

The presence of an 11% negative score for both sound law regularity and conceptual similarity indicates an improvement requirement of at least 6% before the machine can be considered relevant (95%). The 6% attestation of false friend discovery, however, displays an already existing accuracy in our algorithm.

5 Conclusions and Future Work

In this paper, we have shown that using a character-based NMT is a feasible way of expanding a list of cognates by training the model mostly on the cognate pairs for North Sami words in languages other than Skolt Sami. Furthermore, we have shown that an SMT model can be used to generate synthetic parallel data by pushing the model more towards the direction of Skolt Sami by introducing a Skolt Sami language model and tuning the model with Skolt Sami - North Sami parallel data.

In our evaluation, we have only considered the best cognate produced by the NMT model with the idea of one-to-one mapping. However, it is possible to make the NMT model output more than one possible translation. In the future, we can conduct more evaluation for a list of top candidates to see whether the model is able to find more than one cognate for a given word and whether the overall recall can be improved for the words where the top candidate has been rejected by the dictionary check as a non-word.

We have currently limited our research in cognates between Skolt Sami and North Sami where the translation direction of the NMT model has been towards North Sami. An interesting future direction would be to change the translation direction. In addition to that, we are also interested in trying this method out on other languages recorded in the Álgu database.

We are also interested in conducting research that is more linguistic in its nature based on the cognate list produced in this paper. This will shed more light in the current linguistic knowledge of cognates in the Sami languages. The current results of the better working NMT model are released in the Online Dictionary for Uralic Languages[3].

References

Ante Aikio. 2009. *The Saami Loan Words in Finnish and Karelian*, first edition. Faculty of Humanities of the University of Oulu, Oulu. Dissertation.

Alina Maria Ciobanu and Liviu P Dinu. 2014. Automatic detection of cognates using orthographic alignment. In *Proceedings of the 52nd Annual Meeting of the Association for Computational Linguistics (Volume 2: Short Papers)*, volume 2, pages 99–105.

Mika Hämäläinen and Jack Rueter. 2018. Advances in Synchronized XML-MediaWiki Dictionary Development in the Context of Endangered Uralic Languages. In *Proceedings of the Eighteenth EURALEX International Congress*, pages 967–978.

Mika Hämäläinen, Tanja Säily, Jack Rueter, Jörg Tiedemann, and Eetu Mäkelä. 2018. Normalizing early english letters to present-day english spelling. In *Proceedings of the Second Joint SIGHUM Workshop on Computational Linguistics for Cultural Heritage, Social Sciences, Humanities and Literature*, pages 87–96.

Kenneth Heafield, Ivan Pouzyrevsky, Jonathan H Clark, and Philipp Koehn. 2013. Scalable modified Kneser-Ney language model estimation. In *Proceedings of the 51st Annual Meeting of the Association for Computational Linguistics (Volume 2: Short Papers)*, volume 2, pages 690–696.

Guillaume Klein, Yoon Kim, Yuntian Deng, Jean Senellart, and Alexander M. Rush. 2017. OpenNMT: Open-Source Toolkit for Neural Machine Translation. In *Proc. ACL*.

---

[3]http://akusanat.com/

Philipp Koehn, Hieu Hoang, Alexandra Birch, Chris Callison-Burch, Marcello Federico, Nicola Bertoldi, Brooke Cowan, Wade Shen, Christine Moran, Richard Zens, et al. 2007. Moses: Open source toolkit for statistical machine translation. In *Proceedings of the 45th annual meeting of the ACL on interactive poster and demonstration sessions*, pages 177–180. Association for Computational Linguistics.

Eino Koponen and Jack Rueter. 2016. The first complete scientific skolt sami grammar in english. *FUF 63: 254344*, pages 254–266. Pp. 261–265.

Mikko Korhonen. 1981. *Johdatus lapin kielen historiaan*, volume 370 of *Suomalaisen Kirjallisuuden Seuran toimituksia*. Suomalaisen Kirjallisuuden Seura, Helsinki.

Kotus. 2006. Álgu-tietokanta. Saamelaiskielten etymologinen tietokanta. http://kaino.kotus.fi/algu/.

Juhani Lehtiranta. 2001. *Yhteissaamelainen sanasto*, second edition, volume 200 of *Suomalais-Ugrilaisen Seuran toimituksia*. Suomalais-Ugrilainen Seura, Helsinki.

Sjur N. Moshagen, Tommi A. Pirinen, and Trond Trosterud. 2013. Building an open-source development infrastructure for language technology projects. In *Proceedings of the 19th Nordic Conference of Computational Linguistics (NODALIDA 2013); May 22-24; 2013; Oslo University; Norway. NEALT Proceedings Series 16*, 85, pages 343–352. Linköping University Electronic Press.

Franz Josef Och and Hermann Ney. 2003. A systematic comparison of various statistical alignment models. *Computational Linguistics*, 29(1):19–51.

Yves Peirsman and Sebastian Padó. 2010. Cross-lingual induction of selectional preferences with bilingual vector spaces. In *Human Language Technologies: The 2010 Annual Conference of the North American Chapter of the Association for Computational Linguistics*, pages 921–929. Association for Computational Linguistics.

Taraka Rama. 2016. Siamese convolutional networks for cognate identification. In *Proceedings of COL-ING 2016, the 26th International Conference on Computational Linguistics: Technical Papers*, pages 1018–1027.

Taraka Rama, Johannes Wahle, Pavel Sofroniev, and Gerhard Jäger. 2017. Fast and unsupervised methods for multilingual cognate clustering. *arXiv preprint arXiv:1702.04938*.

Rico Sennrich, Barry Haddow, and Alexandra Birch. 2015. Improving neural machine translation models with monolingual data. *arXiv preprint arXiv:1511.06709*.

Adam St. Arnaud, David Beck, and Grzegorz Kondrak. 2017. Identifying cognate sets across dictionaries of related languages. In *Proceedings of the 2017 Conference on Empirical Methods in Natural Language Processing*, pages 2519–2528.

Linda Wiechetek
UiT The Arctic University of Norway
linda.wiechetek@uit.no

Kevin Brubeck Unhammer
Trigram AS
kevin@trigram.no

Sjur Nørstebø Moshagen
UiT The Arctic University of Norway
sjur.n.moshagen@uit.no

Abstract

Communities of lesser resourced languages like North Sámi benefit from language tools such as spell checkers and grammar checkers to improve literacy. Accurate error feedback is dependent on well-tokenised input, but traditional tokenisation as shallow preprocessing is inadequate to solve the challenges of real-world language usage. We present an alternative where tokenisation remains *ambiguous* until we have linguistic context information available. This lets us accurately detect sentence boundaries, multiwords and compound error detection. We describe a North Sámi grammar checker with such a tokenisation system, and show the results of its evaluation.

1 Introduction

Bilingual users frequently face bigger challenges regarding literacy in the lesser used language than in the majority language due to reduced access to language arenas (Outakoski, 2013; Lindgren et al., 2016). However, literacy and in particular writing is important in today's society, both in social contexts and when using a computer or a mobile phone. Language tools such as spellcheckers and grammar checkers therefore play an important role in improving literacy and the quality of written text in a language community.

North Sámi is spoken in Norway, Sweden and Finland by approximately 25,700 speakers (Simons and Fennig, 2018), and written in a number of institutions like the daily Sámi newspaper (*Ávvir*[1]), a few Sámi journals, websites and social media of the Sámi radio and TV (e.g. *YleSápmi*[2]). In addition, the Sámi parliaments, the national governments, and a Sámi university college produce North Sámi text.

An open-source spellchecker for North Sámi has been freely distributed since 2007 (Gaup et al.,

2006).[3] However, a spellchecker is limited to looking only at one word contexts. It can only detect non-words, i.e. words that cannot be found in the lexicon. A grammar checker, however, looks at contexts beyond single words, and can correct misspelled words that are in the lexicon, but are wrong in the given context. In addition, a grammar checker can detect grammatical and punctuation errors.

A common error in North Sámi and other compounding languages is to spell compound words as separate words instead of one. The norm typically requires them to be written as one word, with the non-final components being in nominative or genitive case if they are nouns. This reflects a difference in meaning between two words written separately and the same two words written as a compound. Being able to detect and correct such compounding errors is thus important for the language community.

This paper presents and evaluates a grammar checker framework that handles ambiguous tokenisation, and uses that to detect compound errors, as well as improve sentence boundary detection after abbreviations and numeral expressions. The framework is completely open source, and completely rule-based. The evaluation is done manually, since gold standards for North Sámi tokenisation have not been developed prior to this work.

2 Background

The system we present is part of a full-scale grammar checker (Wiechetek, 2017, 2012). Before this work, there were no grammar checkers for the Sámi languages although some grammar checker-like work has been done in the language learning platform *Oahpa* (Antonsen, 2012). However, there have been several full-scale grammar checkers for

---

[1]https://avvir.no/ (accessed 2018-10-08)
[2]https://yle.fi/uutiset/osasto/sapmi/ (accessed 2018-10-08)

[3] In addition to that, there are syntactic disambiguation grammars, machine translators, dictionaries and a tagged searchable online corpus.

Proceedings of the 3rd Workshop on the Use of Computational Methods in the Study of Endangered Languages: Vol. 1 Papers, pages 46–55,
Honolulu, Hawai'i, USA, February 26–27, 2019.

other Nordic languages, most of them implemented in the rule-based framework Constraint Grammar (CG). *Lingsoft* distributes grammar checkers for the Scandinavian languages,[4] some of which are or have been integrated into *MS Word*; a stand-alone grammar checker like *Grammatifix* (Arppe, 2000) is also available from *Lingsoft*. Another widely used, mostly rule-based and free/open-source system is *LanguageTool* (Milkowski, 2010), though this does not yet support any Nordic languages. Other CG-based checkers are *OrdRet* (Bick, 2006) and *DanProof* (Bick, 2015) for Danish.

2.1 Framework

The central tools used in our grammar checker are *finite state transducers* (FST's) and *CG* rules. CG is a rule-based formalism for writing disambiguation and syntactic annotation grammars (Karlsson, 1990; Karlsson et al., 1995). The *vislcg3* implementation[5] we use also allows for dependency annotation. CG relies on a bottom-up analysis of running text. Possible but unlikely analyses are discarded step by step with the help of morpho-syntactic context.

All components are compiled and built using the *Giella* infrastructure (Moshagen et al., 2013). This infrastructure helps linguists coordinate resource development using common tools and a common architecture. It also ensures a consistent build process across languages, and makes it possible to propagate new tools and technologies to all languages within the infrastructure. That is, the progress described in this paper is immediately available to all languages in the *Giella* infrastructure, barring the necessary linguistic work.

The North Sámi CG analysers take morphologically ambiguous input, which is the output from analysers compiled as FST's. The source of these analysers is written in the Xerox *twolc*[6] and *lexc* (Beesley and Karttunen, 2003) formalisms, compiled and run with the free and open source package HFST (Lindén et al., 2011).

We also rely on a recent addition to HFST, *hfst-pmatch* (Hardwick et al., 2015) (inspired by Xerox pmatch (Karttunen, 2011)) with the runtime tool *hfst-tokenise*. Below we describe how this lets us analyse and tokenise in one step, using FST's to identify regular words, multiword expressions and potential compound errors.

It should be noted that the choice of rule-based technologies is not accidental. The complexity of the languages we work with, and the general sparsity of data, makes purely data-driven methods inadequate. Additionally, rule-based work leads to linguistic insights that feed back into our general understanding of the grammar of the language. We chose a Constraint Grammar rule-based system since it is one we have long experience with, and it has proven itself to be competitive both in high- and low-resource scenarios. For example, *DanProof* (Bick, 2015, p.60) scores more than twice that of *Word2007* on the F1 measure (72.0% vs 30.1%) for Danish grammar checking. CG also compares favourably to modern deep learning approaches, e.g. *DanProof*'s F0.5 (weighting precision twice as much as recall) score is 80.2%, versus the 72.0% reported by Grundkiewicz and Junczys-Dowmunt (2018).

In addition, most current approaches rely very much on large-scale manually annotated corpora,[7] which do not exist for North Sámi. It makes sense to reuse large already existing corpora for training language tools. However, in the absence of these, it is more economical to write grammars of handwritten rules that annotate a corpus linguistically and/or do error detection/correction. As no other methods for developing error detection tools exist for North Sámi or similar languages in comparable situations (low-resourced in terms of annotated corpus, weak literacy, higher literacy in the majority languages), it is impossible for us to provide a comparison with other technologies.

2.2 Motivation

This section describes some of the challenges that lead to the development of our new grammar checker modules.

A basic feature of a grammar checker is to correct spelling errors that would be missed by a spell checker, that is, orthographically correct words that are nevertheless wrong in the given context.

(1) Beroštupmi **gáktegoarrun|gursii**
     interest   costume.sewing|course.ILL
     'An interest in a costume sewing course'

---

[4] `http://www2.lingsoft.fi/doc/swegc/errtypes.html` (accessed 2018-10-08)

[5] `http://visl.sdu.dk/constraint_grammar.html` (accessed 2018-10-08), also Bick and Didriksen (2015)

[6] Some languages in the Giella infrastructure describe their morphophonology using Xfst rewrite rules; both *twolc* and *rewrite rules* are supported by the Giella infrastructure.

[7] "Automatic grammatical error correction (GEC) progress is limited by corpora available for developing and evaluating systems." (Tetreault et al., 2017, p.229)

In the North Sámi norm, generally (nominal) compounds are written as one word; it is an error to insert a space at the compound border. Ex. (1) marks the compound border with a pipe.

(2) *Beroštupmi **gáktegoarrun gursii**

If the components of a compound are separated by a space as in ex. (2) (cf. the correct spelling in ex (1)), the grammar checker should detect a compound spacing error.

Compound errors can not be found by means of a non-contextual spellchecker, since adjacent nominals are not automatically compound errors. They may also have a syntactic relation. Our lexicon contains both the information that *gáktegoarrun-gursii* would be a legal compound noun if written as one word, and the information needed to say that *gáktegoarrun gursii* may have a syntactic relation between the words, that is, they are independent tokens each with their own analysis.[8] We therefore assume ambiguous tokenisation. In order to decide which tokenisation is the correct one, we need context information.

In addition, there is the issue of combinatorial explosion. For example, the bigram *guhkit áiggi* 'longer time' may be a compound error in one context, giving an analysis as a single noun token. But it is also ambiguous with *sixteen* two-token readings, where the first part may be adjective, adverb or verb. We want to include these as alternative readings.

A naïve solution to getting multiple, ambiguous tokenisations of a string like *guhkit áiggi* would be to insert an optional space in the compound border in the entry for dynamic compounds, with an error tag. But if we analyse by longest match, the error reading would be the only possible reading. We could make the error tag on the space be optional, which would make the entry ambiguous between adjective+noun and compound, but we'd still be missing the adverb/verb+noun alternatives, which do not have a compound border between them. To explicitly encode all correct alternatives to compound errors in the lexicon, we would need to enter readings for e.g. verb+noun bigrams simply because they happen to be ambiguous with an error reading of a nominal compound.

Manually adding every bigram in the lexicon

that happens to be ambiguous with an error would be extremely tedious and error-prone. Adding it automatically through FST operations turns out to quickly exhaust memory and multiply the size of the FST. Our solution would need to avoid this issue.

(3) **omd.** sámeskuvllas
for.example Sámi.school.LOC
'for example in the Sámi school'

(4) **omd.** Álttás sámeskuvllas
for.example Alta.LOC Sámi.school.LOC
'for example in Alta in the Sámi school'

In the fragment in ex. (3)–(4) above, the period after the abbreviation *omd.* 'for example' is ambiguous with a sentence boundary. In the first example, we could use the local information that the noun *sámeskuvllas* 'Sámi school (Loc.)' is lowercase to tell that it is not a sentence boundary. However, the second sentence has a capitalised proper noun right after *omd.* and the tokenisation is less straightforward. We also need to know that, if it is to be two tokens instead of one, the form splits before the period, and the tags belonging to "<omd>" go with that form, and the tags belonging to "<.>" go with that form. That is, we need to keep the information of which substrings of the form go with which readings of the whole, ambiguously-tokenised string.

As this and the previous examples show, we need context information to resolve the ambiguity; this means we need to *defer the resolution of ambiguous tokenisation* until after we have some of the morphological/syntactic/semantic analysis available.

(5) **Itgo** don muitte
not.SG2.Q you remember
'Don't you remember'

(6) **It** **go** don muitte
not.SG2 Q you remember
'Don't you remember'

Ex. (5) and (6) above are equivalent given the context – the space is just a matter of style, when used in this sense – but *go* appearing as a word on its own is locally ambiguous, since the question particle *go* may in other contexts be a conjunction (meaning 'when, that'). We want to treat *Itgo* 'don't you' as two tokens *It+go*; having equal analyses for the equal alternatives (after disambiguation) would simplify further processing. This can be encoded in the lexicon as one entry which we might be able to

---

[8] The non-head noun sometimes has an epenthetic only when used as a compound left-part, information which is also encoded in the lexicon.

split with some postprocessing, but before the current work, our tools gave us no way to show what parts of the form corresponded to which tokens. A typical FST entry (here expanded for simplicity) might contain

```
ii+V+Sg2+TOKEN+go+Qst:itgo
```

Now we want to encode that the form splits between 'it' and 'go', and that 'ii+V+2Sg' belongs to 'it', and that 'go+Qst' belongs to 'go'. But inserting a symbol into the form would mean that the form no longer analyses; we need to somehow mark the split-point.

Our system solves all of the above issues – we explain how below.

3   Method

Below we present our grammar checker pipeline, and our method to analyse and resolve ambiguous tokenisation. We first describe the system architecture of the North Sámi grammar checker, then our morphological analysis and tokenisation method, and finally our method of finding errors by disambiguating ambiguous tokenisation.

3.1   System architecture

The North Sámi grammar checker consists of different modules that can be used separately or in combination, cf. Figure 1.

The text is first tokenised and morphologically analysed by the descriptive morphological analyser *tokeniser-gramcheck-gt-desc.pmhfst*, which has access to the North Sámi lexicon with both error tags and lexical semantic tags. The following step, *analyser-gt-whitespace.hfst*, detects and tags whitespace errors. It also tags the first words of paragraphs and other whitespace delimited boundaries, which can then be used by the boundary detection rules later on, which enables detecting e.g. headers based on their surrounding whitespace.

The valency annotation grammar *valency.cg3* adds valency tags to potential governors. Then follows the module that disambiguates ambiguous tokenisation, *mwe-dis.cg3*, which can select or remove compound readings of multi-word expressions based on the morpho-syntactic context and valencies. It can also decide whether punctuation is a sentence boundary or not. The next module, *divvun-cgspell*, takes unknown words and runs them through our spell checker, where suggestions include morphological analyses.

The next module is the CG grammar *grc-disambiguator.cg3*, which performs morpho-syntactic analysis and disambiguation, except for the speller suggestions, which are left untouched. The disambiguator is followed by a CG module, *spellchecker.cg3*, which aims to reduce the suggestions made by the spellchecker by means of the grammatical context. The context is now partly disambiguated, which makes it easier to decide which suggestions to keep, and which not.[9]

The last CG module is *grammarchecker.cg3*, which performs the actual error detection and correction – mostly for other error types than spelling or compound errors. The internal structure of *grammarchecker.cg3* is more complex; local case error detection takes place after local error detection, governor-argument dependency analysis, and semantic role mapping, but before global error detection.

Finally, the correct morphological forms are generated from tag combinations suggested in *grammarchecker.cg3* by means of the normative morphological generator *generator-gt-norm.hfstol*, and suggested to the user along with a short feedback message of the identified error.

3.2   Ambiguous tokenisation

A novel feature of our approach is the support for different kinds of ambiguous tokenisation in the analyser, and how we disambiguate ambiguous tokens using CG rules.

We do tokenisation as part of morphological analysis using the *hfst-tokenise* tool, which does a left-to-right longest match analysis of the input, where matches are those given by a *pmatch* analyser. This kind of analyser lets us define tokenisation rules such as "a word from our lexicon may appear surrounded by whitespace or punctuation". The *pmatch* analyser imports a regular lexical transducer, and adds definitions for whitespace, punctuation and other tokenisation hints; *hfst-tokenise* uses the analyser to produce a stream of tokens with their morphological analysis in CG format.

As an example, *hfst-tokenise* will turn the input *ii, de* 'not, then' into three CG cohorts:

<hr>

[9] In later work done after the submission, we tried using *grc-disambiguator.cg3* again after applying *spellchecker.cg3*, this time allowing it to remove speller suggestions. Given that the context was now disambiguated, and problematic speller suggestion cases had been handled by *spellchecker.cg3*, it disambiguated the remaining speller suggestions quite well, and left us with just one or a few correct suggestions to present to the user.

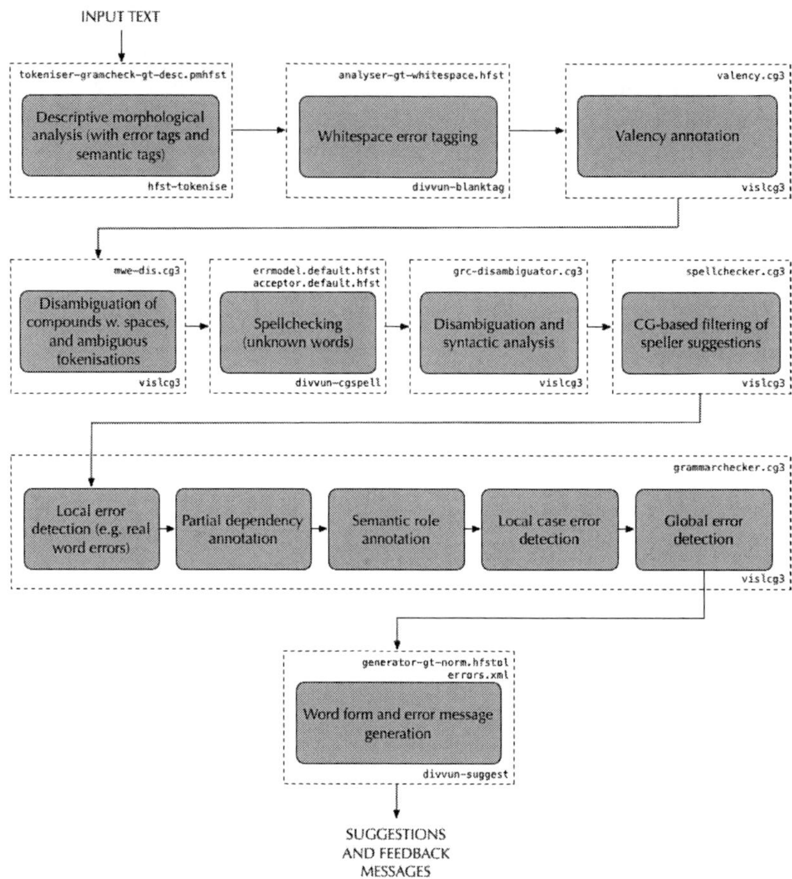

Figure 1: System architecture of the North Sámi grammarchecker

```
"<ii>"
        "ii" V IV Neg Ind Sg3 <W:0>
"<,>"
        "," CLB <W:0>
:
"<de>"
        "de" Adv <W:0>
        "de" Pcle <W:0>
```

The space between the words is printed after the colon. The analyses come from our lexical transducer.

```
Define morphology @bin"analyser.hfst" ;
Define punctword  morphology &
                  [ Punct:[?*] ] ;
Define blank      Whitespace |
                  Punct ;
Define morphoword morphology
                  LC([blank | #])
                  RC([blank | #]) ;
regex [ morphoword | punctword ];
```

The above *pmatch* rules say that a word from the lexicon (*analyser.hfst*) has to be surrounded by a "blank", where a blank is either whitespace or punc-tuation. The LC/RC are the left and right context conditions. We also extract (intersect) the subset of the lexicon where the form is punctuation, and allow that to appear without any context conditions.

We insert *re-tokenisation* hints in the lexicon at places where we assume there is a possible tokeni-sation border, and our changes to *hfst-tokenise* let the analyser backtrack and look for other tokenisa-tions of the same input string. That is, for a given longest match tokenisation, we can force it to *redo* the tokenisation so we get other multi-token read-ings with shorter segments alongside the longest match. This solves the issue of combinatorial ex-plosion.

As a simple example, the ordinal anal-ysis of *17.* has a backtracking mark be-tween the number and the period. If the lexicon contains the symbol-pairs/arcs:

```
1:1 7:7 ε:@PMATCH_BACKTRACK@
ε:@PMATCH_INPUT_MARK@ .:A ε:Ord
```

then, since the form-side of this analysis is `17.`, the input *17.* will match, but since there was a backtrack-symbol, we trigger a retokenisation. The input-mark symbol says where the form should be split.[10] Thus we also get analyses of *17* and *.* as two separate tokens.

```
"<17.>"
        "17" A Ord Attr
        "." CLB "<.>"
                "17" Num "<17>"
```

To represent tokenisation ambiguity in the CG format, we use *vislcg3 subreadings*,[11] where deeper (more indented) readings are those that appeared first in the stream, and any reading with a word-form-tag (`"<.>"` above) should (if chosen by disambiguation) be turned into a cohort of its own. Now we may run a regular CG rule to pick the correct reading based on context, e.g. `SELECT (".") IF (1 some-context-condition) ...;` which would give us

```
"<17.>"
        "." CLB "<.>"
                "17" Num "<17>"
```

Then a purely mechanical reformatter named *cg-mwesplit* turns this into separate tokens, keeping the matching parts together:

```
"<17>"
        "17" Num
"<.>"
        "." CLB
```

We also handle possible compound errors with the above scheme. When compiling the lexical transducer, we let all compound boundaries optionally be realised as a space. Two successive nouns like *illu sáhka* 'happiness news (i.e. happy news)' will be given a compound analysis which includes an error tag. We also insert a backtracking symbol with the space, so that the tokenisation tool knows that the compound analysis is not necessarily the only one (but without having to explicitly list all possible alternative tokenisations). If the retokenisation finds that the nouns can be analysed and tokenised independently, then those tokens and analyses are also printed.

```
"<illu sáhka>"
```

---

[10]This also means we cannot reshuffle the input/output side of the FST. In practice, we use a flag diacritic in the lexicon, which will keep its place during minimisation, and after the regular lexicon is compiled, we turn the flag into the ε:@PMATCH_INPUT_MARK@ symbol-pair.

[11]`https://visl.sdu.dk/cg3/chunked/ subreadings.html` (accessed 2018-10-10)

```
        "illusáhka" N Sg Nom Err/SpaceCmp
        "sáhka" N Sg Nom "< sáhka>"
                "illu" N Sg Nom "<illu>"
```

Given such an ambiguous tokenisation, CG rules choose between the compound error and the two-token readings, using context information from the rest of the sentence. If the non-error reading was chosen, we get:

```
"<illu sáhka>"
        "sáhka" N Sg Nom "< sáhka>"
                "illu" N Sg Nom "<illu>"
```

which *cg-mwesplit* reformats to two cohorts:

```
"<illu>"
        "illu" N Sg Nom
"< sáhka>"
        "sáhka" N Sg Nom
```

3.3 Rule-based disambiguation of ambiguous tokenisation

As mentioned above, disambiguation of ambiguous tokenisation is done after morphological analysis. Consequently, this step has access to undisambiguated morphological (but not full syntactical) information. In addition, lexical semantic tags and valency tags are provided. The rules that resolve sentence boundary ambiguity are based on transitivity tags of abbreviations, lexical semantic tags, and morphological tags. Some of them are specific to one particular abbreviation.

Bi- or trigrams given ambiguous tokenisation can either be misspelled compounds (i.e. in North Sámi typically two-part compounds are the norm) or two words with a syntactic relation. The assumption is that if a compound is lexicalised, two or more adjacent words may be analysed as a compound and receive an errortag (*Err/SpaceCmp*), using a CG rule such as the following:

```
SELECT SUB:* (Err/SpaceCmp) IF (NEGATE
    0/* Err/MissingSpace OR Ess);
```

This rule selects the error reading unless any subreading of this reading (`0/*`) already has another error tag or is an essive case form.

This is the case unless any other previously applied rule has removed the error reading. Version r172405 of the tokenisation disambiguation grammar *mwe-dis.cg3* has 40 REMOVE rules and 8 SELECT rules.

Compound errors are ruled out for example if the first word is in genitive case as it can be the first part of a compound but also a premodifier. The simplified CG rule below removes the compound error reading if the first component is in genitive unless it receives a case error reading (nominative/accusative or nominative/genitive) or it is a lesser used possessive reading and a non-human noun. The rule makes use of both morphological and semantic information.

```
REMOVE (Err/SpaceCmp) IF (0/1 Gen -
    Allegro - Err/Orth-nom-acc - Err/
    Orth-nom-gen - PX-NONHUM);
```

(7) **Gaskavahku   eahkeda**
Wednesday.GEN evening.ACC
'Wednesday evening'

(8) **áhpehis nissonolbmuid**
pregnant woman.ACC.PL
'pregnant women'

In ex. (7), *gaskavahku* 'Wednesday' is in genitive case. The context to rule out a compound error is very local. In ex. (8), *áhpehis* 'pregnant' the first part of the potential compound is an attributive adjective form. Also here compound errors are categorically discarded.

(9) Paltto lea **riegádan jagi**   1947
Paltto is born.PRFPRC year.ACC 1947
'Paltto was born in 1947'

(10) galggai buot báikkiin   **dárogiella**
should all   place.LOC.PL Norwegian.NOM
oahpahusgiellan
instructing.language in all places
'Norwegian had to be the instructing language'

Other cases of compound error disambiguation, however, are more global. In ex. (9), *riegádan jagi* 'birth year (Acc.)' is a lexicalized compound. However as it is preceded by a finite verb, which is also a copula, i.e. *lea* 'is', the perfect participle form *riegádan* 'born' is part of a past tense construction ('was born'), and the compound error needs to be discarded.

In ex. (10), on the other hand, the relation between the first part of the bigram (*dárogiella* 'Norwegian') and the second part (*oahpahusgiellan* 'instructing language (Ess.)') is that of a subject to a subject predicate. The disambiguation grammar refers to a finite copula (*galggai* 'should') preceding the bigram.

4 Evaluation

In this section we evaluate the previously described modules of the North Sámi grammar checker.

Firstly, we evaluate the disambiguation of compound errors in terms of precision and recall. Then we compare our system for sentence segmentation with an unsupervised system. Since a corpus with correctly annotated compound and sentence boundary tokenisation for North Sámi is not available, all evaluation and annotation is done from scratch. We use the *SIKOR* corpus (SIKOR2016)),[12] a descriptive corpus which contains automatic annotations for linguistic research purposes, but no manually checked/verified tags. We selected a random corpus of administrative texts for two reasons. We had a suspicion that it would have many abbreviations and cases of ambiguous tokenisation. Secondly, administrative texts stand for a large percentage of the total North Sámi text body, and the genre is thus important for a substantial group of potential users of our programs.

4.1 Compound error evaluation

For the quantitative evaluation of the disambiguation of potential compound errors we calculated both precision (correct fraction of all marked errors) and recall (correct fraction of all errors). The corpus used contains 340,896 space separated strings, as reported by the Unix tool `wc`. The exact number of tokens will vary depending on tokenisation techniques, as described below.

The evaluation is based on lexicalised compounds as potential targets of ambiguous tokenisation. A previous approach allowed ambiguous tokenisation of dynamic compounds too, solely using syntactic rules to disambiguate. However, this led to many false positives (which would require more rules to avoid). Since our lexicon has over 110,000 lexicalised compounds (covering 90.5 % of the compounds in the North Sámi *SIKOR* corpus) coverage is acceptable without the riskier dynamic compound support.[13]

Table 1 contains the quantitative results of the compound error evaluation. Of the 340.895 running bigrams in the text, there were a total of 4.437 potential compound errors, i.e. 1.30 % of running bigrams are analysed as possible compounds by our lexicon. On manually checking, we found 458 of these to be true compound errors (0.13 % of running bigrams, or 10.3 % of potential compound errors as marked by the lexicon). So the table

---

[12] *SIKOR* contains a range of genres; the part used for evaluation contains bureaucratic texts.

[13] For less developed lexicons, the trade-off may be worth it.

True positives	360
False positives	110
True negatives	3,869
False negatives	98
Precision	76.6%
Recall	78.6%

Table 1: Qualitative evaluation of CG compound error detection

indicates how well our Constraint Grammar disambiguates compound errors from words that are supposed to be written apart, and tells nothing of the work done by the lexicon in selecting possible compound errors (nor of possible compound errors missed by the lexicon).[14]

Precision for compound error detection is well above the 67% threshold for any error type in a commercial grammar checker mentioned by Arppe (2000, p.17), and the F0.5 (weighting precision twice as much as recall) score is 77.0%, above e.g. Grundkiewicz and Junczys-Dowmunt (2018)'s 72.0%.[15]

False positives occur for example in cases where there is an internal syntactic structure such as in the case of ex. (11), where both *bálvalus* 'service' and *geavaheddjiide* 'user (Ill. Pl.)' are participants in the sentence's argument structure. Since there is no finite verb, the syntactic relation could only be identified by defining the valency of *bálvalus* 'service'.

(11)   Buoret **bálvalus**   **geavaheddjiide**
        Better service.NOM.SG user.ILL.PL
        'Better service to the users'

A number of the false negatives (cf. ex. (12)) are due to frequent expressions including *lágan* (i.e. *iešgudetlagan* 'different', *dánlágan* 'this kind of', etc.), which need to be resolved by means of an idiosyncratic rule. *Dan* and *iešgudet* are genitive or attributive pronoun forms and not typically part of a compound, so a syntactic rule only does not resolve the problem.

(12)   *****iešgudet lágan** molssaeavttut
        different kinds alternative.PL
        'Different kinds of alternatives'

(13)   *****Láhka**   **rievdadusaid**
        law.NOM;lacquer.GEN changing.ACC.PL
        birra
        about
        'About the law alterations'

In ex. (13), there is a compound error. However, one of the central rules in the tokeniser disambiguation grammar removes the compound error reading if the first part of the potential compound is in the long genitive case form. However, in this case *láhka* can be both the genitive form of *láhkka* 'lacquer' and the nominative form of *láhka* 'law'. This unpredictable lexical ambiguity had not been taken into account by the disambiguation rule, which is why there is a false negative. In the future it can be resolved by referring to the postposition *birra* 'about', which asks for a preceding genitive.

4.2   Sentence boundary evaluation

A common method for splitting sentences in a complete pipeline (used e.g. by *LanguageTool*) is to tokenise first, then do sentence splitting, followed by other stages of linguistic analysis. Here a standalone tokeniser would be used, e.g. PUNKT (Kiss and Strunk, 2006), an unsupervised model that uses no linguistic analysis, or GATE[16] which uses regex-based rules. The Python package SpaCy[17] on the other hand trains a supervised model that predicts sentence boundaries jointly with dependency structure. Stanford CoreNLP[18] uses finite state automata to tokenise, then does sentence splitting.

In contrast, our method uses no statistical inference. We tokenise as the first step, but the tokenisation remains ambiguous until part of the linguistic analysis is complete.

Below, we make a comparison with PUNKT[19], which, although requiring no labelled training data, has been reported[20] to perform quite well compared to other popular alternatives.

As with the above evaluation, we used bureaucratic parts of the *SIKOR* corpus. We trained the PUNKT implementation that comes with NLTK on

---

[14]We have also not calculated the number of actual compounds in the evaluation corpus, so the ratio of compound errors to correct compounds is unknown.

[15] We would like to compare performance on this task with a state-of-the-art machine learning method, but have seen no references for this particular task to use as an unbiased baseline. However, the gold data set that was developed for evaluating our method is freely available to researchers who would like to experiment with improving on the results.

[16]`http://gate.ac.uk/` (accessed 2018-10-08)

[17]`https://spacy.io/` (accessed 2018-10-08)

[18]`http://www-nlp.stanford.edu/software/corenlp.shtml` (accessed 2018-10-08)

[19]`https://www.nltk.org/_modules/nltk/tokenize/punkt.html` (accessed 2018-10-08)

[20]`https://tech.grammarly.com/blog/how-to-split-sentences` (accessed 2018-10-08)

System	PUNKT	Divvun
True pos.	1932	1986
False pos. (split mid-sent)	39	29
True neg.	474	484
False neg. (joined sents)	55	1
Precision	98.02%	98.56%
Recall	97.23%	99.95%

Table 2: Sentence segmentation errors per system on 2500 possible sentences.[22]

287.516 "words" (as counted by `wc`), and manually compared the differences between our system (named *divvun* below) and PUNKT. We used a trivial `sed` script `s/[.?:!] */&\n/g` to create a "baseline" count of possible sentences, and ran the evaluation on the first 2500 potential sentences given by this script (as one big paragraph), counting the places where the systems either split something that should have been one sentence, or treated two sentences as one; see table 2.

Of the differences, we note that PUNKT often treats abbreviations like *nr* or *kap.* as sentence boundaries, even if followed by lower-case words or numbers (*st. meld. 15* as three sentences). Our system sometimes makes this mistake too, but much more rarely. Also, PUNKT never treats colon as sentence boundaries. The colon in Sámi is used for case endings on names, e.g. *Jönköping:s*, but of course also as a clause or sentence boundary. Thus many of the PUNKT errors are simply *not* marking a colon as a sentence boundary. On the other hand, our system has some errors where an unknown word led to marking the colon (or period) as a boundary. This could be fixed in our system with a simple CG rule.

There are also some odd cases of PUNKT not splitting on period even with following space and title cased word, e.g. *geavahanguovlluid. Rádjegeassin*. Where the baseline *sed* script creates the most sentence boundaries in our evaluation test set (2500), our system creates 2015 sentences, and *PUNKT* 1971.

Our system is able to distinguish sentence boundaries where the user forgot to include a space, e.g. *buorrin.Vuoigatvuođat* is correctly treated as a sentence boundary. This sort of situation is hard to distinguish in general without a large lexicon. Our system does make some easily fixable errors, e.g. *kap.1* was treated as a sentence boundary due to a wrongly-written CG rule (as such, this evaluation

has been helpful in uncovering silly mistakes). Being a rule-based system, it is easy to support new contexts when required.

5 Conclusion

We have introduced the North Sámi grammar checker presenting its system architecture and described its use and necessity for the North Sámi language community. Tokenisation is the first step in a grammar checker when approaching frequent spelling error types that cannot be resolved without grammatical context. We are questioning the traditional concept of a token separated by a space, not only in terms of multiwords, but also in terms of potential compound errors. Our experiment showed that our system outperforms a state-of-the-art unsupervised sentence segmenter. Disambiguation of compound errors and other two-word combinations give good results both in terms of precision and recall, i.e. both are above 76%. Our method of ambiguous tokenisation and ambiguity resolution by means of grammatical context allows us to improve tokenisation significantly compared to the standard approaches. The integration of the grammar checker framework in the *Giella* infrastructure ensures that this approach to tokenisation is directly available to all other languages using this infrastructure.

Acknowledgments

We especially would like to thank Thomas Omma for testing rules and checking examples within the above discussed modules, and our colleagues in *Divvun* and *Giellatekno* for their daily contributions to our language tools and the infrastructure.

References

Lene Antonsen. 2012. Improving feedback on l2 misspellings - an fst approach. In *Proceedings of the SLTC 2012 workshop on NLP for CALL; Lund; 25th October; 2012*, 80, pages 1–10. Linköping University Electronic Press; Linköpings universitet.

Antti Arppe. 2000. Developing a grammar checker for Swedish. In *Proceedings of the 12th Nordic Conference of Computational Linguistics (NoDaLiDa 1999)*, pages 13–27, Department of Linguistics, Norwegian University of Science and Technology (NTNU), Trondheim, Norway.

Kenneth R. Beesley and Lauri Karttunen. 2003. *Finite State Morphology*. CSLI Studies in Computational Linguistics. CSLI Publications, Stanford.

Eckhard Bick. 2006. A constraint grammar based spellchecker for Danish with a special focus on dyslexics. In Mickael Suominen, Antti Arppe, Anu Airola, Orvokki Heinämäki, Matti Miestamo, Urho Määttä, Jussi Niemi, Kari K. Pitkänen, and Kaius Sinnemäki, editors, *A Man of Measure: Festschrift in Honour of Fred Karlsson on his 60th Birthday*, volume 19/2006 of *Special Supplement to SKY Jounal of Linguistics*, pages 387–396. The Linguistic Association of Finland, Turku.

Eckhard Bick. 2015. DanProof: Pedagogical spell and grammar checking for Danish. In *Proceedings of the 10th International Conference Recent Advances in Natural Language Processing (RANLP 2015)*, pages 55–62, Hissar, Bulgaria. INCOMA Ltd.

Eckhard Bick and Tino Didriksen. 2015. CG-3 – beyond classical Constraint Grammar. In *Proceedings of the 20th Nordic Conference of Computational Linguistics (NoDaLiDa 2015)*, pages 31–39. Linköping University Electronic Press, Linköpings universitet.

Børre Gaup, Sjur Moshagen, Thomas Omma, Maaren Palismaa, Tomi Pieski, and Trond Trosterud. 2006. From Xerox to Aspell: A first prototype of a north sámi speller based on twol technology. In *Finite-State Methods and Natural Language Processing*, pages 306–307, Berlin, Heidelberg. Springer Berlin Heidelberg.

Roman Grundkiewicz and Marcin Junczys-Dowmunt. 2018. Near human-level performance in grammatical error correction with hybrid machine translation. *arXiv preprint arXiv:1804.05945*.

Sam Hardwick, Miikka Silfverberg, and Krister Lindén. 2015. Extracting semantic frames using hfst-pmatch. In *Proceedings of the 20th Nordic Conference of Computational Linguistics, (NoDaLiDa 2015)*, pages 305–308.

Fred Karlsson. 1990. Constraint Grammar as a Framework for Parsing Running Text. In *Proceedings of the 13th Conference on Computational Linguistics (COLING 1990)*, volume 3, pages 168–173, Helsinki, Finland. Association for Computational Linguistics.

Fred Karlsson, Atro Voutilainen, Juha Heikkilä, and Arto Anttila. 1995. *Constraint Grammar: A Language-Independent System for Parsing Unrestricted Text*. Mouton de Gruyter, Berlin.

Lauri Karttunen. 2011. Beyond morphology: Pattern matching with FST. In *SFCM*, volume 100 of *Communications in Computer and Information Science*, pages 1–13. Springer.

Tibor Kiss and Jan Strunk. 2006. Unsupervised multilingual sentence boundary detection. *Computational Linguistics*, 32(4):485–525.

Krister Lindén, Miikka Silfverberg, Erik Axelson, Sam Hardwick, and Tommi Pirinen. 2011.

Hfst—framework for compiling and applying morphologies. In Cerstin Mahlow and Michael Pietrowski, editors, *Systems and Frameworks for Computational Morphology*, volume Vol. 100 of *Communications in Computer and Information Science*, pages 67–85. Springer-Verlag, Berlin, Heidelberg.

Eva Lindgren, Kirk P H Sullivan, Hanna Outakoski, and Asbjørg Westum. 2016. Researching literacy development in the globalised North: studying trilingual children's english writing in Finnish, Norwegian and Swedish Sápmi. In David R. Cole and Christine Woodrow, editors, *Super Dimensions in Globalisation and Education*, Cultural Studies and Transdiciplinarity in Education, pages 55–68. Springer, Singapore.

Marcin Milkowski. 2010. Developing an open-source, rule-based proofreading tool. *Softw., Pract. Exper.*, 40(7):543–566.

Sjur N. Moshagen, Tommi A. Pirinen, and Trond Trosterud. 2013. Building an open-source development infrastructure for language technology projects. In *NODALIDA*.

Hanna Outakoski. 2013. Davvisámegielat čálamáhtu konteaksta [The context of North Sámi literacy]. *Sámi dieđalaš áigečála*, 1/2015:29–59.

SIKOR2016. 2016-12-08. SIKOR UiT The Arctic University of Norway and the Norwegian Saami Parliament's Saami text collection. **URL:** *http://gtweb.uit.no/korp (Accessed 2016-12-08)*.

Gary F. Simons and Charles D. Fennig, editors. 2018. *Ethnologue: Languages of the World*, twenty-first edition. SIL International, Dallas, Texas.

Joel R. Tetreault, Keisuke Sakaguchi, and Courtney Napoles. 2017. JFLEG: A fluency corpus and benchmark for grammatical error correction. In *Proceedings of the 15th Conference of the European Chapter of the Association for Computational Linguistics, EACL 2017, Valencia, Spain, April 3-7, 2017, Volume 2: Short Papers*, pages 229–234.

Linda Wiechetek. 2012. Constraint Grammar based correction of grammatical errors for North Sámi. In *Proceedings of the Workshop on Language Technology for Normalisation of Less-Resourced Languages (SALTMIL 8/AFLAT 2012)*, pages 35–40, Istanbul, Turkey. European Language Resources Association (ELRA).

Linda Wiechetek. 2017. *When grammar can't be trusted – Valency and semantic categories in North Sámi syntactic analysis and error detection*. PhD thesis, UiT The arctic university of Norway.

Corpus of usage examples: What is it good for?

Timofey Arkhangelskiy

Universität Hamburg / Alexander von Humboldt Foundation

timarkh@gmail.com

Abstract

Lexicography and corpus studies of grammar have a long history of fruitful interaction. For the most part, however, this has been a one-way relationship. Lexicographers have extensively used corpora to identify previously undetected word senses or find natural usage examples; using lexicographic materials when conducting data-driven investigations of grammar, on the other hand, is hardly commonplace. In this paper, I present a Beserman Udmurt corpus made out of "artificial" dictionary examples. I argue that, although such a corpus can not be used for certain kinds of corpus-based research, it is nevertheless a very useful tool for writing a reference grammar of a language. This is particularly important in the case of underresourced endangered varieties, which Beserman is, because of the scarcity of available corpus data. The paper describes the process of developing the Beserman usage example corpus, explores its differences compared to traditional text corpora, and discusses how those can be beneficial for grammar research.

1 Introduction

Following a widely acknowledged idea that the language above the phonological level can be roughly split into lexicon and grammar, language documentation is divided into two interconnected subfields, lexicography and grammar studies. Corpora have been used since their advent in both these domains; one of the first studies of English based on the Brown corpus (Francis and Kučera, 1982) contained frequency analysis for both words and parts of speech. It was recognized early on in the history of corpora that they are an excellent source of usage examples for both dictionaries and reference grammars. This gave rise to a data-driven approach to language documentation, which prescribes using only "real" examples taken from corpora in descriptive work (Francis, 1993). Corpora have become standard providers of dictionary examples, which can even be searched for automatically (Kilgarriff et al., 2008). However, this approach can hardly be applied to underresourced endangered languages because it relies on large representative corpora, which are normally unavailable for such languages. Grammatical studies based on small spoken corpora with minimal help of additional elicitation are often possible and have been conducted, e.g. by Khanina (2017) for Enets or by Klumpp (2005) for Kamas. The same cannot be said about lexicography. While even small corpora are a valuable source of usage examples for dictionaries, the lexicographer has to elicit examples for non-frequent or obsolete entries or word senses. These examples usually stay in the dictionary and are not used for any non-lexicographic research.

I argue that such elicited usage examples can be turned into a corpus, which can actually prove to be helpful for a variety of grammar studies, especially in the absence of large "natural" corpora. An example of a feature that cannot be available in traditional corpora, but can appear in elicited examples, is negative linguistic material. The paper describes a corpus of usage examples I developed for the documentation of Beserman Udmurt. It presents the data and the methods I used to develop the corpus. After that, its frequency characteristics are compared to those of traditional spoken corpora. Finally, its benefits and disadvantages for certain kinds of grammar research are discussed.

2 The data

Beserman is classified by Kelmakov (1998) as one of the dialects of Udmurt (Uralic > Permic). It is spoken by approximately 2200 people who belong to the Beserman ethnic group, mostly in North-

Proceedings of the 3rd Workshop on the Use of Computational Methods in the Study of Endangered Languages: Vol. 1 Papers, pages 56–63,
Honolulu, Hawai'i, USA, February 26–27, 2019.

Western Udmurtia, Russia. Having no official orthography, it remains almost entirely spoken. This, together with the fact that transmission to children has virtually stopped, makes it an endangered variety. It differs significantly from Standard Udmurt in phonology, lexicon and grammar, which justifies the need for separate dictionaries and grammatical descriptions. The two existing grammatical descriptions, by Teplyashina (1970) and Lyukina (2008), deal primarily with phonology and morphemics, leaving out grammatical semantics and syntax.

Beserman is the object of an ongoing documentation project, whose goal is to produce a dictionary and a reference grammar, accompanied by a spoken corpus. The dictionary, which nears completion, contains approximately 5500 entries, most of which have elaborate descriptions of word senses and phraseology, and illustrated with examples. The annotated texts currently count about 103,000 words, which are split into two collections, sound-aligned corpus (labeled further SpC) and not sound-aligned corpus.[1]

3 Development of the corpus

The Beserman usage example corpus (labeled further ExC) currently contains about 82,000 words in 14,000 sentences. Each usage example is aligned with its translation into Russian[2] and comments. The comments tier contains the information about the number of speakers the example was verified with, and remarks on possible meanings or context. The main source of examples for the corpus was the dictionary, however a small part (5% of the corpus) comes from grammatical questionnaires. The dictionary examples were collected using several different techniques. First, there are translations from Russian (often modified by the speakers in order to be more informative and better describe their culture). Second, many examples were generated by the speakers themselves, who were trained to do so by the linguists. Finally, some of the examples were pro-

duced by the linguists (none of who is a native Beserman speaker) and subsequently checked and corrected by the speakers. The development of the corpus included filtering and converting the source data, performing automatic morphological annotation, and indexing in a corpus platform with a web interface.

3.1 Data preparation

The dictionary is stored in a database created by the TLex dictionary editor, which allows export of the data to XML. The XML version of the dictionary was used as the source file for filtering and conversion.

The filtering included three steps. First, the Beserman dictionary contains examples taken from the spoken corpus. Such examples had to be filtered out to avoid duplicate representation of the same data in the two corpora. Identifying such examples might be challenging because they are not consistently marked in the dictionary database, and because some of them were slightly changed (e.g. punctuation was added or personal data was removed). To find usage examples that come from the spoken corpus, each of them was compared to the sentences of the corpus. Before the comparison, all sentences were transformed to lowercase, and all whitespaces were removed. If no exact matches were found, the Levenshtein distance to the corpus sentences of comparable length was measured. The cut-off parameters were obtained empirically to achieve a balance between precision and recall. If a corpus sentence with a distance of $max(2, len/8)$ was found, where len is the length of the example in question, the example was discarded. Additionally, the "comment" field was checked. The example was discarded if it contained an explicit indication that it had been taken from a text.

Second part of the filtering involved deduplication of examples. Deduplication was necessary because some usage examples appeared in multiple entries. In this case, their versions could have minor differences as well, e.g. because of typo corrections that were made in only one of them. Two sentences were considered identical if both their lowercase versions and their lowercase translations had the Damerau–Levenshtein distance not greater than $len/10$.

Finally, the dictionary is a work in progress. As such, it contains a number of examples that

---

[1] Both the dictionary in its current version and the corpora are publicly accessible at `http://beserman.ru` and `http://multimedia-corpus.beserman.ru/search`.

[2] Since the native speakers, including heritage speakers, are the primary target audience of the dictionary, and they are bilingual in Russian, the examples are translated into Russian. Translation of the dictionary into English has started recently, but no English translations of examples are available at the moment.

have not been proofread or have not passed sufficient verification, which means checking with three speakers, as a rule. The goal of the third step of filtering was to include in the corpus only reliable examples that do not require additional verification. This was done using a combination of comments and available metadata. The examples from the sections that have been entirely proofread for publishing were all included. Examples from other sections were only included if they had indication in the comment that they have been checked with at least two speakers. This excluded a considerable number of examples from the verbal part of the dictionary, which is under construction now. The total share of examples that come from the verbal part is currently just above 9%, despite the fact that verbal examples in the dictionary actually outnumber examples from all other parts taken together. As a consequence, the total size of the corpus is likely to increase significantly after the verbal part has been finalized, probably reaching 150,000 words.

An important difference between a traditional corpus and a collection of usage examples is that the latter may contain negative examples, i.e. sentences which are considered ungrammatical by the speakers. About 9.5% of sentences in the Beserman corpus of usage examples contain negative material. Following linguistic tradition, the sentences or ungrammatical parts of sentences are marked with asterisks. Other gradations of grammatical acceptability include *? (ungrammatical for most speakers) and ?? (marginal / ungrammatical for many speakers). Negative examples are identified by the converter based on the presence of such marks in their texts and by the metadata.

The resulting examples are stored as tab-delimited plain text files. Each file contains examples from one dictionary entry or one grammatical questionnaire; positive and negative examples are kept in separate files. Each example is stored on a separate line and contains the original text, its Russian translation, and comments. Additionally, all filenames are listed in a tab-delimited file together with their metadata.

3.2 Morphological annotation

A workflow used in the Beserman documentation project prior to 2017 involved transcription of recordings for the spoken corpus in a simple text editor and manual annotation in SIL FLEX. That workflow was abandoned, mainly because manual annotation required too much resources, given the amount of recorded data that had to be processed. The new workflow comprises transcription, translation and alignment of recordings in ELAN, subsequent automatic morphological annotation and automatic disambiguation. Such an approach has been demonstrated to be well suited for processing spoken corpora of comparable size by Gerstenberger et al. (2017).

Developing a rule-based morphological analyzer would be a time-consuming task in itself, which is why Waldenfels et al. (2014) and Gerstenberger et al. (2017) advocate for transcribing in standard orthography and applying an analyzer for the standardized variety of the language. The Beserman case is different though because there already exists a digital dictionary. Using the dictionary XML as a source, I was able to produce a grammatical dictionary with the description of lemmata and inflection types. The dictionary was manually enhanced with additional information relevant for disambiguation, such as animacy for nouns or transitivity for verbs. Apart from that, several dozen frequent Russian borrowings, absent from the dictionary, were added to the list. Coupled with a formalized description of morphology, which I compiled manually, it became the basis for the automatic Beserman morphological analyzer. This analyzer is used for processing both new transcriptions in ELAN and usage examples.

After applying the analyzer to the texts, each token is annotated with a lemma, a part of speech, additional dictionary characteristics, and all inflectional morphological features, such as case and number. Annotated texts are stored in JSON. If there are several analyses possible for a token, they are all stored. The resulting ambiguity is then reduced from 1.7 to 1.35 analyses per analyzed token by a set of 87 Constraint Grammar rules (Bick and Didriksen, 2015). The idea was to apply only those rules which demonstrate near-absolute precision (at least 98%), while leaving more complex ambiguity cases untouched. The resulting coverage of the analyzer is 96.3% on the corpus of usage examples. While this number might look unusually high, it is in fact quite expected, given that there should be a dictionary entry for any non-borrowed word that occurs in any dictionary example.

3.3 Indexing

The annotated texts are uploaded to a server and indexed, after which they are available for search through a web interface using an open-source Tsakoprus corpus platform.[3] The interface allows making simple and multiword queries. The queries may include constraints on word, lemma, part of speech, morphological tags, glosses, or any combinations. In word and lemma search, wildcards and regular expressions are available. The search can produce a list of sentences or a list of words that conform to the query, together with some statistical data. The Russian translations are also morphologically analyzed and searchable. The interface is available in English and Russian, and several transliteration options are available for displaying the texts.

4 Differences from spoken corpora

For comparison, I will use the sound-aligned part of the Beserman spoken corpus (SpC), which was morphologically annotated and indexed the same way the Corpus of usage examples (ExC) was processed. At the moment, it contains about 38,000 words in monologues, natural dialogues and dialogues recorded during referential communication experiments. To account for the difference in size, all frequencies will be presented in items per million (ipm).

Two obvious factors make ExC quite different from SpC frequency-wise. First, the former contains comparable amount of usage examples for both frequent and non-frequent words. As a consequence, it has a different frequency distribution of words and lemmata. Its lexical diversity, measured as overall type/token ratio, is visibly higher than that of SpC (0.224 vs. 0.179), despite the fact that it is more than twice as large.

Second, elicited examples constitute a genre very different from natural narratives and dialogues. For example, they contain a much smaller number of discourse particles or personal pronouns. Table 1 demonstrates how different the frequencies of certain lexical classes are in the two corpora.

Additionally, there are more different forms attested for a single lemma on average in ExC than in SpC (Table 2). Although unequal size of the corpora being compared could play a role here, the

POS / Lexical class	SpC	ExC
noun	206K	**400K**
verb	213K	**289K**
adjective	52K	**68K**
pronoun	**177K**	123K
discourse ptcl.	**72K**	22K

Table 1: Frequencies (in ipm) of certain parts of speech and lexical classes in SpC and ExC.

POS	SpC	ExC
noun	3.15	**4.44**
verb	4.75	**6.08**
adjective	2.16	**2.56**
pronoun	2.72	**2.92**

Table 2: Average number of different forms per lemma for certain parts of speech in SpC and ExC.

difference could be explained at least in part by the fact that the lexicographers had a goal of providing each word with a handful of examples containing that word in different forms and in different syntactic positions.

However, the analysis of value distributions of individual grammatical categories within a given part of speech reveals that they are usually not drastically different in the two corpora. Let us take nouns as an example. Nominal categories in Udmurt are case, number and possessiveness. Table 3[4] shows the distribution of case forms in the two corpora (all 8 spatial cases were collated in the last row). Table 4 shows the distribution of number forms. Table 5 shows the distribution of possessive suffixes.[5]

Case and number distributions only have minor differences in SpC and ExC. Moreover, an analysis of combinations of case and number suffixes shows that the distributions of their combinations also look very much alike. Possessiveness presents a somewhat different picture. Although not entirely different from SpC, the distribution in ExC shows lower figures for 2sg, 3pl, and especially 3sg, and higher ones for the first person possessors. Lower numbers for 3sg and 2sg have a straightforward explanation. Apart from being

---

[4] The numbers in each column add up to slightly more than 100% because of the remaining ambiguity.

[5] Nouns may occur without possessive marking; only nouns marked for possessiveness were included. Figures for 2pl were verified manually because of large-scale ambiguity between nom,2pl and pl,acc.

case	SpC	ExC
nominative / unmarked	60%	65.7%
accusative (marked)	4.7%	9.9%
dative	2%	1.2%
genitive	1.8%	2.2%
2nd genitive (ablative)	0.74%	1.6%
instrumental	7%	4.7%
caritive	0.025%	0.024%
adverbial	0.25%	0.13%
all spatial cases	24.6%	20%

Table 3: Share of different case forms for nouns in SpC and ExC.

number	SpC	ExC
sg	94.6%	92.7%
pl	5.4%	7.3%

Table 4: Share of different number forms for nouns in SpC and ExC.

possessor	SpC	ExC
1sg	13.2%	28.2%
1pl	1.7%	5.6%
2sg	13.5%	7.7%
2pl	0.2%	0.4%
3sg	63%	54.8%
3pl	8.4%	3.3%

Table 5: Share of different possessive forms for possessive-marked nouns in SpC and ExC.

used in the direct, possessive sense, these particular suffixes have a range of "discourse", non-possessive functions. This is also true for Standard Udmurt (Winkler, 2001) and other Uralic languages (Simonenko, 2014). The 3sg possessive marks, among other things, contrastive topics and semi-activated topics that have to be reactivated in the discourse. The 2sg possessive is also used with non-possessive meanings, although less often, only in dialogues and in other contexts than the 3sg. Its primary discourse function is marking a new referent that is located physically or metaphorically in the domain of the addressee. Example 1, taken from a dialogue, shows both suffixes in non-possessive functions:

(1) Vaj   so-ize=no
     bring.IMP that-P.3SG.ACC=ADD
     gozâ-de!
     rope-P.2SG.ACC

'Bring me that rope as well!'

tense	SpC	ExC
present	43.8%	39.4%
past (direct)	30%	43.2%
future	26.2%	17.4%

Table 6: Share of different tense forms for finite verbs in SpC and ExC.

The 3sg possessive on "that" marks contrast: another rope was discussed earlier in the conversation. The 2sg possessive on "rope" indicates that this particular rope has not been mentioned in the previous discourse and should be identified by the addressee. The rope is located next to the addressee. That the direct possessive sense is ruled out here follows from the fact that the whole dialogue happens on the speaker's property, so the rope belongs to him, rather than to the addressee. Such "discourse" use of the possessives in elicited examples is quite rare because they normally require a wider context to appear. A possible explanation for the lower 3pl figure in ExC is that it is often used when the plural possessor was mentioned earlier and is recoverable from the context.

A quick look at the distribution of verbal tenses in Table 6[6] shows a picture similar to that of the possessives. The distributions are not wildly different, but the past tense is clearly more frequent in ExC. This is expected because a lot of usage examples, especially for obsolete words, contain information about cultural practices connected to the item being described that are no longer followed. In this respect, the tense distribution in ExC resembles the one in the narratives, which usually describe past events.

5 Fitness for grammar studies

The way a corpus of usage examples is different from traditional corpora makes it unfit for some kinds of linguistic research. It cannot be used in any study that looks into long-range discourse effects, requires a context or a conversation involving several participants. This includes, for example, studies of discourse particles, use of anaphoric pronouns, or information structure (topic/comment; given/new information, etc.). Similarly, it is useless for studies that rely on

---

[6]Only finite forms were counted. The fourth tense, the second (evidential) past, was not included because most of its forms are ambiguous with a much more frequent nominalization, to which it is historically related.

word or lemma frequency counts, or on type/token ratios, as those may differ significantly from traditional corpora.

All downsides listed above are quite predictable; in fact, it was hardly necessary to build a corpus of usage examples to arrive at those conclusions. Whether such a corpus could be of any value in other kinds of linguistic research, is a less trivial question. The observations in Section 4 suggest that the answer to that question is positive. While the Beserman corpus of usage examples differs from the spoken corpus in the places where it could be predicted to differ, it is remarkable how statistically similar the two corpora are in all other respects. The relative frequencies of grammatical forms are only different (although not extremely different) if these forms convey deictic or discourse-related meanings. In other cases, the forms have very similar distributions. This means that corpora of examples in principle can be used in linguistic research that involves comparing frequencies of certain grammatical forms or constructions, with necessary precautions.

Only research that involves comparing frequency counts or distributions of linguistic phenomena has been discussed so far. A lot of grammar studies, however, only or primarily need the information about (un)grammaticality or productivity of a certain phenomenon. It turns out that a corpus of usage examples could be actually superior to a traditional corpus of a comparable size for such studies. The reason for that is higher lexical diversity and more uniform frequency distribution of lemmata. This means that for any form or construction being studied, the researcher will see more *different* contexts involving it than in a traditional corpus, on average.

Let us take the approximative case as an example. This case, which has the marker *-lań* in all Udmurt varieties where it exists, marks the Ground in the approximate direction of which the Figure is moving. Although it is claimed to exist in literary Udmurt by all existing grammars, corpus studies reveal that it only functions as an unproductive derivational suffix compatible with a handful of nominal, pronominal and adjectival stems. To learn whether it can be considered a productive case suffix in Beserman, its compatibility with a wider range of nouns should be established.

The approximative has similar relative frequencies in ExC and SpC: 1858 ipm and 1750 ipm, re-

spectively. In both corpora, the approximative was not a primary focus of investigation. The number of different contexts it is encountered in, however, is much higher in ExC. In SpC, there are 16 different types that contain an approximative suffix, featuring 10 different stems. Only one of those stems (*ulća* 'street') does not attach the derivational approximative suffix in Standard Udmurt. This is definitely insufficient to establish its productiveness in Beserman. ExC, however, contains 32 different types that belong to 25 different stems. Such a difference can hardly be ascribed to the larger size of ExC because the number of different types is expected to have slower-than-linear growth with respect to the corpus size, and the type/stem ratio is expected to go up rather than down. Out of these stems, at least 5 are incompatible with the approximative in Standard Udmurt, including *reka* 'river', *korka* 'house' and *šundə* 'sun'.[7] Another 5 come from negative examples that highlight the incompatibility of the approximative with certain inflected postpositions (relational nouns). All this proves that it is most probably a productive suffix, while outlining the limits of its productivity.

Comparison of the figures for the recessive suffix, which also was not the focus of investigation in either corpus, yields similar results. The recessive case, with a marker *-laśen*, is the semantic opposite of the approximative and does not exist in the literary language even as a derivational suffix. In SpC, there are 7 different types that contain it. All of them have different lemmata, but again, only one of the types (*kətlaśen* 'from the side of the belly') suggests that they might not constitute a closed set of denominal adverbs. By contrast, ExC has 26 different types, containing 26 different stems, 4 out of which come from negative examples.

The skewed distribution of parts of speech could be beneficial too. For example, there is a construction in Udmurt that involves juxtaposition of an unmarked nominal stem to another noun, e.g. *t'ir nəd* 'axe handle'. It exists in other Uralic languages and has been analyzed as compounding by Fejes (2005). However, its productivity, allowed

---

[7]The 65,000-word FLEX part of the spoken corpus, not counted here, contains 21 different stems. However, this is only because it includes transcriptions of referential communication experiments specifically designed to make the participants use spatial cases and postpositions with a variety of nouns.

possessive relations and constraints on the dependent noun (animacy, referential status, etc.) vary significantly across Uralic languages and dialects. A detailed investigation of that construction would therefore require looking at a large number of instances featuring a variety of dependent nouns. A search for such a construction yields 77 different dependent nouns in SpC (total frequency 7525 ipm) and 449 different nouns in ExC (total frequency 25132 ipm).[8] In this case, the tremendous increase in numbers stems from the increased share of nouns in ExC, rather than from an increased lexical diversity. Nouns are almost twice as likely to appear in ExC than in SpC. Therefore meeting a sequence of two nouns would be almost 4 times higher if they were generated independently. The independence condition does not hold for words in a sentence, of course, but the observed factor of 3.34 is still large enough to make the corpus of examples a more attractive tool for studying the juxtaposition construction.

Research questions that arise when writing a reference grammar mostly belong to the type discussed above. Concise description of morphological and syntactic properties of an affix or a construction mostly require looking at a range of diverse examples to determine their productivity and constraints. The three case studies above show that this is exactly the situation where a corpus of usage examples could outperform a similarly sized spoken corpus.

Apart from the aforementioned considerations, which would probably be valid for a corpus based on any comprehensive dictionary, there are specific features of the Beserman usage example corpus that may become beneficial for research. Most importantly, it contains elicited examples from grammatical questionnaires, both positive and negative. Although their share is too small to reach any conclusions about their usefulness at the moment, this could be a first step to the reuse of elicited data in subsequent research. Currently, data collected through questionnaires is virtually always used only once. At best, the examples are archived to support the analysis based on them and ensure that the findings are reproducible; at worst, they are discarded and forgotten. Of course, each questionnaire is tailored to the particular research question of its author. However, it is probable that

if the corpus is large enough, it will contain examples that could prove useful for the research questions other than their author had in mind. Presence of negative material could partially reduce the general aversion to corpora that the linguists working in the generative paradigm tend to have. Availability of such corpora for multiple languages will also facilitate typologically oriented research on syntax, which otherwise relies on manual work with reference grammars and other secondary sources.

Finally, the Beserman corpus of usage examples, as well as any corpus based on a bilingual dictionary, is in essence a parallel corpus. This could be used for both linguistic needs (see e.g. Volk et al. (2014) for the list of possibilities) and for developing or evaluating machine translation systems.

6 Conclusion

Having a comprehensive dictionary in a machine-readable form and a morphological analyzer allows one to create a corpus of usage examples rather quickly. Its size could be comparable to those of large spoken corpora, which tend to have a maximum of 150,000 tokens for unwritten endangered languages. Even if a spoken corpus is available, this is a significant addition. Sometimes, however, dictionary examples could be the only large source of linguistic data, e.g. in the case of extinct languages. It is therefore important to know how the data of usage examples corresponds to that of spoken texts, and for what kind of linguistic research they are suitable. An analysis of the Beserman corpus of usage examples reveals that it can actually be used as a reliable tool in a wide range of research on grammar. Obvious limitations prevent its use in studies that involve word and lemma counts, discourse or information structure. However, outside of these areas, usage examples are quite similar to natural texts, which justifies use of such corpora. Increased lexical diversity and more uniform word distributions make corpora of usage examples even more useful for some kinds of research than traditional corpora of similar size. Finally, such corpora can additionally contain data from questionnaires and negative material, which could facilitate their reuse.

Acknowledgements

I am grateful to all my colleagues who have worked on the documentation of Beserman Ud-

---

[8]To avoid as much ambiguity as possible without manual filtering, the search was narrowed down to unambiguously annotated tokens.

murt and especially to Maria Usacheva. This research would have not been possible without their prolonged lexicographic work.

References

Eckhard Bick and Tino Didriksen. 2015. CG–3 - Beyond Classical Constraint Grammar. In *Proceedings of the 20th Nordic Conference of Computational Linguistics (NODALIDA 2015)*, pages 31–39. Linköping University Electronic Press.

László Fejes. 2005. *Összetett szavak finnugor nyelvekben [Compound words in Finno-Ugric languages]*. PhD, Eötvös Loránd Tudományegyetem, Budapest.

Gill Francis. 1993. A corpus-driven approach to grammar: Principles, methods and examples. In Mona Baker, Gill Francis, and Elena Tognini-Bonelli, editors, *Text and technology: In honour of John Sinclair*, pages 137–156. John Benjamins, Amsterdam & Philadelphia.

W. Nelson Francis and Henry Kučera. 1982. *Frequency Analysis of English Usage: Lexicon and Grammar*. Houghton Mifflin, Boston.

Ciprian Gerstenberger, Niko Partanen, and Michael Rießler. 2017. Instant annotations in ELAN corpora of spoken and written Komi, an endangered language of the Barents Sea region. In *Proceedings of the 2nd Workshop on the Use of Computational Methods in the Study of Endangered Languages*, pages 57–66. Association for Computational Linguistics.

Valentin Kelmakov. 1998. *Kratkij kurs udmurtskoj dialektologii [Brief course of Udmurt dialectology]*. Izdatel'stvo Udmurtskogo Universiteta, Izhevsk.

Olesya Khanina. 2017. Digital resources for Enets: A descriptive linguist's view. *Acta Linguistica Academica*, 64(3):417–433.

Adam Kilgarriff, Miloš Husák, Katy McAdam, Michael Rundell, and Pave Rychlý. 2008. GDEX: Automatically finding good dictionary examples in a corpus. In *Proceedings of the XIII EURALEX International Congress*, pages 425–432, Barcelona.

Gerson Klumpp. 2005. Aspect markers grammaticalized from verbs in Kamas. *Acta Linguistica Hungarica*, 52(4):397–409.

Nadezhda Lyukina. 2008. *Osobennosti jazyka balezinskix i jukamenskix besermjan [The peculiarities of the language of Balezino and Yukamenskoye Besermans]*. PhD, Udmurt State University, Izhevsk.

Aleksandra Simonenko. 2014. Microvariation in Finno-Ugric possessive markers. In *Proceedings of the Forty-Third Annual Meeting of the North East Linguistic Society (NELS 43)*, volume 2, pages 127–140.

Tamara Teplyashina. 1970. *Jazyk besermjan [The language of the Beserman]*. Nauka, Moscow.

Martin Volk, Johannes Graën, and Elena Callegaro. 2014. Innovations in Parallel Corpus Search Tools. In *LREC 2014 Proceedings*, pages 3172–3178.

Ruprecht von Waldenfels, Michael Daniel, and Nina Dobrushina. 2014. Why standard orthography? Building the Ustya River Basin corpus, an online corpus of a Russian dialect. In *Computational Linguistics and Intellectual Technologies. Papers from the Annual International Conference "Dialogue"*, volume 13, pages 720–728.

Eberhard Winkler. 2001. *Udmurt*. Number 212 in Languages of the world. Lincom Europa, Munich.

A Preliminary Plains Cree Speech Synthesizer

Atticus Harrigan
galvin@ualberta.ca

Timothy Mills
timills@ualberta.ca

Antti Arppe
arppe@ualberta.ca

Alberta Language Technology Laboratory
University of Alberta
Edmonton, Alberta

Abstract

This paper discusses the development and evaluation of a Speech Synthesizer for Plains Cree, an Algonquian language of North America. Synthesis is achieved using Simple4All and evaluation was performed using a modified Cluster Identification, Semantically Unpredictable Sentence, and a basic dichotomized judgment task. Resulting synthesis was not well received; however, observations regarding the process of speech synthesis evaluation in North American indigenous communities were made: chiefly, that tolerance for variation is often much lower in these communities than for majority languages. The evaluator did not recognize grammatically consistent but semantically nonsense strings as licit language. As a result, monosyllabic clusters and semantically unpredictable sentences proved not the most appropriate evaluate tools. Alternative evaluation methods are discussed.

1 Introduction

While majority languages such as English provide ample data for the creation and training of speech recognition, corpus annotation, and general language models, under-resourced languages are in a unique position to benefit greatly from such technologies. Speech Synthesizers, mobile keyboards, in-browser reading guides and smart dictionaries all provide invaluable tools to help aid language learners in gaining proficiency in languages where speaker numbers are falling. With the ubiquity of speech synthesis systems in public transit, emergency broadcast systems, and (most notably) mobile phones, under-resourced language communities often clamour for such technology. In addition to the positive social implications of having your language associated with technological innovation, speech synthesis systems provide a very real benefit in endangered and under-resourced language communities: while it is unfeasible for elders and remaining fluent speakers to detail every possible word and story, an ideal speech synthesizer allows for a learner to hear, on demand, any word, phrase, sentence, or passage. Despite this obvious benefit, endangered language groups rarely have such technology available, especially in the context of North American Indigenous languages.

This paper details the development of an early synthesizer for Plains Cree, an Indigenous language of Canada, and an evaluation of the resulting system. Through synthesis via the Simple4All suite of programs, this paper documents the pros and cons of such a system, and investigates how a speech synthesizer can be evaluated in the context of North American Indigenous languages.

2 Plains Cree Phonology

Plains Cree is a polysynthetic language of the Algonquian family spoken mainly in western Canada. With a recorded speaker count of nearly 35,000[1], Plains Cree is classified as a stage 5 language (or "developing") according to the Expanded Intergenerational Transmission Disruption Scale (Ethnologue, 2016).

Much of the literature on the language has focused on its morphosyntax. The phonetics and phonology have been less well described. Indeed, only five of the 50 pages of Wolfart's (1996) sketch of the language deal with what can be categorized as phonetics or phonology, and only four pages of his earlier, more comprehensive, grammar were dedicated to the topic (Wolfart, 1973). In the former, which is the more phonologically inclined, Wolfart identifies the phoneme inventory

---

[1] Although this is the current cited number of speakers, it is likely that this is an optimistic count of speakers. The true number is likely several thousand speakers lower, though reliable demographics are difficult to obtain.

Proceedings of the 3rd Workshop on the Use of Computational Methods in the Study of Endangered Languages: Vol. 1 Papers, pages 64–73,
Honolulu, Hawai‘i, USA, February 26–27, 2019.

of Plains Cree as containing eight consonants, two semi-vowels/glides, and seven vowels (three short and four long).[2]

Although Plains Cree vowels are distinguished by length, it is also the case that the long vowels are qualitatively different from the short vowels (with the short vowels being less peripheral than their long counterparts (Harrigan and Tucker, 2015; Muehlbauer, 2012)). Further, the issue of quality is exacerbated by the language's system of stress, which is poorly understood. Consonants show similar, though better understood, variation. Stops are generally voiceless word initially, geminated when between two short vowels, and show free-variation between voiced and voiceless realization otherwise (Wolfart, 1996). The affricate /ts/ and fricative /s/ appear in seemingly free variation with [tʃ] and [ʃ], respectively (Wolfart, 1996). Plains Cree also possesses diphthongs, though only as allophonic realizations of vowels adjacent to glides. When either long or short /a/, /o/, or /e/ occur before /j/ the diphthongs [aɪ], [oɪ], [eɪ] occur (respectively). When these come before /w/, the diphthongs [aʊ], [oʊ], and [eʊ] are realized (respectively). When short or long /i/ occurs before /j/, it is lengthened; when short /i/ comes before /w/, [o] is realized, while long /i:/ in the same position produces the diphthong [iʊ]

Possible syllables are described by Wolfart (1996, 431) as having an optional onset composed of a consonant (optionally followed by a /w/ if the consonant is stop, an affricate, or /m/), a vowel nucleus, followed by an optional coda composed of a single consonant or either an /s/ or /h/ followed by a stop/affricate. According to Wolfart (1996, 431) the vast majority of Cree syllables have no coda.

Plains Cree has a standardized orthography referred to as the Standard Roman Orthography (SRO) The standard is best codified by Okimâsis and Wolvengrey (2008) and makes use of a phonemic representation, ignoring allophonic variation such as the stop voicing described above. The standard also offers morphophonological information; for example, although the third-person singular *apiw* ('S/he sits') is pronounced /apo/, it is not written as such, so as to allow the reader to apply morphological rules such as inflecting for the imperative by removing the third-person morpheme, {-w}, and adding {-tân}. Were the third-person form written <apow> or <apo>, one might incorrectly expect the imperative form to be /apota:n/, rather than the correct /apɪta:n/. Vowels in the SRO are marked for length by using either a circumflex or macron over the vowel, and <e> is always to be written as long. When diphthongs are allophonically present, the underlying phonemes are used, as in the example of [apo] being written as <apiw>. The orthography is mostly shallow: the seven consonants (/p, t, k, ts, s, h, m, n/) are represented by single graphemes (< p, t, k , c, s, h, m, n>); short vowels (/a, i, o/) are written without any diacritic (<a, i, o>), while long vowels (/a:, i:, o:, e:/) are written with a circumflex or macron (<â, î, ô, ê>)

While this standard has been codified in Okimâsis and Wolvengrey (2008), it is not universally (or even largely) adopted. While major publications such as Masuskapoe (2010), Minde (1997), or those put out by provincial/federal departments, are written in the SRO, many publications and communications (especially those informal) are done using nonstandard conventions. In the Maskwacîs Dictionary of Cree Words(1997), for example, <ch> is used in place of <c>, <h> is used (in addition to its regular phonemic representation) essentially to impart that a vowel is different than the expected English pronunciation, and vowel length is not identified. The Alberta Elder's Cree Dictionary (LeClaire et al., 1998) does mark vowel length, though <e> is always written without length marking.

These orthographic variations, as well as the paucity of data provide challenges for language technology.

3 Speech Synthesis

Broadly speaking, speech synthesis comes in two main forms: *parametric* and *concatenative*. Parametric synthesis aims to recreate the particular rules and restrictions that exist to manipulate a sound wave as in speech (Jurafsky and Martin, 2009, 249). Concatenative synthesis, rather than focusing on recreating the parameters that produce speech, concerns itself with stitching together pre-existing segments to create a desired utterance (Jurafsky and Martin, 2009, 250).

The contemporary focus of speech synthesis is so-called *text to speech* (TTS) (Jurafsky and Martin, 2009, 249), wherein input text is transformed

---

[2]There is only one /e/ phoneme in the language and it is generally considered long for historical reasons. Initially, Plains Cree did have a short /e/, but this eventually converged with long /i/ (Bloomfield, 1946, 1).

into sound. In this process, text is phonemically represented and then synthesized into a waveform (Jurafsky and Martin, 2009, 250). Phonemic representation is accomplished though various means: dictionaries of pronunciation offer up a transcription of common words and sometimes even names, though these are almost guaranteed to *not* contain every single word a synthesizer could expect to encounter (Jurafsky and Martin, 2009). As a result, other methods such as "letter-to-sound" rules (which aims to provide a phonemic representation for a grapheme given a context) have also been employed (Black et al., 1998). Other units of representation have also been considered, such as those smaller than the phoneme (Prahallad et al., 2006). In general, most contemporary TTS systems generate a phonemic representation through machine learning (Jurafsky and Martin, 2009, 260). Black et al. (1998), for example, instituted a system wherein a computer is fed set of graphemes and a set of allowable pronunciations for each of those graphemes, along with the probabilities of a particular grapheme-to-phoneme pairing. More recent techniques such as those described by Mamiya et al. (2013) instead take a subset of speech and text data that are manually aligned and, using machine learning algorithms, learn the most likely phonemic representation of each grapheme given the context. In any case, grapheme-to-phoneme alignment results in a system that is able to produce sound for a given text sequence. A speech synthesis system will also provide intonational information to best reflect naturalistic speech (Jurafsky and Martin, 2009, 264).

While there have been speech synthesis efforts for minority language (Duddington et al., n.d), little focus has been paid to North American languages. Although there appears to be a Mohawk voice available for the eSpeak open-source software project (Duddington et al., n.d), the only published account of an Indigenous language synthesizer seems to be a 1997 technical report detailing a basic fully-concatenative synthesizer for the Navajo language (Whitman et al., 1997). In this instance, the authors compiled a list of all possible diphones (two-phoneme pairs) and had a Navajo speaker read these in a list (Whitman et al., 1997, 4). These diphones were then manually segmented, concatenated, and adjusted for tone (as Navajo is a tonal language) (Whitman et al., 1997). According to the authors, although the system was small and lacked much of the data one might prefer when building a speech synthesizer, the concatenative method they used managed to produce an intelligible synthesizer (Whitman et al., 1997, 13). Other than this effort, it appears that speech synthesis for North American languages has been largely non-existent. The reason for this is likely due to the lack of resources in these languages. Languages of North America may lack even a grammar, though many will have a variety of recordings of important stories or conversations (Arppe et al., 2016). Few languages of North America have a standard and well established written tradition. As a result, speech synthesis development is necessarily difficult for these languages. Plains Cree, as one of the most widely spoken indigenous languages of North America with roughly 20,000 speakers (Harrigan et al., 2017), provides relatively large amounts of standardized text for a North American language (Arppe et al., forthc.). The sources range from biblical texts (Mason and Mason, 2000), to narratives (Vandall and Douquette, 1987), and even interviews between fluent speakers (Masuskapoe, 2010). The texts used for TTS synthesis in this paper are described in Section 4.

4 Materials

4.1 Training Data

This study uses two varieties of materials: training data and a TTS toolchain. Training data comes in the form of the biblical texts of Psalms from Canadian Bible Society (2005). These texts, narrated by Dolores Sand, are accompanied by transcriptions in the SRO (Canadian Bible Society, 2005). The audio files are uncompressed, stereo audio with a 16 bit depth, 44,100 sampling frequency. Not all Psalms were available as an audio recording, though 52 files totaling 2 hours 24 minutes and 50 seconds in length were available as training data. Because the toolchain discussed below requires files with only a single channel for input, the Psalm recordings were converted into mono-channel files using the *SoX* utility (Bagwell, 1998–2013). Finally, the computation was completed on a virtual server with an Intel 2.67 GHz Xenon X5650 processor and 16 GB of RAM.

4.2 Tool Chain

Simple4All (Simple4All, 2011–2014) aims to develop lightly or unsupervised speech recognition/synthesis (Simple4All, 2011–2014). Two of the major outputs of the project are *ALISA*, a lightly supervised alignment system (Simple4All, 2014), and *Ossian*, a front-end synthesizer (Simple4All, 2013-2014). ALISA aligns based on ten minutes of pre-training data which has been manually segmented (Stan et al., 2013). The system learns and then attempts to align the rest of the training data and text transcript provided to it (Stan et al., 2013) (as detailed later, ALISA alignment was not particularly successful, and so hand alignment was conducted.). Resulting from alignment is a set of utterance sound files and text files with the respective orthographic representation. These files are then fed directly to into Ossian which uses these data to train itself and produces a synthesized voice. Ossian itself is a 'collection of Python code for building text-to-speech (TTS) systems, with an emphasis on easing research into building TTS systems with minimal expert supervision' (Simple4All, 2013-2014).

5 Evaluation

Two iterations of the synthesizer were created. The first iteration was built on alignment from ALISA. In order to evaluate the synthesized voice, a combination of various common metrics was used. Both functional (i.e. intelligibility of the system (Hinterleitner, 2017, 24)) and judgment (i.e. how pleasant the system is to use) tests were implemented. Ideally, at least a dozen participants would be used, but due to the limited number of people who speak and are literate in the language, and being mindful of the need to not bias speakers for future non-pilot level tests, one speaker was deemed appropriate for each iteration of the synthesis[3].

For functional level analysis, a modification of the Cluster Identification Task (Jekosch, 1992) was used. In this modified task, basic V, CV, and CVC syllables (*not* words) were randomly presented (at least twice, but as often as the participant requests) after which the participant was asked to write down what they heard. Although complex onsets and codas exist in Plains Cree, they are certainly less frequent, as discussed above. Although each possible syllable would ideally be presented at least once, the number of evaluations would total nearly 2000 items, a task too onerous for a single session and participant. In order to acclimate the participants, three test scenarios using English syllables from a native English speaker (/skwi/, /cle/, and /ram/) were run.

In addition to the Cluster Identification Task, the participant was asked to take part in a modified Semantically Unpredictable Sentence task (Benoît et al., 1996). In this task the participant was asked to listen to sentences that, while morphosyntactically correct, were semantically unlikely such as *ê-mowat sêhkêw*, 'You eat the car', where *ê-mowat* licenses any grammatically animate noun like *sêhkêw*, 'car,' but is much more likely to refer to food than a vehicle.

After listening to the stimuli at least twice, the participant was asked to write down what they heard. This test produces a situation wherein speakers are less able to rely on context for discrimination (Hinterleitner, 2017) while making use of real words rather than just monosyllables. A total of 5 semantically regular sentences were also presented so as to investigate how well our system works. As we would expect a greater level of comprehension in these sentences, any other result would indicate very poor performance.

To assess the pleasantness of synthesis, a set of scales with opposing metrics was created. Scales where end points fall beyond metric markings were used (see Figures 1 and 2 for an example). This was done so as to avoid the tendency for participants to not rate at the ends of scales and the tendency for individuals to have difficulty in distinguishing a stimuli that is either terrible or very good (Hinterleitner, 2017). The scales were comprised of the following pairs: Natural vs. Unnatural, Pleasant vs. Unpleasant, Quick vs. Slow, and overall Good vs Bad. Judgments were elicited for two utterances: one a an excerpt from the training data, and one a synthesis of an utterance pulled from a corpus (Arppe et al., forthc.; Ahenakew, 2000; Bear et al., 1992; Kâ-Nîpitêhtêw, 1998; Masuskapoe, 2010; Minde, 1997; Vandall and Douquette, 1987; Whitecalf, 1993). The use of non-

---

[3]The second iteration actually contained two evaluations by the same participant due to the initial evaluation tasks containing non standard spellings in the Semanticaly Unpredictable Sentence and Judgment tasks. Only these tasks were re-administered (with new stimuli verified for orthographic consistency). The first evaluation of the second synthesizer was substantially similar to the second evaluation and so will not be detailed in this paper.

synthesized data was used as a point of comparison. The identities of these stimuli were not made known to the participant. Because the participant was a former language instructor, general comments regarding the usefulness of the synthesizer were invited.

6 Results

Although the methodologies described above were carefully considered for the task of evaluation, major modifications had to be made once the evaluation was actually undertaken. The first iteration of the synthesizer proved difficult for evaluation, with the participant barely able to complete most of the tasks. According to the participant, syntheses were unintelligible, unpleasant, too quick, and overall bad. Listening to the syntheses through headphones was so jarring that evaluation was done through basic laptop speakers. Judgment assessment of longer utterances was extremely difficult for the participant, and stimuli were deemed to be too long. The cause of this poor synthesis is likely due to the fact that ALISA managed to align only 24 minutes of nearly 2.5 hours of training data.

To respond to this issue, the entirety of the training data was aligned by hand. This second iteration of the synthesizer was substantially more natural, intelligible, and pleasant. As the first participant's schedule was quite busy, a second participant was recruited. This participant was a male, middle-aged former Cree-language teacher who is proficient in the SRO. The following section details the evaluation of the second iteration of the speech synthesizer. All stimuli were presented in a randomized order.

6.1 Modified Cluster Identification Task

So as not to exhaust the participant, 70 clusters were presented. Of the tested clusters, 21 were identified correctly in their entirety. Another 16 were classified as minor errors (accepted variation in the orthograhy) such as 6 instances of <ê> being written as <î> (likely the result of the two phonemes overlapping in vowel space (Harrigan and Tucker, 2015) as well as perhaps the influence of English orthography) and 7 long vowels being written as short vowels following by an <h> (a common non-standard way of indicating that a vowel is long). These two types make up the majority (13/16) of minor errors. Together, minor errors and correctly identified clusters make up the majority of responses (53%). There were 11 items where the onset was misheard, with the majority of these (6) being <c> misheard as <s>. Given that <c> represents /ts/, this is not wholly surprising. Remaining error types were smaller in their tokens: 3 clusters had a vowel identified correctly, but the participant missed the onset entirely; 4 vowels were identified with the correct quality but the wrong length; 6 clusters showed the wrong quality but the correct length; and 4 clusters were heard as incorrect vowel with incorrect lengths. See Table 6.1 for a full list of stimuli and results. A highlighted row indicates a sentence where the participant's transcription deviated from the input. Boldface letters indicate where the deviance occurred.

6.2 Semantically Unpredictable Sentences

Semantically Unpredictable sentences showed similar results. All sentences where the participant's transcriptions varied from the SRO input were semantically unpredictable. The differences in transcription were nearly always restricted to differences in vowel length. In the one case where vowel quality differed (*kikî-sîkinik minôs*), the error was an instance of input <î> being written by the participant as <ê>. As mentioned previously, this variation is unsurprising due to overlapping vowel spaces. Table 6.2 summarizes the evaluation of the SUS task. Those sentences preceded by a hash-mark are semantically unpredictable, while those without are semantically predictable. As above, a highlighted row indicates a sentence where the participant's transcription deviated from the input, and boldface letters indicate where the deviance occurred.

6.3 Judgment Tasks

Impressionistic judgment of the synthesizer shows that the system performed worse than an actual native-speaker production. Figure 1 represent the evaluation of the synthesizer, and Figure 2 the representation of the natural utterance. Unlike the first iteration of the synthesizer (which was almost entirely rated as negatively as possible on all scales), the second synthesizer was rated as somewhat *unnatural, unpleasant* and *bad*, but not drastically so. The synthesizer was rated as only slightly slower than the middle ground between *quick* and *slow*. The naturally produced stimuli

Stimulus	Heard	Stimulus	Heard
kit	kit	yit	it
tit	kit	wiit	wiit
coot	ot	moot	moht
sat	sat	wot	wot
woot	rot	niit	neet
maat	maat	siit	seet
miit	miit	soot	sat
wit	wit	hot	hot
taat	taat	sit	sit
hat	hat	seet	seet
keet	kit	naat	naat
kot	pat	mot	not
kiit	keet	pot	pat
pat	at	yeet	yit
teet	NA	sot	sot
cot	sot	cit	sit
wat	wat	paat	paat
noot	not	heet	hiht
kaat	kaat	toot	toht
not	not	ceet	siht
haat	hat	hiit	neht
yaat	yaat	pit	pit
yot	eewt	kat	kat
ciit	seet	piit	peet
koot	pat	mat	mat
tiit	teet	yat	yeet
peet	peet	tot	tot
hoot	hoht	cat	set
neet	neet	hit	ahiht
weet	weet	nit	nit
nat	nat	poot	poht
tat	tat	caat	saht
yiit	eet	waat	waht
yoot	eewt	meet	miht
mit	mit	saat	seht

Table 1: Cluster Identification Results

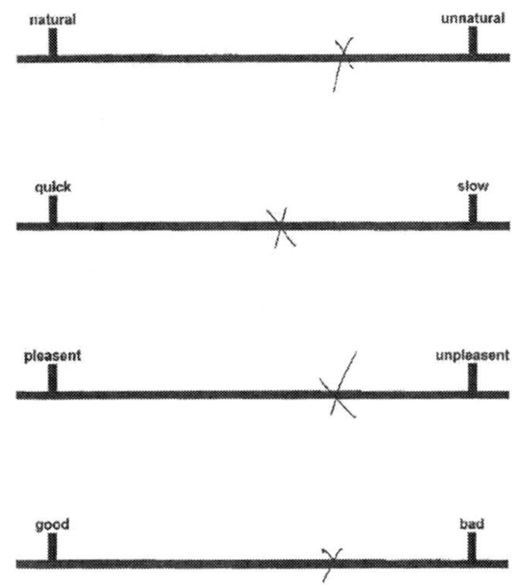

Figure 1: Synthesized Voice Judgment Task Evaluation

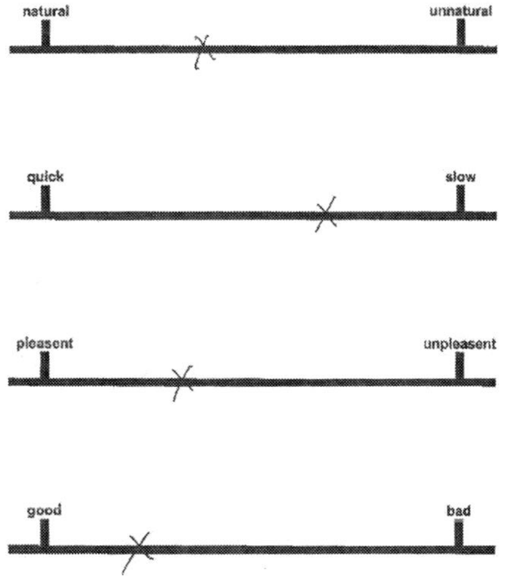

Figure 2: Naturally Produced Voice Judgment Task Evaluation

showed almost the opposite pattern, being modestly *natural*, *pleasant*, *good*, and *slow*.

Interestingly, the naturally produced utterance was not judged to be maximally *natural, pleasant,* or *good*. This is likely due to the fact that the utterance was not of quick or conversational speech, but rather a *performed* recording of biblical text.

7 Discussion

Although a synthesizer was developed, alignment through ALISA was unsuccessful, with just 24 minutes of roughly 2.5 hours correctly aligned (19%). According to the developer, Adriana Stan, despite attempting to create an alignment system for a wide variety of languages, polysynthetic languages such as Plains Cree were not considered or tested; as a result, ALISA's parameters disprefer very long words, instead assuming an error in processing (p.c. Adriana Stan, Jan 31, 2018). Although ALISA allowed for some adjustment in this respect, changing the average acceptable length for a word to any extent did not produce any significant increase in alignment (either by lowering or raising this threshold). Further, ALISA

Input	Participant Transcription	English Gloss
# ê-pâhpisit sêhkêw	ê-pahpisit sêhkêw	'The car laughs.'
# sîwinikan pimohtêw	sîwinikan pimohtêw	'Sugar walks.'
# ê-postiskawacik kinosêwak	ê-postiskawacik kinosêwak	'You put the fishes on.'
awâsis wâpahtam masinahikan	awâsis wâpahtam masinahikan	'A child sees a book'
ê-wiyâtikosit iyiniw	ê-wiyâtikosit iyiniw	'The Indigenous person is happy'
nâpêw ê-mîcisot	nâpêw ê-mîcisot	'The man is eating'
kinêpik nipâw	kinêpik nipâw	'A snake is sleeping'
#atim kiwî-saskamohitin	atim kiwî-saskamôhîtin	'I am going to put a dog in your mouth.'
#kikî-sîkinik minôs	kikî-sêkinik minôs	'The cat poured you.'
iskwêw pîkiskâtisiw	iskwêw pîkiskâtisiw	'A woman is sad.'

Table 2: Evaluated Sentences

seemed relatively successful for other agglutinating languages such as Finnish and Turkish with similarly long words; this suggests that the issue with alignment may be more complex than just word length.

The evaluation of hand-aligned data with Ossian synthesizer showed promising results. The second iteration of the synthesis was relatively well received by the second participant, who remarked that the speech synthesizer, while not perfect, was serviceable and represented an exciting opportunity for language learners. Despite this, multiple issues arose throughout the evaluation process. Most significant was the issue of orthographic proficiency. Because the tasks selected for this evaluation relied on written responses, only participants with strong literacy in SRO could be considered. This is especially problematic for Indigenous languages of Canada, as many of these varieties are historically oral languages. Few fluent speakers of Plains Cree actually possess the level of literacy needed for the evaluation tasks. This severely restricts who can participate in evaluation of the synthesizer. A side effect of this restriction was the scarce availability of a native speaker to review the stimuli (as one would prefer not to have reviewers act as participants in the study), leading to the several orthographic inconsistencies in the first evaluation for both iterations of the speech synthesizer. For the second iteration of the synthesizer, evaluation was re-administered for those items with orthographic inconsistencies. One solution to this issue is to eschew the need for writing. Instead of writing down what they hear, participants could be asked to provide word-to-word translations (insofar as possible) and to compare these with the intended meaning of the stimuli. Though this would not address the participants' ability to recognize particular graphemes, the lack of a need for literacy would allow for a signficantly larger number of participants than what would be available when requiring literacy in the SRO. Alternatively, participants could be asked to repeat what they have heard, though this would likely require a complete reworking of stimuli.

In building a synthesizer for Plains Cree, the full Simple4All toolchain proved unreliable. In addition to the issues faced in ALISA alignment for Plains Cree, documentation installation of the software provided multiple challenges with little documentation for support. Future endeavors should consider newer systems such as the Merlin project (Wu et al., 2016) which has been using Deep Neural Nets (DNN), a form of machine learning that seem to provide better results than the Hidden Markov Models (HMMs) used in the Simple4All project. Although no such comparison of DNN vs. other machine learning methods has been reported for synthesis of North American languages, DNN based systems such as Google's WaveNet report significantly better results than other techniques such as HMMs (van den Oord et al., 2016). If continuing to use Simple4All, the results of this evaluation suggest that one should not use ALISA for text alignment. In addition, researchers should consider the use of prebuilt aligners for languages with similar phoneme inventories. In the case of Plains Cree, given that the phoneme inventory is a subset of English's, one could consider the use of force aligners built for English with a modified dictionary specific to Plains Cree. This should be feasible in theory, though it remains to be seen whether it is useful in practice.

In regards to evaluation, the SUS task might best be abandoned altogether in assessing future Plains Cree synthesizers. Results showed very little difference between semantically unpredictable sentences and semantically predictable ones. Both participants noted that the 'unpredictable' sentences were, in fact, ungrammatical: the line between unlikely and allowable is very thin. It would be interesting to repeat this task with other native speakers, as it may be a participant-specific attribute (though this study's participants had experience as second-language instructors and were likely far more familiar with listening, identifying and interpreting odd, infelicitous, and/or mispronounced utterances than the average speaker). If this is a tendency that holds across native speakers of Plains Cree, it may be worth investigating the factors influencing these attitudes (such as a tendency for speakers of the language to be either very novice or very fluent, perhaps leading to a lack of familiarity or tolerance of variation as seen in the SUS task). Assuming this attitude holds for the general population, it would be best to choose somewhat semantically predictable, but less frequent, stimuli (e.g. *I ate the zebra*, where *zebra* is more predictable than *car*, but less predictable than *rabbit*) or avoid the SUS task entirely. Of course, this means the confound of semantic predictability endures, though this might be addressed presenting words in isolation (accepting that this does not allow for sentence level prosody to be assessed).

Based on the feedback from the participant, reducing the number of syllables presented would be beneficial, though the details of how to do so remain unclear, especially considering that this study ignored a large portion of possible syllables. Random sampling could be used by selecting simply one type of each sound in each syllable position (e.g. ensuring there is tested at least one syllable starting with a stop and ending with a fricative). Spreading out the set over many participants, such that every syllable is evaluated the same number of times but not by each participant, is perhaps a better solution as it allows every syllable to be evaluated; in this case, one would have to analyze results via some sort of mixed-effects model (where *speaker* acts as a random effect) to account for the variation between speakers. Further, this method requires many participants, an inherent restriction in working with minority languages, especially those of North America. Finally, the first participant indicated that a few of the monosyllables, while unattested in dictionaries, were actually vulgarities. As this task was meant to assess only syllable intelligibility separately from word-level intelligibility, and due to their offensive nature, it is important that future studies remove these words or at least warn participants of their possible presence.

8 Conclusion

This paper presents one of the first parametric syntheses of an Indigenous language of Canada, using the Simple4All packages ALISA and Ossian. Based on roughly 2.5 hours of speech, this method of speech synthesis makes use of lightly supervised forced alignment to ease the workload required by the researcher. Although Simple4All has been used with a variety of languages (Simple4All, 2011–2014), the forced alignment was largely unsuccessful with the Plains Cree data. No conclusive reason could be found to account for this, though it may be that word length played a factor. In contrast, the results of the second synthesizer based on hand-aligned training data present promising results, with many of the stimuli being understood in their entirety. Although this second synthesizer was clearly identified as non-natural speech, its output was intelligible and relatively well received by the participant. Where the participant's transcription of stimuli deviated from the input, deviations generally concerned different vowel lengths. The results of this paper also indicate that careful consideration must be given to the evaluation frameworks, since those techniques that have become established and applied successfully for majority languages may not be suitable for Indigenous languages, at least for those in the Canadian context.

Acknowledgements

The authors of this paper would like to thank Dolores Sand, the speaker on whom the synthesis was based for here willingness to have her data used in this project. We would also like to thank Martti Vainio, Antti Suni, and Adriana Stan for not only their work in developing Simple4All, but their generosity in helping to troubleshoot throughout the synthesis. This research was supported by the Social Sciences and Humanities Research Council of Canada (Grants 890-2013-0047 and 611-2016-0207), the University of Alberta Kule Institute for Advanced Study Research Cluster Grant, and a Social Sciences and Humanities Research Council of Canada Doctoral Fellowship. We would also like to thank Arok Wolvengrey and Jean Okimâsis for their help in reviewing stimuli, Arden Ogg for helping to facilitate our relationship with Dolores Sand, and community members of Maskwacîs, Alberta for their input throughout the process of developing the synthesizer. Finally, we would like to thank our anonymous participants for their expertise, patience, and participation.

References

Alice Ahenakew. 2000. âh-âyîtaw isi ê-kî-kiskêyihtahkik maskihkiy/They knew both sides of medicine: Cree tales of curing and cursing told by Alice Ahenakew, edited by HC Wolfart and F Ahenakew. *Publications of the Algonquian Text Society. Winnipeg: University of Manitoba Press.*

Antti Arppe, Jordan Lachler, Trond Trosterud, Lene Antonsen, and Sjur N Moshagen. 2016. Basic language resource kits for endangered languages: A case study of plains Cree. *CCURL*, pages 1–8.

Antti Arppe, Katherine Schmirler, Atticus G. Harrigan, and Arok Wolvengrey. forthc. A morphosyntactically tagged corpus for Plains Cree. In *Papers of the 49th Algonquian Conference.*

Chris Bagwell. 1998–2013. Sox – sound exchange, the swiss army knife of audio manipulation. `http://sox.sourceforge.net/sox.html`.

Glecia Bear, Minnie Fraser, Irene Calliou, Mary Wells, Alpha Lafond, and Rosa Longneck. 1992. *kôhkominawak otâcimowiniwâwa/Our Grandmothers' Lives: As Told In Their Own Words, edited by F Ahenakew and HC Wolfart,* volume 3. University of Regina Press.

Christian Benoît, Martine Grice, and Valérie Hazan. 1996. The SUS test: A method for the assessment of text-to-speech synthesis intelligibility using semantically unpredictable sentences. *Speech Communication*, 18:381 – 392.

Alan W. Black, Kevin A. Lenzo, and Vincent Pagel. 1998. Issues in building general letter to sound rules. In *The Third ESCA/COCOSDA Workshop on Speech Synthesis, Blue Mountains, Australia, November 26-29, 1998,* pages 77–80.

Leonard Bloomfield. 1946. Algonquian. In *Linguistic structures of Native America,* volume 6, pages 85–129. Viking Fund Publications in Anthropology, New York.

Canadian Bible Society. 2005. *kihci-masinahikan nikamowina: âtiht kâ-nawasônamihk.* Toronto: Canadian Bible Society.

Jonathan Duddington, Martin Avison, Reece Dunn, and Valdis Vitolins. n.d. eSpeak speech synthesizer.

Ethnologue. 2016. Plains Cree.

Atticus Harrigan and Benjamin Tucker. 2015. Vowels spaces and reduction in Plains Cree. *Journal of the Canadian Acoustics Association,* 43(3).

Atticus G. Harrigan, Katherine Schmirler, Antti Arppe, Lene Antonsen, Trond Trosterud, and Arok Wolvengrey. 2017. Learning from the computational modelling of Plains Cree verbs. *Morphology,* 27(4):565–598.

Florian Hinterleitner. 2017. *Quality of Synthetic Speech: Perceptual Dimensions, Influencing Factors, and Instrumental Assessment,* 1st edition. Springer Publishing Company, Incorporated.

Ute Jekosch. 1992. The cluster-identification test. In *CSLP-1992.*

Dan Jurafsky and James H. Martin. 2009. *Speech and language processing : An introduction to natural language processing, computational linguistics, and speech recognition.* Pearson Prentice Hall, Upper Saddle River, N.J.

Jim Kâ-Nîpitêhtêw. 1998. *Counselling Speeches of Jim Kâ-Nîpitêhtêw, edited by F Ahenakew and HC Wolfart.* University of Manitoba Press.

Nancy LeClaire, George Cardinal, Emily Hunter, and Earle G. Waugh. 1998. *Alberta Elders' Cree Dictionary: Alperta ohci kehtehayak nehiyaw otwestamâkewasinahikan,* 1st edition. Edmonton: University of Alberta Press.

Yoshitaka Mamiya, Junichi Yamagishi, Oliver Watts, Robert A.J. Clark, Simon King, and Adriana Stan. 2013. Lightly Supervised GMM VAD to use Audiobook for Speech Synthesiser. In *Proc. ICASSP.*

Maskwachees Cultural College. 1997. *Maskwacîs Dictionary of Cree Words/Nehiyaw Pîkiskwewinisa.* Maskwachees Cultural College.

William Mason and Sophia Mason. 2000. *Oski Testament.* Toronto: Canadian Bible Society.

Cecilia Masuskapoe. 2010. *piko kîkway ê-nakacihtât: kêkêk otâcimowina ê-nêhiyawastêki, edited by HC Wolfart and F Ahenakew.* Algonquian and Iroquoian Linguistics.

Emma Minde. 1997. *kwayask ê-kî-pê-kiskinowâpahtihicik/Their Example Showed Me the Way, edited by F Ahenakew and HC Wolfart.* Edmonton: University of Alberta Press.

Jeffrey Muehlbauer. 2012. Vowel Spaces in Plains Cree. *Journal of the International Phonetic Association*, 42(1):91–105.

Jean Okimâsis and Arok Wolvengrey. 2008. *How to Spell it in Cree*. Regina : Miywâsin Ink.

Aäron van den Oord, Sander Dieleman, Heiga Zen, Karen Simonyan, Oriol Vinyals, Alexander Graves, Nal Kalchbrenner, Andrew Senior, and Koray Kavukcuoglu. 2016. Wavenet: A generative model for raw audio. In *Arxiv*.

Kishore Prahallad, Alan W. Black, and Mosur Ravishankar. 2006. Sub-phonetic modeling for capturing pronunciation variations for conversational speech synthesis. In *2006 IEEE International Conference on Acoustics Speech and Signal Processing, ICASSP 2006, Toulouse, France, May 14-19, 2006*, pages 853–856.

Simple4All. 2011–2014. Simple4all: developing automatic speech synthesis technology. `http:// simple4all.org`.

Simple4All. 2013-2014. Ossian speech synthesis toolkit. `http://homepages.inf.ed.ac. uk/owatts/ossian/html/index.html`.

Simple4All. 2014. Alisa: An automatic lightly supervised speech segmentation and alignment tool. `http://simple4all.org/product/ alisa/`.

A. Stan, P. Bell, J. Yamagishi, and S. King. 2013. Lightly supervised discriminative training of grapheme models for improved sentence-level alignment of speech and text data. In *Proceedings of the Annual Conference of the International Speech Communication Association, INTERSPEECH*, INTERSPEECH 2013 - 14th Annual Conference of the International Speech Communication Association, pages 1525–1529, (1)Communications Department, Technical University of Cluj-Napoca.

Peter Vandall and Joe Douquette. 1987. *wâskahikaniwiyiniw-âcimowina/Stories of the House People, edited by F Ahenakew*. University of Manitoba Press.

Sarah Whitecalf. 1993. kinêhiyâwiwininaw nêhiyawêwin/The Cree language is our identity: The La Ronge lectures of Sarah Whitecalf, edited and translated by HC Wolfart and F Ahenakew. *Publications of the Algonquian Text Society / Collection de la Société d'édition des textes algonquiennes. Winnipeg: University of Manitoba Press*.

Robert Whitman, Chilin Shih, and Richard Sproat. 1997. A navajo language text-to-speech synthesizer. Technical report, AT&T Bell Laboratories.

H. Christoph Wolfart. 1973. *Plains Cree: a grammatical study*. Transactions of the American Philosophical Society: new ser., v. 63, pt. 5. Philadelphia, American Philosophical Society, 1973.

H. Christoph Wolfart. 1996. Sketch of Cree, an Algonquian Language. In *Handbook of American Indians. Volume 17: Languages*, volume 17, pages 390–439. Smithsonian Institute, Washington.

Zhizheng Wu, Oliver Watts, and Simon King. 2016. Merlin: An open source neural network speech synthesis system. In *9th ISCA Speech Synthesis Workshop (2016)*, pages 218–223.

A biscriptual morphological transducer for Crimean Tatar

Francis M. Tyers
Department of Linguistics
Indiana University
ftyers@iu.edu

Jonathan North Washington
Linguistics Department
Swarthmore College
jonathan.washington@swarthmore.edu

Darya Kavitskaya
Slavic Languages and Literatures
U.C. Berkeley
dkavitskaya@berkeley.edu

Memduh Gökırmak
ÚFAL
Univerzita Karlova in Prague
memduhg@gmail.com

Nick Howell
Faculty of Mathematics
Higher School of Economics
nlhowell@gmail.com

Remziye Berberova
Department of Crimean Tatar[*]
Crimean Tavrida University
bra.berberova@yandex.ua

Abstract

This paper describes a weighted finite-state morphological transducer for Crimean Tatar able to analyse and generate in both Latin and Cyrillic orthographies. This transducer was developed by a team including a community member and language expert, a field linguist who works with the community, a Turkologist with computational linguistics expertise, and an experienced computational linguist with Turkic expertise.

Dealing with two orthographic systems in the same transducer is challenging as they employ different strategies to deal with the spelling of loan words and encode the full range of the language's phonemes and their interaction. We develop the core transducer using the Latin orthography and then design a separate transliteration transducer to map the surface forms to Cyrillic. To help control the non-determinism in the orthographic mapping, we use weights to prioritise forms seen in the corpus. We perform an evaluation of all components of the system, finding an accuracy above 90% for morphological analysis and near 90% for orthographic conversion. This comprises the state of the art for Crimean Tatar morphological modelling, and, to our knowledge, is the first biscriptual single morphological transducer for any language.

1   Introduction

This paper presents the development and evaluation of a free/open-source finite-state morphological transducer for Crimean Tatar that is able to analyse and generate both Latin and Cyrillic orthographies.[1] As an example, this transducer can map between the analysis köy<n><px3sp><loc> 'in the village of' and both of the possible orthographic forms, in Latin *köyünde* and in Cyrillic *коюнде*.

This paper is structured as follows: Section 2 presents background on Crimean Tatar and its orthographic systems; Section 3 gives an overview of the current state of computational analysis of Crimean Tatar morphology; Section 4 presents certain challenging aspects of Crimean Tatar morphology and their implementation; and Section 5 evaluates the transducer. Finally, Section 6 summarises possible directions for future work, and Section 7 provides concluding remarks.

2   Crimean Tatar

2.1   Context

Crimean Tatar ([quɾumtɑtɑrʧɑ], ISO 639-3: crh) is an understudied Turkic language of the Northwestern Turkic (Kypchak) subgroup (Johanson and Csató, 1998).[2] The language also shows a considerable influence from the Southwestern Turkic (Oghuz) subgroup, acquired via contact with Turkish, as well as more recent influence from the Southeastern Turkic subgroup, due to the nearly 5-decade-long resettlement of the entire Crimean Tatar population of Crimea to Central Asia (predominantly to Uzbekistan) by the Soviet government in 1944. It shares some level of mutual intelligibility with other languages in these subgroups, but is an independent language. The geographical location of Crimean Tatar in reference to other NW (Kypchak) and SW (Oghuz) varieties is shown in Figure 1.

Currently, about 228,000 speakers of Crimean Tatar have returned to Crimea, and another 313,000 live in diaspora (Simons and Fennig, 2018). Almost all speakers of Crimean Tatar are bilingual or multilingual in Russian and the language of the place of their exile, such as Uzbek, Kazakh, or Tajik.

---

[*]Emerita

[1]The transducer is available in a publicly accessible repository at http://github.com/apertium/apertium-crh.

[2]Crimean Tatar and [Kazan] Tatar (tat) happen to share a name, but are only related in that they are both Northwestern Turkic languages—though members of different subsubgroups.

Proceedings of the 3rd Workshop on the Use of Computational Methods in the Study of Endangered Languages: Vol. 1 Papers, pages 74–80,
Honolulu, Hawai'i, USA, February 26–27, 2019.

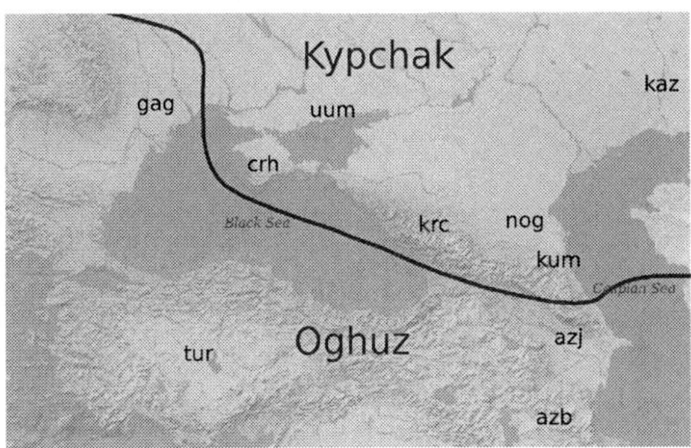

Figure 1: Location of the Crimean Tatar speaking area (crh) within the Black Sea region, relative to other Kypchak (Urum – uum, Karachay-Balkar – krc, Nogay – nog, Kumyk – kum and Kazakh – kaz) and Oghuz languages (Gagauz – gag, Turkish – tur, and Azerbaijani – azb and azj).

Crimean Tatar is spoken mostly by the older population, but the usage may be rising, due to the increasing efforts in the community to teach the language to the younger generation, despite impedance caused by the generally unfavourable sociolinguistic situation.

2.2 Orthographic systems

As previously mentioned, Crimean Tatar can be written with two orthographic systems, one based on the Latin alphabet and one based on the Cyrillic alphabet. Both orthographies are widely used and have varying degrees of official support. They have different ways of treating phenomena such as front rounded vowels, the uvular/velar contrast in obstruents, and loanwords from Russian.

The Latin orthography contains 31 characters, and uses no digraphs except for foreign sounds in borrowings. Each phoneme is implemented using a distinct character; for example ‹o› for the non-high back rounded vowel and ‹ö› for its front counterpart. The diacritics tilde (‹ñ› for [ŋ]), cedilla (e.g., ‹ş› for [ʃ]) and diaeresis (e.g., ‹ö› for [ø]) are used as components of characters for sounds that are not covered in a straightforward way by the basic Latin alphabet. In the Latin orthography, Russian words can be treated as adapted to the phonology of Crimean Tatar, such as *bücet* ‘budget’—as opposed to **byudjet*, a more faithful rendering in the Latin orthography of the pronunciation of the Russian *бюджет*. However, most loanwords are pronounced as in Russian, yet are rendered more faithfully to their Russian spelling than to their Russian pronunciation; for example, *konki* for Russian *коньки* [kɐnʲˈkʲi] ‘skates’ is pronounced as in Russian and not **[konki] as its Latin-orthography spelling would suggest.

The Cyrillic orthography contains the 33 characters of the Russian alphabet and four diagraphs for sounds not found in Russian: ‹дж› [ʤ], ‹гъ› [ʁ], ‹къ› [q], and ‹нъ› [ŋ]. The additional sounds [ø] and [y] are implemented by either the use of the “soft sign” ‹ь› in conjunction with the letters for [o] ‹о› and [u] ‹у› or by using the corresponding “yoticised” vowel letters ‹ё› and ‹ю›, respectively; the particular system is clarified below. Russian words are spelled as in Russian, including the use of hard and soft signs and Russian phonological patterns. An example is *коньки* ‘skates’, in which the ‹ь› indicates that the [n] is palatalised.

Table 1 shows the basic mapping between the two orthographic systems.

b	c	ç	d	f	g	ğ	h	j	k	l
б	дж	ч	д	ф	г	гъ	х	ж	к	л

m	n	ñ	p	q	r	s	t	v	y	z
м	н	нъ	п	къ	р	с	т	в	й	з

a	â	ı	o	u	e	i	ö	ü
а, я	я	ы	о, ё	у, ю	э, е	и	о, ё	у, ю

Table 1: The basic correspondences between the characters of the two Crimean Tatar orthographies.

While the Latin orthography represents the front vowels [ø] and [y] simply as ‹ö› and ‹ü›, in the Cyrillic orthography they are represented in one of the following ways.

With the letters ‹о› and ‹у›:

- With a front-vowel character (‹и›, ‹е›) or one of the “yoticised” vowels (‹ё›, ‹ю›) following the subsequent consonant. This strategy is usually limited to the first syllable of a [multisyllable] word when in certain consonant contexts, and is more prevalent in open syllables. Examples include *учюнджи* [yʧ-ynʤi] ‘third’, *кунюнде* [kyn-yn-de] ‘on the day of’, *болип* [bøl-ip] ‘having divided’, and *муче* [myʧe] ‘body part’.

- Either with the “soft sign” ‹ь› following the subsequent consonant or without if a “soft consonant” (i.e., velar pair to a uvular consonant), like [k] or [g], follows the vowel. This strategy is generally used only in the first syllable of a word when there is a following coda consonant. Examples include *учь* [yʧ] ‘three’, куньлери [kyn-ler-i] 'days of', больмеди [bøl-me-di] 'did not divide', кок [køk] 'sky', and букти [byk-ti] 'he/she/it bent'.

With the "yoticised" vowel letters «ё» and «ю»:

- When not in the first syllable of a word. Examples include юзю [jyz-y] 'his/her face', тёксюн [tøk-syn] 'let it spill', and мумкюн [mymkyn] 'possible'. Note that [ø] almost never occurs outside of the first syllable of a word.

- When in the first syllable of a word and preceded by a consonant. Examples include тюшти [tyʃ-ti] 'fell', дёрт [dørt] 'four', and чёпке [tʃøp-ke] 'to the rubbish'.

The difference between when the letters «о» or «у» are used as opposed to «ё» or «ю» in first syllables of words seems to in part depend on the values of surrounding consonants. However, a certain level of idiosyncrasy exists, as seen in pairs like козь [køz] 'eye' and сёз [søz] 'word', кёр [kør] 'blind' and корь [kør] 'see', or юз [jyz] 'hundred' and юзь [jyz] 'face'.

The "yoticised" vowel letters «ё» and «ю» also represent the vowels [o] and [u] when following [j] as well as [ø] and [y] when following [j]—sound combinations that can occur word-initially or after another vowel (usually rounded and of corresponding backness, though note that [ø] and [o] are extremely uncommon outside of the first syllable of a word). Hence there is in principle the potential for systematic ambiguity between rounded back vowels preceded by [j] («ё» [jo] and «ю» [ju]) and rounded front vowels preceded by [j] («ё» [ø] and «ю» [y]). In practice it is difficult to identify examples of this, but pairs like ют [jut] 'swallow' and юз [jyz] 'hundred' demonstrate the concept.

Furthermore, [j] is represented in the Cyrillic orthography either by й (e.g., къой [qoj] [put]), or with a yoticised vowel letter (e.g., къоюл [qoj-ul] 'be put'); i.e., these letters are involved in a many-to-many mapping with the phonology.

3 Prior work

Altıntaş and Çiçekli (2001) present a finite-state morphological analyser for Crimean Tatar. Their morphological analyser has a total of 5,200 stems and the morphotactics[3] are based on a morphological analyser of Turkish. They explicitly cover only

---

[3]The morphotactics of a language is the way in which morphemes can be combined to create words.

the native part of the vocabulary, excluding loan words, and use an ASCII representation for the orthography. Their analyser is not freely available for testing so unfortunately we could not compare its performance to that of ours.

4 Methodology

To implement the transducer we used the Helsinki Finite-State Toolkit, HFST (Lindén et al., 2011). This toolkit implements the `lexc` and `twol` formalisms and also natively supports weighted FSTs. The former implements morphology, or mappings between analysis and morphological form, such as `köy<n><px3sp><loc> : köy>{s}{I}{n}>{D}{A}`, while the latter is used to ensure the correct mapping between morphological form and orthographic (or "phonological") form, such as `köy>{s}{I}{n}>{D}{A} : köyünde`. When compose-intersected, the transducers generated from these modules result in a single transducer mapping the two ends with no intermediate form, e.g., `köy<n><px3sp><loc> : köyünde`.

The choice to model the morphophonology using `twol` as opposed to using a formalism that implements sequential rewrite rules may be seen as controversial. Two-level phonological rules are equivalent in expressive power to sequential rewrite rules (Karttunen, 1993); however, from the point of view of linguistics, they present some differences in terms of how phonology is conceptualised. Two-level rules are viewed as constraints over a set of all possible surface forms generated by expanding the underlying forms using the alphabet, and operate in parallel. Sequential rewrite rules, on the other hand, are viewed as a sequence of operations for converting an underlying form to a surface form. As such, sequential rules result in intermediate forms, whereas the only levels of representation relevant to two-level rules are the morphological (underlying) form and the phonological (surface) form. While it may not be relevant from an engineering point of view, we find more cognitive plausibility in the two-level approach. Furthermore, the computational phonologist on our team finds the two-level model much less cumbersome to work with for modelling an entire language's phonology than sequential rewrite rules. Readers are encouraged to review Karttunen (1993) for a more thorough comparison of the techniques.

4.1 Lexicon

The lexicon was compiled semi-automatically. We added words to the lexicon by frequency, based on frequency lists from Crimean Tatar Bible[4] and Wikipedia[5] corpora (see Section 5.1 for sizes). Table 2 gives the number of lexical items for each of the major parts of speech. The proper noun lexicon includes a list of toponyms extracted from the Crimean Tatar Wikipedia.

Part of speech	Number of stems
Noun	6,271
Proper noun	4,123
Adjective	1,438
Verb	1,007
Adverb	87
Numeral	40
Pronoun	31
Postposition	21
Conjunction	20
Determiner	16
Total:	13,054

Table 2: Number of stems in each of the main categories.

4.2 Tagsets

The native tagset of the analyser is based on the tagsets used by other Turkic-language transducers[6] in the Apertium platform.[7] In addition we provide a mapping from this tagset to one compatible with Universal Dependencies (Nivre et al., 2016) based on 125 rules and a set overlap algorithm.[8] The rules are composed of triples of (lemma, part of speech, features) and are applied deterministically longest-overlap first over the source language analyses.

4.3 Morphotactics

The morphotactics of the transducer are adapted from those of the Kazakh transducer described by Washington et al. (2014). The nominal morphotactics are almost identical between Kazakh and Crimean Tatar. The verbal morphotactics are rather different, and we here followed Kavitskaya (2010).

4.4 Transliterator

The transliterator is implemented as a separate substring-to-substring `lexc` grammar and `twol` ruleset.

The `lexc` grammar defines a transducer which converts from the Latin orthography to a string where placeholders are given for the hard sign, soft sign, and some digraphs which are single characters in the Cyrillic orthography (e.g., *ts* = ц). The output may be ambiguous, for example the input string *şç* produces both şç (analysis, preceding transliteration) and a special symbol щ (also analysis) standing for Cyrillic щ (surface form). This is necessary because *şç* may map to either щ (*borşç* = борщ [borç] 'borsch') or шч (*işçi* = ишчи [iʃtʃi] 'worker').

The `twol` ruleset defines a transducer which then maps the Latin string produced to strings in Cyrillic via the alphabet, and applies a set of constraints to restrict the possible combinations. All remaining theoretically valid mappings are kept. An example of one of these constraints is shown in Figure 2.

```
"e as э"
e:э <=> .#. _ ;
        [ e: | a: | i: | ü: ] _ ;
```

Figure 2: An example of a `twol` constraint used in the mapping of Latin strings to Cyrillic strings. This constraint forces Latin ‹e› [e] to be realised as Cyrillic ‹э› instead of Cyrillic ‹e› (which would in turn stand for [je]) at the beginning of the word and after certain vowels.

The resulting transducer takes surface forms in Latin script, and outputs surface forms in Cyrillic script. In order to get an analyser which analyses Cyrillic, we then composed the original [Latin] transducer with the transliteration transducer.

In order to be able to choose the orthographically correct variant for generation in the case of ambiguity in the conversion, we tried two corpus-based methods.

The first method we tried was simply to weight surface forms we saw in the corpus with a negative weight; since our transducer interprets lower weights as better, forms which were previously seen would always be given preference over those generated by the model *on the fly*. This was done by making a negative-weight identity transducer of the surface forms, composing with the transliteration transducer, and taking the union with the transliteration transducer alone.

The second method was to estimate probabilities for the generated transliterations using character *n*-

---

[4]Compiled by IBT Russia/CIS, `https://ibt.org.ru`

[5]Content dump from the Crimean Tatar Wikipedia, `https://crh.wikipedia.org`, dated 2018-12-01.

[6]See for example Washington et al. (2016) for a description.

[7]Available online at `http://www.apertium.org`.

[8]Available in the repository as `texts/crh-feats.tsv`.

gram frequencies from the corpus. We used a particularly simplistic estimation technique: fix $n \geq 1$. We collect k-grams for $k \leq n$, the collections of size n_k with redundancy. The probability assigned to the k-gram x is $\#x/n_k$. Weights are chosen to be the negative logarithm of the probability. The unaugmented transliteration transducer is then composed with this new weighted transducer before being composed with the morphological transducer.

Transducers produced by the two methods are unioned; the result is then composed with the morphological transducer. Generated transliterations thus have many paths which they can follow to acceptance, assigning various weights. If the transliteration is a surface form observed in the training corpus, it is assigned a negative weight (given absolute preference). Unobserved transliterations are assigned positive weights based on possible segmentations; k-character segments are assigned weights from the k-gram counters, and the weight of a segmentation is the sum of the weights of the segments.

4.5 Error model

While working on morphological models for languages with a less-than-stable written norm, or where there is little support for proofing tools or keyboards, it is desirable to be generous with what forms are accepted while being conservative with what forms are generated. Orthographic variation is inevitable, and if we want to create a high coverage resource, then we should also take this variation into account. For example, in the corpus the locative of *Belarus* (the country) is written *Belarusde* 4 times, *Belarusta* twice and *Belaruste* 1 time. The normative spelling, to fit with the pronunciation [belarus] should be *Belarusta*; however, we would also like to be able to provide an analysis for the other variants. Based on an informal examination of $1,000$ random tokens in the news and encyclopaedic corpora, we estimate that at least 0.8% of tokens in these corpora constitute non-normative orthographic forms of this type.

Our approach again is to use `twol`. First the rules for vowel harmony and other phonological phenomena were removed from the `twol` transducer that implements the normative orthography, leaving only unconstrained symbol mappings. This was then composed with the lexicon to produce a transducer which has all of the possible phonological variants (much like a fully expanded version of the `lexc` transducer). This was then sub-

tracted from the normative transducer and a tag `<err_orth>` was appended to the analysis side of all remaining forms to indicate orthographic error, This was output into a transducer which accepts any phonological variant that was not normative and give an analysis with an extra tag. This was unioned with the normative transducer to produce the final analyser. This approach allows us to analyse prescriptively incorrect variants like *Belaruste* as `Belarus<np><top><loc><err_orth>`.

5 Evaluation

We have evaluated the morphological transducer in several ways. We computed the naïve coverage and the mean ambiguity of the analyser on freely available corpora (Section 5.1) as well as its accuracy (precision and recall) against a gold standard (Section 5.2). Additionally, we evaluated the accuracy of the transliteration transducer (Section 5.3).

5.1 Analyser coverage

We determined the naïve coverage and mean ambiguity of the morphological analyser. Naïve coverage is the percentage of surface forms in a given corpus that receive at least one morphological analysis. Forms counted by this measure may have other analyses which are not delivered by the transducer. The mean ambiguity measure was calculated as the average number of analyses returned per token in the corpus. These measures for three corpora, spanning both orthographies, are presented in Table 3.[9]

Corp.	Orthog.	Tokens	Cov.	Ambig.
Bible	Cyr	217,611	90.9%	1.86
Wiki	Lat	214,099	92.1%	1.86
News	Lat	1,713,201	93.7%	2.12

Table 3: Naïve coverage and mean ambiguity of the analyser on three corpora.

The transducer provides analyses for over 90% of tokens in each corpus, with each token receiving an average of around two analyses.

5.2 Transducer accuracy

Precision and recall are measures of the average accuracy of analyses provided by a morphological transducer. Precision represents the number of the

---

[9]The Bible and Wikipedia corpora are those described in Section 4.1, and the News corpus is content for the years 2014–2015 extracted from `http://ktat.krymr.com/`.

analyses provided by the transducer for a form that are correct. Recall is the percentage of analyses that are deemed correct for a form that are provided by the transducer.

To calculate precision and recall, it was necessary to create a hand-verified list of surface forms and their analyses. We extracted around 2,000 unique surface forms at random from the Wikipedia corpus, and checked that they were valid words in the languages and correctly spelled. When a word was incorrectly spelled or deemed not to be a form used in the language, it was discarded.[10]

This list of surface forms was then analysed with the most recent version of the analyser, and around 500 of these analyses were manually checked. Where an analysis was erroneous, it was removed; where an analysis was missing, it was added. This process gave us a 'gold standard' morphologically analysed word list of 448 forms.[11]

We then took the same list of surface forms and ran them through the morphological analyser once more. Precision was calculated as the number of analyses which were found in both the output from the morphological analyser and the gold standard, divided by the total number of analyses output by the morphological analyser. Recall was calculated as the total number of analyses found in both the output from the morphological analyser and the gold standard, divided by the number of analyses found in the morphological analyser plus the number of analyses found in the gold standard but not in the morphological analyser.

After comparing with the gold-standard in this way, precision was 94.98% and recall was 81.32%.

Most of the issues with recall were due to missing stems in the lexicon, primarily nouns and proper nouns.[12] Regarding the precision, common issues included incorrect categorisation in the lexicon, and dubious forms, such as the imperative of *kerek-* 'need', which is in the analyser and is a hypothetically possible form, but appears not to be possible in practice.

5.3 Transliterator accuracy

We evaluated the transliteration component on the headwords from a bilingual Crimean Tatar–Russian dictionary that has been published in both Cyrillic and Latin orthographies.[13] We created a list of Cyrillic–Latin correspondences by aligning the headwords automatically based on an automated word-by-word comparison of the definitions in Russian, for a total of $14,905$ unique entries.

141 entries (~1%) had comments which did not match word-for-word; while it is possible that these could be corrected by hand, we discarded them. We then fed the Latin entries to the full transliteration transducer and evaluated against the corresponding Cyrillic entry.

Table 4 shows the performance of the transliterator for the different methods. In this case, precision is the percentage of predictions which are correct, recall is the percentage of words for which a correct transliteration is predicted, and the F-score is the harmonic mean of the two: $F^{-1} = \mathrm{mean}(\mathrm{Prec}^{-1}, \mathrm{Rec}^{-1})$.

Method	States	Precision	Recall	F-score
–	114	53.0	98.4	68.9
1-gram	2,030	93.4	93.5	93.5
2-gram	17,382	94.1	94.2	94.1
3-gram	99,761	94.0	94.1	94.1
4-gram	290,201	94.4	94.6	94.5
5-gram	577,926	95.1	95.2	95.2
6-gram	924,719	95.5	95.6	95.5
7-gram	1,282,917	95.4	95.6	95.0

Table 4: Performance of the transliterator using different methods. States gives a measure of the size of the generated FST.

Without n-grams, there is no attempt to filter proposed transliterations; that is, this "null" method generates all possible transliterations according to the combined phonological-morphological transducer. It demonstrates the theoretical limit of recall. Precision dramatically increases with the introduction of n-grams, as expected. Precision increases with more n-grams, levelling off at just over 95%. Recall drops from the maximum of 98.4% (the theoretical maximum the n-gram system can hope to attain); as the quality of the statistical filter increases, so does recall, until it levels off at 95.6%.

The problems with the transliteration model consist almost entirely of issues related to the presence of hard and soft signs in Cyrillic spellings (accounting for 492 of 1007, or 48.9%, of errors), incorrect vowels, mostly related to yoticisation (accounting for 469, or 46.6%, of errors), and issues correctly

---

[10]Available in the repository as dev/annotate.txt.

[11]Available in the repository as dev/annotate.all.txt.

[12]However, note that the recall number may be somewhat inflated, as thinking of missing analyses for already analysed words is particularly difficult.

[13]Available from http://medeniye.org/node/984.

predicting "ц" versus "тс" (accounting for 40, or 4% of errors). These errors typically arise in loanwords, where the correct Cyrillic spelling is often impossible to predict from the Latin orthography. Accuracy regarding these issues could likely be improved by having a larger and more representative corpus of Crimean Tatar in Cyrillic with which to train the n-gram models, or by attempting to model the loanword system.

6 Future work

The performance of the n-gram model could be improved by modelling the predictability of the orthography in n-grams and with a sliding window to filter out unlikely concatenations of common n-grams.

Aside from expanding the lexicon, the transducer forms part of a machine translation system from Crimean Tatar to Turkish being developed in the Apertium platform. There is also the prospect of applying it to dependency parsing for Crimean Tatar, and there have been some preliminary experiments in this direction (Ageeva and Tyers, 2016). We would also like to apply the approach for dealing with multiple scripts to other Turkic languages, such as Uzbek, Kazakh, or Karakalpak, where more than one widely-used normative orthography is in use. An additional advantage of our approach is that when orthographic systems are replaced, as is currently occurring in Kazakhstan for Kazakh, there is no need to completely rewrite an existing mature transducer; instead, a supplemental transliteration transducer can be constructed.

7 Concluding remarks

The primary contributions of this paper are a wide-coverage morphological description of Crimean Tatar able to analyse and generate both Cyrillic and Latin orthographies, and a general approach to building biscriptual transducers.

Acknowledgements

This work was made possible in part by Google's Summer of Code program, the Swarthmore College Research Fund, and the involvement of the Apertium open source community. We also very much appreciate the thoughtful, constructive comments from several anonymous reviewers.

References

Ekaterina Ageeva and Francis M. Tyers. 2016. Combined morphological and syntactic disambiguation for cross-lingual dependency parsing. In *Proceedings of TurkLang 2016*, Bishkek, Kyrgyzstan.

Kemal Altıntaş and İlyas Çiçekli. 2001. A morphological analyser for Crimean Tatar. In *Turkish Symposium on Artificial Intelligence and Neural Networks (TAINN2001)*.

Lars Johanson and Éva Á. Csató. 1998. *The Turkic Languages*. Routledge.

Lauri Karttunen. 1993. *The Last Phonological Rule: Reflections on constraints and derivations*, chapter Finite-state constraints. University of Chicago Press.

Darya Kavitskaya. 2010. *Crimean Tatar*. LINCOM Europa.

Krister Lindén, Miikka Silfverberg, Erik Axelson, Sam Hardwick, and Tommi Pirinen. 2011. *HFST—Framework for Compiling and Applying Morphologies*, volume 100 of *Communications in Computer and Information Science*. Springer.

Joakim Nivre, Marie-Catherine de Marneffe, Filip Ginter, Yoav Goldberg, Jan Hajič, Chris Manning, Ryan McDonald, Slav Petrov, Sampo Pyysalo, Natalia Silveira, Reut Tsarfaty, and Dan Zeman. 2016. Universal Dependencies v1: A Multilingual Treebank Collection. In *Proceedings of Language Resources and Evaluation Conference (LREC'16)*.

Gary F. Simons and Charles D. Fennig, editors. 2018. Twenty-first edition edition. SIL International, Dallas, Texas. Crimean Tatar: https://www.ethnologue.com/language/crh.

Jonathan North Washington, Aziyana Bayyr-ool, Aelita Salchak, and Francis M. Tyers. 2016. Development of a finite-state model for morphological processing of Tuvan. *Родной Язык*, 1(4):156–187.

Jonathan North Washington, Ilnar Salimzyanov, and Francis M. Tyers. 2014. Finite-state morphological transducers for three Kypchak languages. In *Proceedings of the 9th Conference on Language Resources and Evaluation, LREC2014*.

Improving Low-Resource Morphological Learning with Intermediate Forms from Finite State Transducers

Sarah Moeller and **Ghazaleh Kazeminejad** and **Andrew Cowell** and **Mans Hulden**
Department of Linguistics
University of Colorado
`first.last@colorado.edu`

Abstract

Neural encoder-decoder models are usually applied to morphology learning as an end-to-end process without considering the underlying phonological representations that linguists posit as abstract forms before morphophonological rules are applied. Finite State Transducers for morphology, on the other hand, are developed to contain these underlying forms as an intermediate representation. This paper shows that training a bidirectional two-step encoder-decoder model of Arapaho verbs to learn two separate mappings between tags and abstract morphemes and morphemes and surface allomorphs improves results when training data is limited to 10,000 to 30,000 examples of inflected word forms.

1 Introduction

A morphological analyzer is a prerequisite for many NLP tasks. A successful morphological analyzer supports applications such as speech recognition and machine translation that could provide speakers of low-resource languages access to online dictionaries or tools similar to Siri or Google Translate and might support and accelerate language revitalization efforts. This is even more crucial for morphologically complex languages such as Arapaho, an Algonquian language indigenous to the western USA. In polysynthetic languages such as Arapaho, inflected verbal forms are often semantically equivalent to whole sentences in morphologically simpler languages. A standard linguistic model of morphophonology holds that multiple morphemes are concatenated together and then phonological rules are applied to produce the inflected forms. The operation of phonological rules can reshape the string of fixed morphemes considerably, making it difficult for learners, whether human or machines, to recreate correct forms (generation) from the morpheme sequence or to analyze the reshaped inflected forms into their individual morphemes (parsing).

In this paper we describe an experiment in training a neural encoder-decoder model to replicate the bidirectional behavior of an existing finite state morphological analyzer for the Arapaho verb (Kazeminejad et al., 2017). When a language is low-resource, natural language processing needs strategies that achieve usable results with less data. We attempt to replicate a low-resource context by using a limited number of training examples. We evaluate the feasibility of learning abstract intermediate forms to achieve better results on various training set sizes. While common wisdom regarding neural models has it that, given enough data (Graves and Jaitly, 2014), end-to-end training is usually preferable to pipelined models, an argument can be made that morphology is an exception to this: learning two regular mappings separately *may* be easier than learning a single complex one. In Liu et al. (2018), adressing a related task, noticeably better results were reached for German, Finnish, and Russian when a neural system was first tasked to learn morphosyntactic tags than when it was tasked to produce an inflected form directly from uninflected forms and context. These three languages are morphologically complex or unpredictable, but marginally better results were achieved for the less complex languages.

2 Arapaho Verbs

Arapaho is a member of the Algonquian (and larger Algic) language family; it is an agglutinating, polysynthetic language, with free word order (Cowell and Moss Sr, 2008). The language has a very complex verbal inflection system, with a number of typologically uncommon elements. A given verb stem is used either with animate or inanimate subjects for intransi-

Proceedings of the 3rd Workshop on the Use of Computational Methods in the Study of Endangered Languages: Vol. 1 Papers, pages 81–86,
Honolulu, Hawai'i, USA, February 26–27, 2019.

tive verbs (*tei'eihi-* 'be strong.animate' vs. *tei'oo-* 'be strong.inanimate'), and with animate or inanimate objects for transitive verbs (*noohow-* 'see s.o.' vs. *noohoot-* 'see s.t.'). For each of these categories, the pronominal affixes/inflections vary in form. For example, 2SG with intransitive, animate subject is */-n/*, while for transitive, inanimate object it is */-ow/* (*nih-tei'eihi-n* 'you were strong' vs. *nih-noohoot-ow* 'you saw it').

All stem types can occur in four different verbal orders, whose function is primarily modal. These verbal orders each use different pronominal affixes/inflections as well. Thus, with four different verb stem types and four different verbal orders, there are a total of 16 different potential inflectional paradigms for any verbal root, though there is some overlap in the paradigms, and not all stem forms are possible for all roots.

Arapaho also has a proximate/obviative system, which designates pragmatically more- and less-prominent participants. "Direction-of-action" markers included in inflections do not correspond to true pronominal affixes. Thus *nih-noohow-oot* 'more important 3SG saw less important 3S/PL' vs. *nih-noohob-eit* 'less important 3SG/PL saw more important 3S'. The elements *-oo-* and *-ei-* specify direction of action, not specific persons or numbers of participants.

Arapaho has both progressive and regressive vowel harmony, operating on */i/* and */e/* respectively. This results in alternations in both the inflections themselves, and the final elements of stems, such as *noohow-un* 'see him!' vs. *niiteheib-in* 'help him!', or *nih-ni'eeneb-e3en* 'I liked you' vs. *nih-ni'eenow-oot* 'he liked her'.

The Arapaho verb, then, is subject to complicated morphophonological processes. For example, the underlying form of the word 'we see you' concatenates the transitive verb stem with animate object (TA) *noohow* 'see' and the '1PL.EXCL.SUBJ.2SG.OBJ' suffix *-een*. This underlying form undergoes significant transformation after morphophonological rewrite rules are applied. An initial change (IC) epenthesizes *-en* before the first vowel in the verb stem because it is a long vowel and because the verb is affirmative present. Then vowel harmony is at work, changing *n-en-oohow-een* to *n-on-oohow-een*. Finally a consonant mutation rule changes *w* to *b*, producing the surface form *nonoohobeen* (cf. Figure 1).

3   Finite State Model

One of the clear successes in computational modeling of linguistic patterns has been finite state transducer (FST) models for morphological analysis and generation (Koskenniemi, 1983; Beesley and Karttunen, 2003; Hulden, 2009; Lindén et al., 2009). An FST is bidirectional, able to both parse inflected word forms and generate all possible word forms for a given stem (Beesley and Karttunen, 2003). Given enough linguistic expertise and time investment, FSTs provide the capability to analyze any well-formed word in a language.

The Arapaho FST model used in this paper was constructed with the *foma* finite-state toolkit (Hulden, 2009). It used 18,559 verb stems taken from around 91,000 lines of natural discourse in a large transcribed and annotated spoken corpus of Arapaho, parts of which are publicly available in the Endangered Languages Archive (ELAR).[1]. All possible basic inflections occur in the corpus. The FST produces over 450,000 inflected forms from the stems.

The FST is constructed in two parts, the first being a specification of the lexicon and morphotactics using the finite-state lexicon compiler (lexc), a high-level declarative language for effective lexicon creation, where concatenative morphological rules and morphological irregularities are addressed (Karttunen, 1993). The first part produces intermediate, abstract "underlying" forms. These forms concatenate the appropriate morphemes from the lexicon in the correct order, (e.g. *noohoween* in Figure 1) but are not well-formed words in the language.

The second part of the FST implements the morphophonological and phonological rules of the language using "rewrite rules". These rules apply the appropriate phonological changes to the intermediate forms in specified contexts. Thus, in generation, the inflected word is not merely a bundle of morphemes, but the completely correct word form in accord with the morphophonological and phonological rules of the language. By composing, in a particular order (specified in the grammar of the language), the FSTs resulting from these rewrite rules to the parsed forms, the result is a single FST able to both generate and parse as shown in Figure 1.

---

[1] https://elar.soas.ac.uk/Collection/MPI189644

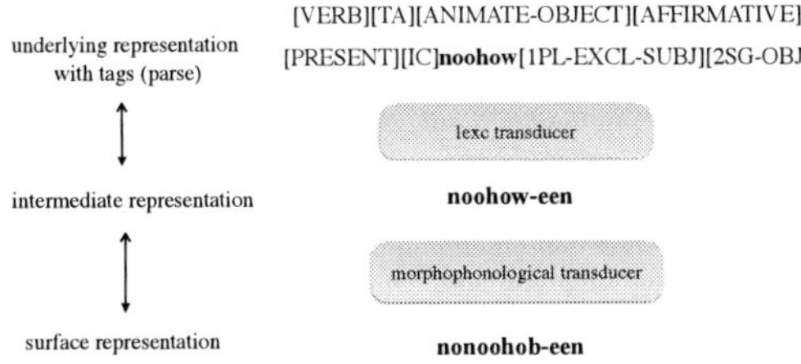

Figure 1: An example of a parsed form with verb stem and morphosyntactic tags (top left) and inflected surface form (bottom left) for the Arapaho FST. The intermediate underlying phonological forms (middle left) are accessible to the FST before/after applying morphophonological alternations.

4 Training the LSTM

Although an extensive finite state morphological analyzer is an extremely useful resource, neural models are much better able to analyze to unseen forms than finite state machines are. However, neural models are hampered in low-resource contexts by their data greediness. In order to see whether this limitation could be addressed we simulated training a neural model in low-resource contexts using output from the Arapaho FST. Since the currently strongest performing models for morphological inflection (Cotterell et al., 2017; Kann and Schütze, 2016; Makarov et al., 2017) use an LSTM-based sequence-to-sequence (seq2seq) model (Sutskever et al., 2014), we follow this design in our work. We implement the seq2seq model with OpenNMT's (Klein et al., 2018) default parameters of 2 layers for both the encoder and decoder, a hidden size of 500 for the recurrent unit, and a maximum batch size of 64.

Training corpora of various sizes are created by randomly selecting examples of inflected word forms and their corresponding intermediate and parsed forms from the bidirectional output of the Arapaho FST. This results in triplets like in Figure 1. The triplets are arranged into three pairs—inflected "surface" forms (SF) & intermediate forms (IF), IF & parsed forms (PF), and SF & PF. Re-using the pairs for both parsing and generation gives six data sets. For simplicity's sake, since the primary aim is to compare the two strategies' performance and not to measure accuracy, forms with ambiguous inflected forms, parses, or intermediate forms were filtered. Other experiments (Moeller et al., 2018) indicate that pre-processing the data to account for ambiguous forms would not greatly affect accuracy.

We treat the intermediate strategy of parsing as a translation task of input character sequences from the fully-inflected surface forms to an output of character sequences of the intermediate forms, and then from the intermediate forms to a sequence of morphosyntactic tags plus the character sequences of the verbal root. Generation follows the same model in the opposite direction.

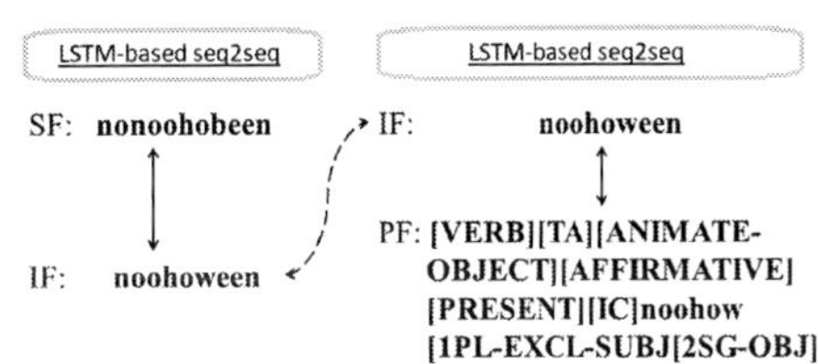

Figure 2: An example from training/test sets. In parsing, surface forms (SF) predict intermediate forms (IF). The output trains another encoder-decoder to predict parsed forms (PF). Generation follows the same steps but proceeding from the PF instead.

The selected data is divided roughly in half. The first half serves as training and development and the second half as testing data in the first step of the intermediate training strategy (SF⇔IF or PF⇔IF). In order to compare the two training strategies, the output of this intermediate step trains and tests the second step of the intermediate strategy. The original second half also serves to train and test the direct strategy (SF-PF or PF-SF). Symbol prediction degrades at the end of a sequence. Best results are achieved when each character/tag sequence is doubled on its line for training and testing (Moeller et al., 2018) and trimmed for evaluation. So, for example, *nonoohobeen* becomes *nonoohobeennonoohobeen* during training and testing but predicted symbols that exceed the length of the original string are deleted and the first half of the predicted string is evaluated against the original string.

5 Experiment and Results

We compare two strategies to train a neural model to generate inflected verbs from morphosyntactic tags with verb stem or to parse inflected verb forms. First, we train the neural model to learn correct output forms directly from the parsed or inflected input. Second, we added an intermediate step where the model first learns the mapping to intermediate forms and, from there, the mapping to the correct parsed or inflected form. We measure the final accuracy score and the average Levenshtein distance and compare the performance of the two strategies in generation and in parsing. Accuracy is measured as the fraction of correct generated/parsed forms in the output compared to complete gold inflected or parsed forms.

5.1 Generation

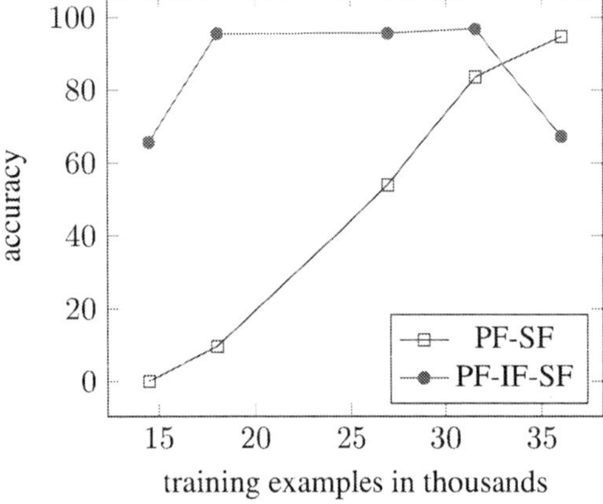

Figure 3: Generation - accuracy scores

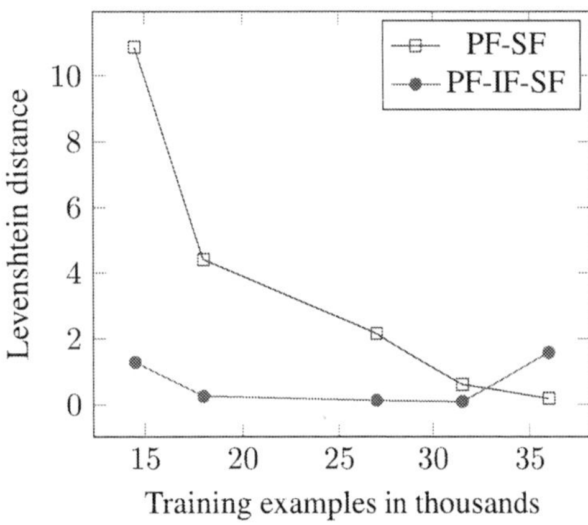

Figure 4: Generation - average Levenshtein distances

We trained a bidirectional LSTM encoder-decoder with attention (Bahdanau et al., 2015) to generate Arapaho verbs using five training sets with approximately 14.5, 18, 27, 31.5, and 36 thousand examples. The direct strategy trains on the morphosyntactic tags and verb stem. Each tag occurs in the same order as its corresponding morpheme appears in the intermediate form. Only

"direction-of-action" tags/morphemes come after the stem.

The accuracy scores in Figure 3 and the Levenshtein distance measures in 4 show that the intermediate strategy performs better than the direct strategy in low-resource settings. Starting at about 14,500 training examples, where the direct strategy produces barely any inflected forms (SF) correctly, the intermediate strategy achieves nearly 69% accuracy. As the training size approaches 36,000, the advantage of the intermediate step is lost. Indeed, the intermediate strategy begins to perform worse while the direct strategy continues to improve. The intermediate strategy seems to peak at 30,000 training examples.

5.2 Parsing

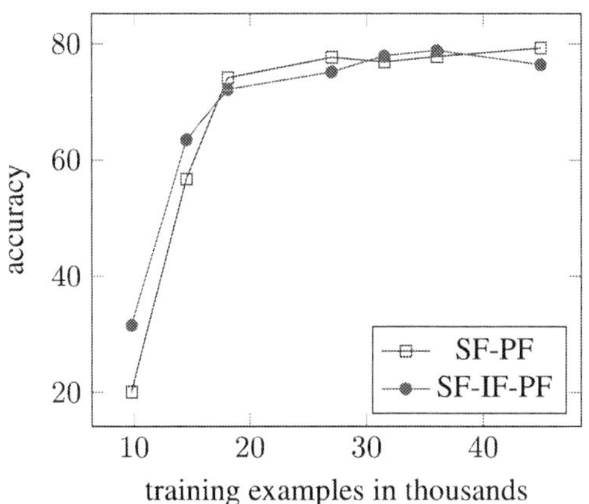

Figure 5: Parsing - accuracy scores

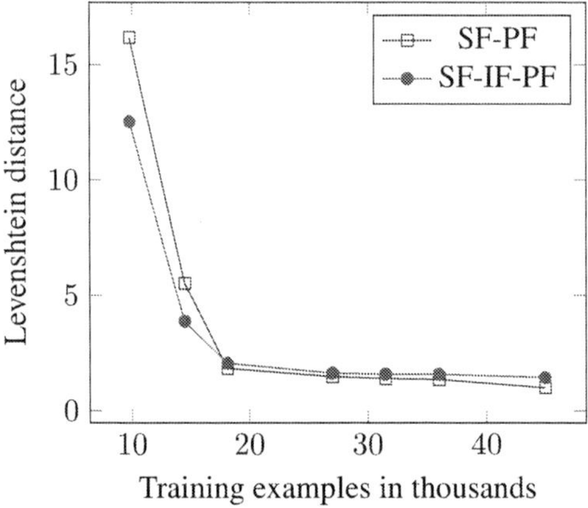

Figure 6: Parsing - average Levenshtein distances

The parsing trend is less clear when compared to morphological generation. We compare seven training sets of approximately 10, 14.5, 18, 31.5, 36, and 45 thousand examples. As in morphological generation, at the lowest data settings the intermediate learning strategy is preferable to the direct strategy, though it has a less dramatic performance difference. The accuracy scores in Figure 5 show that with 14,000 training examples, the intermediate strategy performs only about 10 points higher. The advantage of the intermediate strategy is less noticeable in parsing, nor does its advantage decrease as quickly. With 36,000 examples barely one point separates the two strategies and the intermediate strategy performs slightly better. The intermediate strategy performance does not begin to reduce until 45,000 examples. The average Levenshtein distances in Figure 6, however, show that the direct strategy improves more consistently, though it is still only slightly better as training size increases.

5.3 Discussion

An end-to-end neural model demands quite a bit of data in order to learn patterns. It appears that, for languages with complicated morphophonological alternations, if an intermediate model is trained on a simple concatenation of morphemes, these disadvantages may be counterbalanced. The morpheme substrings in the intermediate forms correspond predictably to morphosyntactic tags in the parsed form. Subsequent alternations are less predictable. This may explain the intermediate strategy's difference in performance between parsing and generation. A pipelined approach with intermediate training is generally not preferable to end-to-end training. The intermediate step inevitably introduces errors into the training of the second neural model. The intermediate strategy's performance degradation beyond 35 or 40 thousand examples might indicate that the errors become too dominant.

Comparing our results to the recent CoNLL-SIGMORPHON shared tasks (Cotterell et al., 2016, 2017, 2018), it is surprising that the Arapaho direct generation results at 10,000 examples are so low. However, polysynthetic languages are rare in the shared task—only one, Navajo, was available in 2016 and 2017–making it difficult to compare results on such complicated and varied morphologies. In addition, our data included phenomena which could be considered derivational, such as verbal stems signaling animacy and modality (cf.

Sect. 2). Also, since the data was selected randomly from the full FST output, the neural model may simply have not seen enough repeated stems in the low settings. Our results are not very good at the lowest settings but, in future, more in-depth pre-processing and filtering of the data could improve overall performance.

The varying results from morphological parsing shown in Figures 5 and 6 demonstrate the preliminary nature of this study. The trend between the two strategies seems indicative but several more comparisons should be conducted on similar languages. We hope to conduct a similar study on other low-resource languages for which an FST exists in order to determine whether the trend will reappear.

6 Conclusion

A sweet spot exists between 10,000 and 30,000 randomly selected training examples of Arapaho verbs where better results are achieved in morphological generation by first training an encoder-decoder to produce the intermediate forms from an FST than by learning the inflected or parsed form directly. For generation, the intermediate strategy achieves the strongest results around 30,000 examples. The results of morphological parsing vary, with the intermediate strategy outperforming the direct strategy at very low settings but achieving similar results with 18,000 and 36,000 training examples. Overall, the intermediate strategy appears to produce reliably better results at low-resource settings than the direct strategy.

Acknowledgements

NVIDIA Corp. donated the Titan Xp GPU used in this research.

References

Dzmitry Bahdanau, Kyunghyun Cho, and Yoshua Bengio. 2015. Neural machine translation by jointly learning to align and translate. In *ICLR*.

Kenneth R. Beesley and Lauri Karttunen. 2003. *Finite State Morphology*. CSLI Publications, Stanford, CA.

Ryan Cotterell, Christo Kirov, John Sylak-Glassman, Géraldine Walther, Ekaterina Vylomova, Arya D. McCarthy, Katharina Kann, Sebastian Mielke, Garrett Nicolai, Miikka Silfverberg, David Yarowsky,

Jason Eisner, and Mans Hulden. 2018. The CoNLL–SIGMORPHON 2018 shared task: Universal morphological reinflection. In *Proceedings of the CoNLL SIGMORPHON 2018 Shared Task: Universal Morphological Reinflection*, pages 1–27, Brussels. Association for Computational Linguistics.

Ryan Cotterell, Christo Kirov, John Sylak-Glassman, Gèraldine Walther, Ekaterina Vylomova, Patrick Xia, Manaal Faruqui, Sandra Kübler, David Yarowsky, Jason Eisner, and Mans Hulden. 2017. CoNLL-SIGMORPHON 2017 shared task: Universal morphological reinflection in 52 languages. In *Proceedings of the CoNLL SIGMORPHON 2017 Shared Task: Universal Morphological Reinflection*, pages 1–30. Association for Computational Linguistics.

Ryan Cotterell, Christo Kirov, John Sylak-Glassman, David Yarowsky, Jason Eisner, and Mans Hulden. 2016. The SIGMORPHON 2016 shared task—morphological reinflection. In *Proceedings of the 14th SIGMORPHON Workshop on Computational Research in Phonetics, Phonology, and Morphology*, pages 10–22, Berlin, Germany. Association for Computational Linguistics.

Andrew Cowell and Alonzo Moss Sr. 2008. *The Arapaho Language*. University Press of Colorado.

Alex Graves and Navdeep Jaitly. 2014. Towards end-to-end speech recognition with recurrent neural networks. In *International Conference on Machine Learning*, pages 1764–1772.

Mans Hulden. 2009. Foma: a finite-state compiler and library. In *Proceedings of the 12th Conference of the European Chapter of the Association for Computational Linguistics*, pages 29–32. Association for Computational Linguistics.

Katharina Kann and Hinrich Schütze. 2016. Single-model encoder-decoder with explicit morphological representation for reinflection. In *Proceedings of the 54th Annual Meeting of the Association for Computational Linguistics (Volume 2: Short Papers)*, pages 555–560, Berlin, Germany. Association for Computational Linguistics.

Lauri Karttunen. 1993. *Finite-state lexicon compiler*. Xerox Corporation. Palo Alto Research Center.

Ghazaleh Kazeminejad, Andrew Cowell, and Mans Hulden. 2017. Creating lexical resources for polysynthetic languages—the case of Arapaho. In *Proceedings of the 2nd Workshop on the Use of Computational Methods in the Study of Endangered Languages*, pages 10–18, Honolulu. Association for Computational Linguistics.

Guillaume Klein, Yoon Kim, Yuntian Deng, Vincent Nguyen, Jean Senellart, and Alexander Rush. 2018. OpenNMT: Neural machine translation toolkit. In *Proceedings of the 13th Conference of the Association for Machine Translation in the Americas (Volume 1: Research Papers)*, pages 177–184. Association for Machine Translation in the Americas.

Kimmo Koskenniemi. 1983. *Two-level morphology: A general computational model for word-form recognition and production*. Publication 11, University of Helsinki, Department of General Linguistics, Helsinki.

Krister Lindén, Miikka Silfverberg, and Tommi Pirinen. 2009. HFST tools for morphology—an efficient open-source package for construction of morphological analyzers. In *International Workshop on Systems and Frameworks for Computational Morphology*, pages 28–47. Springer.

Ling Liu, Ilamvazhuthy Subbiah, Adam Wiemerslage, Jonathan Lilley, and Sarah Moeller. 2018. Morphological reinflection in context: CU Boulder's submission to CoNLL-SIGMORPHON 2018 shared task. In *Proceedings of the CoNLL SIGMORPHON 2018 Shared Task: Universal Morphological Reinflection*, pages 86–92, Brussels. Association for Computational Linguistics.

Peter Makarov, Tatiana Ruzsics, and Simon Clematide. 2017. Align and copy: UZH at SIGMORPHON 2017 shared task for morphological reinflection. In *Proceedings of the CoNLL SIGMORPHON 2017 Shared Task: Universal Morphological Reinflection*, pages 49–57, Vancouver. Association for Computational Linguistics.

Sarah Moeller, Ghazaleh Kazeminejad, Andrew Cowell, and Mans Hulden. 2018. A neural morphological analyzer for Arapaho verbs learned from a finite state transducer. In *Proceedings of the Workshop on Computational Modeling of Polysynthetic Languages*, pages 12–20. Association for Computational Linguistics.

Ilya Sutskever, Oriol Vinyals, and Quoc V. Le. 2014. Sequence to sequence learning with neural networks. In *Advances in Neural Information Processing Systems (NIPS)*, pages 3104–3112.

Bootstrapping a Neural Morphological Analyzer for
St. Lawrence Island Yupik from a Finite-State Transducer

Lane Schwartz
University of Illinois
at Urbana-Champaign
lanes@illinois.edu

Emily Chen
University of Illinois
at Urbana-Champaign
echen41@illinois.edu

Benjamin Hunt
George Mason University
bhunt6@gmu.edu

Sylvia L.R. Schreiner
George Mason University
sschrei2@gmu.edu

Abstract

Morphological analysis is a critical enabling
technology for polysynthetic languages. We
present a neural morphological analyzer for
case-inflected nouns in St. Lawrence Island
Yupik, an endangered polysythetic language
in the Inuit-Yupik language family, treating
morphological analysis as a recurrent neural
sequence-to-sequence task. By utilizing an
existing finite-state morphological analyzer to
create training data, we improve analysis coverage on attested Yupik word types from approximately 75% for the existing finite-state
analyzer to 100% for the neural analyzer. At
the same time, we achieve a substantially
higher level of accuracy on a held-out testing
set, from 78.9% accuracy for the finite-state
analyzer to 92.2% accuracy for our neural analyzer.

1 Introduction

St. Lawrence Island Yupik, henceforth Yupik, is
an endangered polysynthetic language spoken on
St. Lawrence Island, Alaska and the Chukotka
Peninsula of Russia. Members of the Yupik community on St. Lawrence Island have expressed interest in language revitalization and conservation.

Recent work by Chen and Schwartz (2018) resulted in a finite-state morphological analyzer for
Yupik implemented in foma (Hulden, 2009). That
analyzer implements the grammatical and morphophonological rules documented in *A Practical
Grammar of the St. Lawrence Island / Siberian
Yupik Eskimo Language* (Jacobson, 2001).

In this work, we test the coverage of the finite-
state analyzer against a corpus of digitized Yupik
texts and find that the analyzer fails to return any
analysis for approximately 25% of word types (see
§2 and Table 1). We present a higher-coverage
neural morphological analyzer for case-inflected
Yupik nouns that involve no derivational mor-

phology, using the previously-developed finite-
state analyzer to generate large amounts of labeled
training data (§3). We evaluate the performance of
the finite-state and neural analyzers, and find that
the neural analyzer results in higher coverage and
higher accuracy (§5), even when the finite-state
analyzer is augmented with a guessing module to
hypothesize analyzes for out-of-vocabulary words
(§4). We thus find that a robust high-accuracy
morphological analyzer can be successfully bootstrapped from an existing lower-coverage finite-
state morphological analyzer (§6), a result which
has implications for the development of language
technologies for Yupik and other morphologically-
rich languages.

2 Evaluation of the FST Analyzer

The finite-state morphological analyzer of Chen
and Schwartz (2018) implements the grammatical and morphophonological rules documented
in *A Practical Grammar of the St. Lawrence Island / Siberian Yupik Eskimo Language* (Jacobson,
2001) using the foma finite-state toolkit (Hulden,
2009).

In order to evaluate the percentage of attested
Yupik word forms for which the finite-state analyzer produces any analysis, we began by digitizing several hundred Yupik sentences presented
in Jacobson (2001) as examples to be translated
by the reader. We next assembled, digitized, and
manually validated seven texts that each consist
of a collection of Yupik stories along with corresponding English translations. The texts include four anthologies of Yupik stories, legends,
and folk tales, along with three leveled elementary
primers prepared by the Bering Strait School District in the 1990s (Apassingok et al., 1993, 1994,
1995). Of the four anthologies, three comprise a
trilogy known as *The Lore of St. Lawrence Is-*

Proceedings of the 3rd Workshop on the Use of Computational Methods in the Study of Endangered Languages: Vol. 1 Papers, pages 87–96,
Honolulu, Hawai'i, USA, February 26–27, 2019.

Text	% Coverage		Corpus size
	Tokens;	Types	(in words)
Ref	98.24	97.87	795
SLI1	79.10	70.62	6859
SLI2	77.14	68.87	11,926
SLI3	76.98	68.32	12,982
Ungi	84.08	73.45	15,766
Lvl1	76.64	70.86	4357
Lvl2	75.42	72.62	5358
Lvl3	77.71	75.19	5731

Table 1: For each Yupik text, the percentage of types and tokens for which the Yupik finite-state analyzer of Chen and Schwartz (2018) returns an analysis, along with the total number of tokens per text. *Ref* refers to Yupik examples taken from the Jacobson (2001) reference grammar, *SLI1 - SLI3* refer to the *Lore of St. Lawrence Island*, volumes 1-3 (Apassingok et al., 1985, 1987, 1989), *Ungi* is an abbreviation for *Ungipaghaghlanga* (Koonooka, 2003), and *Lvl1 - Lvl3* refer to the elementary Yupik primers (Apassingok et al., 1993, 1994, 1995).

land (Apassingok et al., 1985, 1987, 1989), while the last is a stand-alone text, *Ungipaghaghlanga* (Koonooka, 2003; Menovshchikov, 1988). Together, these texts represent the largest known collection of written Yupik.

After digitizing each text, we analyzed each Yupik word in that text using the finite-state morphological analyzer. We then calculated the percentage of tokens from each text for which the finite-state analyzer produced at least one analysis. We call this number *coverage*, and report this result for each text in Table 1. The mean coverage over the entire set of texts was 77.56%. The neural morphological analyzer described in the subsequent section was developed in large part to provide morphological analyses for the remaining 22.44% of heretofore unanalyzed Yupik tokens.

3 Yupik Morphological Analysis as Machine Translation

The task of morphological analysis can be regarded as a machine translation (sequence-to-sequence) problem, where an input sequence that consists of characters or graphemes in the source language (surface form) is mapped to an output sequence that consists of characters or graphemes *and* inflectional tags (underlying form). For example, in English, the sequence of characters representing the surface word form *foxes* can be transformed into a sequence of characters representing the root word *fox* and the inflectional tag indicating plurality:

$$f\,o\,x\,e\,s$$
$$\downarrow$$
$$f\,o\,x\,[\text{PL}]$$

In contrast to English, Yupik is highly productive with respect to derivational and inflectional morphology.[1] See §3.1.1 for noun inflection tags.

(1) **kaviighet**
    kaviigh-   -$\sim_{\text{sf}}$-w:(e)t
    fox-   -ABS.UNPD.PL
    'foxes'

But in much the same way, (1) can be rewritten as a translation process from an input sequence of graphemes that represent the surface form to an output sequence of graphemes and inflectional tags that represent the underlying form:

$$k\,a\,v\,i\,i\,g\,h\,e\,t$$
$$\downarrow$$
$$k\,a\,v\,i\,i\,gh\,[\text{ABS}]\,[\text{UNPD}]\,[\text{PL}]$$

3.1 Generating Data from an FST

Very little Yupik data has previously been manually annotated in the form of interlinear glosses. On the other hand, the finite-state morphological analyzer of Chen and Schwartz (2018) is capable of generating Yupik surface forms from provided underlying forms, and vice versa. In the following sections, bracketed items [..] introduce the inflectional tags that are used in the underlying forms of the finite-state analyzer.

3.1.1 Basic Yupik Nouns

Yupik nouns inflect for one of seven grammatical cases:

1. *ablative-modalis* [ABL_MOD]
2. *absolutive*   [ABS]
3. *equalis*   [EQU]
4. *localis*   [LOC]
5. *terminalis*   [TER]
6. *vialis*   [VIA]
7. *relative*   [REL]

---

[1] Each derivational and inflectional suffix is associated with a series of morphophonological rules. Each rule is represented by a unique symbol such as – or $\sim_{\text{sf}}$ as introduced in Jacobson (2001). This convention is used in the Yupik grammar, in the Yupik-English dictionary (Badten et al., 2008), and by Chen and Schwartz (2018). We therefore follow this convention, employing these symbols in our glosses here. See Table 2 on the following page for more details.

Symbol	Description
~	Drops *e* in penultimate (semi-final) position or *e* in root-final position and *hops* it *e-Hopping* is the process by which vowels *i*, *a*, or *u* in the first syllable of the root are lengthened as a result of dropping semi-final or final-*e*, so termed because it is as if the *e* has "hopped" into the first syllable and assimilated. *e-Hopping* will not occur if doing so results in a three-consonant cluster within the word or a two-consonant cluster at the beginning (Jacobson, 2001).
~$_f$	Drops final *e* and hops it
~$_{sf}$	Drops semi-final *e* and hops it
-w	Drops weak final consonants, that is, *gh* that is not marked with an *. Strong *gh* is denoted *gh**
:	Drops uvulars that appear between single vowels
–	Drops final consonants
—	Drops final consonants and preceding vowel
@	Indicates some degree of modification to root-final *te*, the degree of which is dependent on the suffix
+	Indicates no morphophonology occurs during affixation. This symbol is implicitly assumed if no other symbols are present.

Table 2: List of documented morphophonological rules in Yupik and their lexicalized symbols. For more details see Jacobson (2001) and Badten et al. (2008).

Nouns then remain *unpossessed* [UNPD] and inflect for number (*singular* [SG], *plural* [PL], or *dual* [DU]), or inflect as possessed nouns. Possessed nouns are marked for number, and for the person and number of the possessor. For example, [1SGPOSS][SGPOSD] marks a possessed singular noun with a first person singular possessor.

The Badten et al. (2008) Yupik-English dictionary lists 3873 noun roots, and the Jacobson (2001) reference grammar lists 273 nominal inflectional suffixes. We deterministically generated data by exhaustively pairing every Yupik noun root with every inflectional suffix (ignoring any semantic infelicity that may result). As shown in Table 3 above, the underlying forms that result from

Root		Case		Poss		Posd		*Total*
3873	×	7	×	1	×	3	=	81,333
3873	×	7	×	12	×	3	=	975,996
								1,057,329

Table 3: Extracted training data. The first row counts the total number of *unpossessed* nouns which are marked for number: [SG], [PL], [DU]. The second row counts the total number of *possessed* nouns which are marked for number and also for 12 differing types of possessors, which themselves are marked for person, [1-4], and number, [SG], [PL], [DU].

ble 3 above, the underlying forms that result from these pairings map to just over 1 million inflected Yupik word forms or surface forms. Note that these word forms represent morphologically licit forms, but not all are attested. Even so, we did not exclude unattested forms nor weight them according to plausibility, since we lack sufficient documentation to distinguish the valid forms from the semantically illicit ones. This parallel dataset of inflected Yupik nouns and their underlying forms represents our corpus.

3.1.2 Identified Flaw in Existing Yupik FST

While generating data using the finite-state analyzer, we observed a minor bug. Specifically, the finite-state analyzer fails to account for the allomorphy that is triggered on some noun roots when they are inflected for a subset of the 3rd person possessor forms (root-final -*e* surfaces as -*a*).

(2) **neqangit**
    neqe-   -~:(ng)it
    food-   -ABS.PL.3PLPOSS
    '*their foods*'

As shown in (2), the correct surface form for **neqe**[ABS][PL][3PLPOSS] is **neqangit**, but the analyzer incorrectly generates **neqngit** instead. Due to time constraints and the relatively small estimated impact, we did not modify the analyzer to correct this bug. Though this impacts the training data, having previously evaluated the analyzer, we do not believe this error to be egregious enough to compromise the generated dataset.

3.1.3 Yupik Verbs and Derivational Suffixes

While our training set for this work is the set of inflected Yupik nouns described in §3.1.1, it is important to note that this process could in principle be used to generate a much larger training set. The Badten et al. (2008) Yupik-English dic-

Sequence Type	Tokenize by Character	Tokenize by Grapheme
surface form	q i k m i q	q i k mm i q
underlying form	q i k m i gh [N] [ABS] [UNPD] [SG]	q i k mm i gh [N] [ABS] [UNPD] [SG]

Table 4: Contrasts the two tokenization methods introduced in § 3.2.1 (tokenization by character and tokenization by orthographically transparent Yupik grapheme) on the surface form **qikmiq** (*dog*) and its underlying form **qikmigh**[N][ABS][UNPD][SG].

#	Possible Nouns	Possible Verbs	Both
0	1.06×10^{06}	8.80×10^{06}	9.86×10^{06}
1	1.37×10^{08}	2.04×10^{09}	2.18×10^{09}
2	2.22×10^{10}	4.19×10^{11}	4.41×10^{11}
3	4.03×10^{12}	8.31×10^{13}	8.72×10^{13}
4	7.66×10^{14}	1.63×10^{16}	1.71×10^{16}
5	1.48×10^{17}	3.18×10^{18}	3.33×10^{18}
6	2.88×10^{19}	6.21×10^{20}	6.50×10^{20}
7	5.61×10^{21}	1.21×10^{23}	1.27×10^{23}

Table 5: Number of morphotactically possible Yupik word forms formed using 0-7 derivational suffixes.

tionary and Jacobson (2001) Yupik grammar also list 3762 verb roots along with 180 intransitive and 2160 transitive verbal inflectional morphemes. If one were to naively assume that every Yupik verb can be either transitive or intransitive,[2] another 8.8 million training examples consisting of Yupik verbs could be generated.

Yupik also exhibits extensive derivational morphology. The dictionary lists 89 derivational suffixes that can each attach to a noun root and yield another noun, 58 derivational suffixes that can each attach to a noun root and yield a verb, 172 derivational suffixes that can each attach to a verb root and yield another verb, and 42 derivational suffixes that can each attach to a verb root and yield a noun. Yupik words containing up to seven derivational morphemes have been attested in the literature (de Reuse, 1994). By considering all possible Yupik nouns and verbs with up to seven derivational morphemes, well over 1.2×10^{23} inflected Yupik word forms could be generated as shown in Table 5 above. As before, many of these forms, while morphologically valid, would be syntactically or semantically illicit.

3.2 Neural Machine Translation

In this work, we made use of Marian (Junczys-Dowmunt et al., 2018), an open-source neural ma-chine translation framework that supports bidirectional recurrent encoder-decoder models with attention (Schuster and Paliwal, 1997; Bahdanau et al., 2014). In our experiments using Marian, we trained neural networks capable of translating from input sequences of characters or graphemes (representing Yupik words) to output sequences of characters or graphemes plus inflectional tags (representing an underlying Yupik form).

3.2.1 Data

We began by preprocessing the data described in §3.1.1 by tokenizing each Yupik surface form, either by characters or by orthographically transparent, *redoubled* graphemes. An example can be seen in the transformation of the word *kavi-ighet* at the beginning of §3, where each character and inflectional tag were separated by a space. When tokenizing by redoubled graphemes, orthographically non-transparent graphemes were first replaced following the approach described in Schwartz and Chen (2017) which ensures there is only one way to tokenize a Yupik word form. This approach undoes an orthographic convention that shortens the spelling of words by exploiting the following facts:

- Graphemic doubling conveys voicelessness (*g* represents the voiced velar fricative while *gg* represents the *voiceless* velar fricative)

- Consecutive consonants in Yupik typically agree in voicing, with the exception of voiceless consonants that follow nasals

Yupik orthography undoubles a voiceless grapheme if it co-occurs with a second voiceless grapheme, according to the following three Undoubling Rules (Jacobson, 2001):

1. A fricative is undoubled next to a stop or one of the voiceless fricatives where doubling is not used to show voicelessness (*f*, *s*, *wh*, *h*).

2. A nasal is undoubled after a stop or one of the voiceless fricatives where doubling is not used to show voicelessness.

---

[2] The Yupik-English dictionary does not annotate verb roots with valence information.

3. A fricative or nasal is undoubled when it comes after a fricative where doubling is used to show voicelessness, except that if the second fricative is *ll* then the first fricative is undoubled instead.

These two tokenization methods subsequently produced two parallel corpora, whose training pairs differed as seen in Table 4 on the previous page. Nevertheless, the input data always corresponded to Yupik surface forms, and the output data corresponded to underlying forms. The parallel corpora were then randomly partitioned into a training set, a validation set, and a test set in a 0.8/0.1/0.1 ratio.

3.2.2 Initial Experiment

Using Marian, we used the data tokenized by characters and trained a shallow neural network model that implemented an attentional encoder-decoder model (Bahdanau et al., 2014) with early stopping and holdout cross validation. We used the parameters described in Sennrich et al. (2016), where the encoder and decoder consisted of one hidden layer each, of size 1024. Of the 109,395 items in the final test set, this shallow neural model achieved 100% coverage and 59.67% accuracy on the test set.

Error analysis revealed a substantial amount of underspecification and surface form ambiguity as a result of syncretism in the nominal paradigm. As exemplified in (3a) and (3b), inflectional suffixes in Yupik may share the same underlying phonological form as well as the same morphophonological rules associated with that suffix.

(3a) **ayveghet**
ayvegh-　　-∼_sf-w:(e)t
walrus-　　-**ABS**.UNPD.PL
'*walruses*'

(3b) **ayveghet**
ayvegh-　　-∼_sf-w:(e)t
walrus-　　-**REL**.UNPD.PL
'*of walruses*'

For example, any noun that is inflected for the unpossessed absolute plural, [N][ABS][UNPD][PL], produces a word-form that is identical to the form yielded when the noun is inflected for the unpossessed relative plural, [N][REL][UNPD][PL]. The generated parallel data therefore includes the following two parallel forms, both of which have the exact same surface form. The first is the word in absolutive case:

$$a\ y\ v\ e\ g\ h\ e\ t$$
$$\downarrow$$
$$a\ y\ v\ e\ g\ h\ [\text{N}]\ [\text{ABS}]\ [\text{UNPD}]\ [\text{PL}]$$

The second is the word in relative case:

$$a\ y\ v\ e\ g\ h\ e\ t$$
$$\downarrow$$
$$a\ y\ v\ e\ g\ h\ [\text{N}]\ [\text{REL}]\ [\text{UNPD}]\ [\text{PL}]$$

Since these surface forms are only distinguishable through grammatical context, and our neural analyzer was not trained to consider context, it was made to guess which underlying form to return, and as suggested by the low accuracy score of 59.67%, the analyzer's guesses were often incorrect. We did not think it was proper to penalize the analyzer for wrong answers in instances of syncretism, and consequently implemented a postprocessing step to account for this phenomenon.

This step was performed after the initial calculation of the neural analyzer's accuracy score, and provided an estimated or adjusted accuracy score that considered the syncretic forms equivalent. It iterated through all outputs of the neural analyzer that were initially flagged as incorrect for differing from their test set counterparts. Using the finite-state analyzer, the surface forms for each output and its corresponding test set item were then generated to verify whether or not their surface forms matched. If they matched, the neural analyzer's output was instead counted as correct (see Table 6 on the following page for examples). Assessed in this way, the shallow model achieved an adjusted accuracy score of 99.90%.

3.2.3 Data Revisited

Although the postprocessing step is sufficient to demonstrate the true performance of the neural analyzer, we attempted to resolve this ambiguity issue with a more systematic approach. In their development of a neural morphological analyzer for Arapaho verbs, Moeller et al. (2018) conflated tags that resulted in ambiguous surface forms into a single, albeit less informative, tag, such as [**3-SUBJ**], joined from [3SG-SUBJ] and [3PL-SUBJ]. We attempted to do the same for Yupik by collapsing the tag set, but Yupik presents a somewhat more intricate ambiguity patterning. Syncretic tags can differ in their case markings alone, as in (3a) and (3b), but they can also differ across

Neural Analyzer Output	Surface	Gold Standard	Surface	
anipa[N][ABS][UNPD][PL]	anipat	anipa[N][REL][UNPD][PL]	anipat	✓
wayani[N][LOC][UNPD][PL]	wayani	wayagh[N][LOC][UNPD][PL]	wayani	✓
suflu[N][LOC][UNPD][PL]	sufluni	suflugh[N][ABS][4SGPOSS][SGPOSD]	sufluni	✓
puume[N][LOC][UNPD][DU]	pumegni	puu[N][LOC][4DUPOSS][SGPOSD]	puumegneng	✗

Table 6: An illustration of the process of the post-processing step that was implemented to resolve surface form ambiguity. If the output and its gold standard match in their surface forms, the output is then considered correct, despite the mismatch in the underlying forms.

case, possessor type, *and* number, as seen in (4a) and (4b).

(4a) **neghsameng**
neghsagh- -~f-wmeng
seal- **-ABL_MOD.UNPD.SG**
'*seal* (as indefinite object); *from seal*'

(4b) **neghsameng**
neghsagh- -~f-wmeng
seal- **-REL.PL.4DUPOSS**
'*their₂ (reflexive) seals*'

As a result, we could not conflate our tags in the same way Moeller et al. (2018) did. Instead, for each set of syncretic tags, one string of tags was selected to represent all of the tags in the set, such that [N][ABS][UNPD][PL] denoted both unpossessed absolute plural *and* unpossessed relative plural. The original 273 unique strings of tags (7 cases × 13 possessor types × 3 number markers) were consequently reduced to 170 instead.

Having identified and reduced tag set ambiguity, we retrained the shallow model but only managed to achieved an unadjusted accuracy score of 95.48%. Additional error analysis revealed that some surface form ambiguity remained, but among non-syncretic tags that could not be collapsed. In other words, these tags generated identical surface forms for some nouns but not others. This is shown in (5a) – (5d):

(5a) **sufluni**
suflu- --ni
cave- **-ABS.SG.4SGPOSS**
'*his/her* (reflexive) *own cave*'

(5b) **sufluni**
suflu- -~f-wni
cave- **-LOC.UNPD.PL**
'*in the cave*'

(5c) **sufluni**
suflug- --ni
chimney- **-ABS.SG.4SGPOSS**
'*his/her* (reflexive) *own chimney*'

(5d) **suflugni**
suflug- -~f-wni
chimney- **-LOC.UNPD.PL**
'*in the chimney*'

Thus, despite the identical surface forms shown in (5a) and (5b), these same inflection tags do not result in identical surface forms for the noun root **suflug** in (5c) and (5d), since the underlying inflectional suffixes they represent are distinct: **–ni** versus ~f-**wni**. As such, these two strings of tags, [N][ABS][4SGPOSS][SGPOSD] and [N][LOC][UNPD][PL], cannot be collapsed.

Since the tag set cannot be reduced further than 170 tags, we must invoke the post-processing step introduced in §3.2.2 regardless. Moreover, since our proposed method results in some loss of information with respect to all possible underlying forms, we will have to seek an alternative method for handling syncretism. Nevertheless, after applying the post-processing step, the retrained model also achieved an adjusted accuracy score of 99.90%.

3.2.4 Additional Experiments

We trained four models on the inflected nouns dataset, experimenting with the shallow versus deep neural network architectures and the two tokenization methods: by characters and by redoubled graphemes. The shallow neural models were identical to those described in §3.2.2 and §3.2.3. The deep neural models used four hidden layers and LSTM cells, following Barone et al. (2017). As before, all models were trained to convergence and evaluated with holdout cross validation on the same test set. Results are presented in Table 7 on the next page, along with the accuracy scores before and after resolving all surface ambiguities.

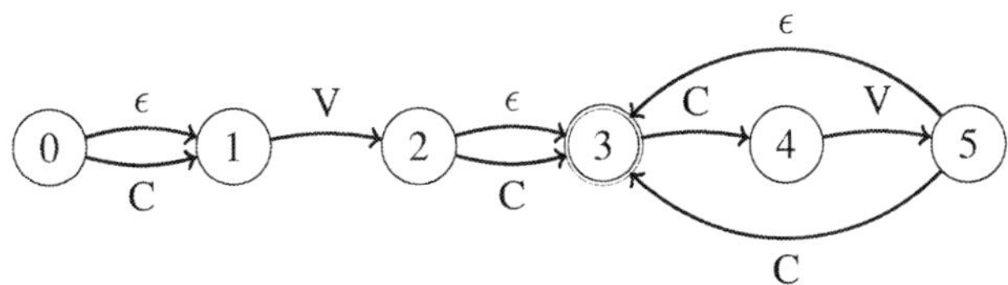

Figure 1: Finite-state diagram depicting legal word structure for nouns in Yupik. Here, **V** may refer to either a short vowel, *-i, -a, -u, -e,* or a long vowel, *-ii, -aa, -uu,* and **C** refers to any consonantal Yupik grapheme. Additionally, any noun-final **C** is restricted to be *-g, -gh, -ghw,* or *-w*.

Model	Tokenization	Accuracy	Adjusted
shallow	char	95.37	99.87
deep	char	95.07	99.95
shallow	redoubled	95.48	99.90
deep	redoubled	95.17	**99.96**

Table 7: Accuracy and adjusted accuracy scores on the generated test data from §3.2.1 (before and after resolving all surface ambiguity) for each model. The bolded percentage indicates the highest-performing model on the heldout test data.

While all models reached over 99% adjusted accuracy, the deep models outperformed their shallow counterparts, and the models trained on data tokenized by redoubled graphemes fared marginally better than those trained on data tokenized by individual characters. The latter may result from the fact that some inflections operate on full graphemes, for instance, **gh#** → **q#** during inflection for the unpossesed absolutive singular. The percentage improvement is so slight, however, that this may not be of much consequence. The deep model trained on redoubled graphemes was most accurate, peaking at 99.96%.

Despite comparable accuracy scores, there did not appear to be a discernible pattern with respect to errors among the four models.

4 Finite-State Guesser

We modified the finite-state analyzer of Chen and Schwartz (2018) by implementing a guesser module; this guesser permits the analyzer to hypothesize possible roots not present in its lexicon that nevertheless adhere to Yupik phonotactics and syllable structure. Noun roots, for example, may only end in a vowel, *-g, -gh, -ghw,* or *-w*, and follow the structural pattern given by the regular expression below:

$$(C)\ V\ (C)\ (C\ V\ (C))*$$

Thus, any guess made for a noun would adhere to this patterning, which the finite-state diagram in Figure 1 above captures visually. Moreover, the guesser was implemented as a backoff mechanism, such that it was only called if no other analysis could be determined. Guesses were also labeled with an additional tag, [GUESS], to distinguish them from the output returned by the finite-state analyzer itself.

5 Comparing Neural vs. Finite-State Analyzers

The final experimental condition involved comparing and quantifying the performance of the neural analyzer against its equivalent finite-state counterpart. Because the test set used in §3 was generated by the finite-state Yupik analyzer, it would be unfair to contrast the performance of the neural analyzer and the finite-state analyzer on this dataset, as the finite-state analyzer would be guaranteed to achieve 100% accuracy.

5.1 Blind Test Set

Instead, we made use of the nouns from a published corpus of Yupik interlinear glosses as an unseen test set: *Mrs. Della Waghiyi's St. Lawrence Island Yupik Texts With Grammatical Analysis by Kayo Nagai* (2001), a collection of 14 orally-narrated short stories that were later transcribed, annotated and glossed by hand. From these stories, we extracted all inflected nouns with no intervening derivational suffixes to form a modest evaluation corpus of 360 words. This was then pared down further to 349 words by removing 11 English borrowings that had been inflected for Yupik nominal cases. Manual examination of the evaluation corpus revealed several problematic items that we believe represent typos or other errors. These were removed from the final evaluation set.

for types	Coverage	Accuracy
FST (No Guesser)	85.78	78.90
FST (w/Guesser)	100	84.86
Neural	100	92.20

for tokens	Coverage	Accuracy
FST (No Guesser)	85.96	79.82
FST (w/Guesser)	100	84.50
Neural	100	91.81

Table 8: Comparison of coverage and accuracy scores on the blind test set (§5.1), contrasting the finite-state and neural analyzers. Accuracy is calculated over all types and tokens.

5.2 Blind Test Results

We analyzed the data from §5.1 using the original finite-state analyzer, the finite-state analyzer with guesser (§4), and the best-performing neural model from §3.2.4 (the deep model trained on graphemes).

Accuracy scores for the neural and finite-state analyzers, when evaluated on this refined corpus, are reported for types and tokens in Table 8 above, where accuracy was calculated over the total number of types and tokens, respectively. On the blind test set, the neural analyzer achieved coverage of 100% and accuracy of over 90%, outperforming both finite-state analyzers.

6 Discussion

Of the two analyzers which manage to achieve maximum coverage by outputting a parse for each item encountered, the neural analyzer consistently outperforms the finite-state analyzer, even when the finite-state analyzer is supplemented with a guesser. Furthermore, as illustrated in Tables 9 and 10, the neural analyzer is also more adept at generalizing.

6.1 Capacity to Posit OOV Roots

Out-of-vocabulary (OOV) roots are those roots that appear in the evaluation corpus extracted from Nagai and Waghiyi (2001) that do not appear in the lexicon of the finite-state analyzer nor in the Badten et al. (2008) Yupik-English dictionary. Of the seven unattested roots identified in the corpus, the neural analyzer returned a correct morphological parse for three of them while the finite-state analyzer only returned two (see Table 9).

Unattested Root	FST	NN
aghnasinghagh	–	–
aghveghniigh	–	✓
akughvigagh	✓	✓
qikmiraagh	–	–
sakara	✓	–
sanaghte	–	–
tangiqagh	–	✓

Table 9: Comparison of finite-state and neural analyzer's performances on unattested roots, which are unaccounted for in both the lexicon of the finite-state analyzer and the Badten et al. (2008) Yupik-English dictionary. A checkmark indicates that the correct morphological analysis was returned by that analyzer.

6.2 Capacity to Handle Spelling Variation

The neural analyzer performed even better with spelling variation in Yupik roots (see Table 10). Of the three spelling variants identified in the corpus, all of them differed from their attested forms with respect to a single vowel, *-i-* versus *-ii-*. The neural analyzer returned the correct morphological parse for all spelling variants, while the finite-state analyzer supplemented with the guesser only succeeded with one, **melqighagh**. Moreover, the neural analyzer even managed to guess at the correct underlying root in spite of a typo in one of the surface forms (*uku̱sumun* rather than *uksumun*).

Root Variant	FST	NN
melqighagh	✓	✓
piitesiighagh	–	✓
uqfiilleghagh	–	✓
*uku̱sumun	–	✓

Table 10: Comparison of finite-state and neural analyzer's performances on root variants, which are spelled differently from their attested counterparts in the lexicon of the finite-state analyzer and Badten et al. (2008). A checkmark implies that the analyzer returned the correct morphological analysis while the asterisk * denotes an item with a typo.

6.3 Implications for Linguistic Fieldwork

The higher-quality performance of the neural analyzer has immediate implications for future computational endeavors and field linguists working in Yupik language documentation and longer-range implications for field linguists in general. With respect to fieldwork, a better-performing analyzer with greater and more precise coverage equates to better real-time processing of data for field linguists performing morphological analysis and interlinear glossing.

The neural analyzer is also immune to overgeneration, since it relies on a machine translation framework that returns the "best" translation for every input sequence; in our case, this equates to one morphological analysis for each surface form. This contrasts with the finite-state analyzer variants that may return hundreds or thousands of analyses for a single surface form if the finite-state network permits. For instance, it was found that within the text corpus of the Jacobson (2001) reference grammar alone (see Table 1), the Yupik finite-state analyzer (without guesser) generated over 100 analyses for each of 16 word types. The word with the greatest number of analyses, **laalighfiknaqaqa**, received 6823 analyses followed by **laalighfikiikut** with 1074 (Chen and Schwartz, 2018). In this way, to have developed a neural analyzer that returns one morphological analysis per surface form is valuable to field linguists as it does not require them to sift through an indiscriminate number of possibilities.

6.4 Application to Other Languages

Aside from our procedure to tokenize Yupik words into sequences of fully transparent graphemes, exceedingly little language-specific preprocessing was performed. Our general procedure consists of creating a parallel corpus of surface and underlying forms by iterating through possible underlying forms and using a morphological finite-state transducer to generate the corresponding surface forms. We believe that this procedure of bootstrapping a learned morphological analyzer through the lens of machine translation should be generally applicable to other languages (especially, but certainly not exclusively, those of similar typology).

6.5 Added Value of FST Analyzers

Finally, the methodology employed here, in which a neural analyzer is trained with data generated from an existing finite-state implementation, is inherently valuable. Though the development of finite-state morphological analyzers demands considerable effort, the fact that their output may be leveraged in the development of better-performing systems is especially practical for under-resourced languages such as Yupik, where any form of training data is scarce. Thus, finite-state analyzers may serve a twofold purpose: that of morphological analysis, as they were intended to be used, but also for the generation of training data to train neural systems.

7 Conclusion

Morphological analysis is a critical enabling technology for polysynthetic languages such as St. Lawrence Island Yupik. In this work we have shown that the task of learning a robust high-accuracy morphological analyzer can be bootstrapped from an existing finite-state analyzer. Specifically, we have shown how this can be done by framing the problem as a machine translation task. We have successfully trained a neural morphological analyzer for derivationally unaffixed nouns in St. Lawrence Island Yupik, and compared its performance with that of its existing finite-state equivalent with respect to accuracy.

This work represents a case where the student truly learns to outperform its teacher. The neural analyzer produces analyses for all Yupik word types it is presented with, a feat that the original finite-state system fails to achieve. At the same time, the neural analyzer achieves higher accuracy than either the original finite-state analyzer or a variant FST augmented with a guesser. The neural analyzer is capable of correctly positing roots for out-of-vocabulary words. Finally, the neural analyzer is capable of correctly handling variation in spelling.

In future work, we plan to explore more thorough methods for handling ambiguous surface forms. We also plan to correct the minor FST error identified in §3.1.2. Most importantly, the training dataset will be extended to include items beyond inflected nouns with no intervening derivational suffixes. Specifically, we intend to increase the training set to include verbs, particles, and demonstratives in addition to nouns, as well as words that include derivational suffixes.

References

Anders Apassingok, (Iyaaka), Jessie Uglowook, (Ayuqliq), Lorena Koonooka, (Inyiyngaawen), and Edward Tennant, (Tengutkalek), editors. 1993. *Kallagneghet / Drumbeats*. Bering Strait School District, Unalakleet, Alaska.

Anders Apassingok, (Iyaaka), Jessie Uglowook, (Ayuqliq), Lorena Koonooka, (Inyiyngaawen), and Edward Tennant, (Tengutkalek), editors. 1994. *Akiingqwaghneghet / Echoes*. Bering Strait School District, Unalakleet, Alaska.

Anders Apassingok, (Iyaaka), Jessie Uglowook, (Ayuqliq), Lorena Koonooka, (Inyiyngaawen), and Edward Tennant, (Tengutkalek), editors. 1995. *Suluwet / Whisperings*. Bering Strait School District, Unalakleet, Alaska.

Anders Apassingok, (Iyaaka), Willis Walunga, (Kepelgu), and Edward Tennant, (Tengutkalek), editors. 1985. *Sivuqam Nangaghnegha — Siivanllemta Ungipaqellghat / Lore of St. Lawrence Island — Echoes of our Eskimo Elders*, volume 1: Gambell. Bering Strait School District, Unalakleet, Alaska.

Anders Apassingok, (Iyaaka), Willis Walunga, (Kepelgu), and Edward Tennant, (Tengutkalek), editors. 1987. *Sivuqam Nangaghnegha — Siivanllemta Ungipaqellghat / Lore of St. Lawrence Island — Echoes of our Eskimo Elders*, volume 2: Savoonga. Bering Strait School District, Unalakleet, Alaska.

Anders Apassingok, (Iyaaka), Willis Walunga, (Kepelgu), and Edward Tennant, (Tengutkalek), editors. 1989. *Sivuqam Nangaghnegha — Siivanllemta Ungipaqellghat / Lore of St. Lawrence Island — Echoes of our Eskimo Elders*, volume 3: Southwest Cape. Bering Strait School District, Unalakleet, Alaska.

Linda Womkon Badten, (Aghnaghaghpik), Vera Oovi Kaneshiro, (Uqiitlek), Marie Oovi, (Uvegtu), and Christopher Koonooka, (Petuwaq). 2008. *St. Lawrence Island / Siberian Yupik Eskimo Dictionary*. Alaska Native Language Center, University of Alaska Fairbanks.

Dzmitry Bahdanau, Kyunghyun Cho, and Yoshua Bengio. 2014. Neural machine translation by jointly learning to align and translate. *arXiv preprint arXiv:1409.0473*.

Antonio Valerio Miceli Barone, Jindřich Helcl, Rico Sennrich, Barry Haddow, and Alexandra Birch. 2017. Deep architectures for neural machine translation. *arXiv preprint arXiv:1707.07631*.

Emily Chen and Lane Schwartz. 2018. A morphological analyzer for St. Lawrence Island / Central Siberian Yupik. In *Proceedings of the 11th Language Resources and Evaluation Conference (LREC'18)*, Miyazaki, Japan.

Mans Hulden. 2009. Foma: a finite-state compiler and library. In *Proceedings of the 12th Conference of the European Chapter of the Association for Computational Linguistics*, pages 29–32. Association for Computational Linguistics.

Steven A. Jacobson. 2001. *A Practical Grammar of the St. Lawrence Island/Siberian Yupik Eskimo Language*, 2nd edition. Alaska Native Language Center, University of Alaska Fairbanks, Fairbanks, Alaska.

Marcin Junczys-Dowmunt, Roman Grundkiewicz, Tomasz Dwojak, Hieu Hoang, Kenneth Heafield, Tom Neckermann, Frank Seide, Ulrich Germann, Alham Fikri Aji, Nikolay Bogoychev, André F. T. Martins, and Alexandra Birch. 2018. Marian: Fast neural machine translation in C++. In *Proceedings of ACL 2018, System Demonstrations*, pages 116–121, Melbourne, Australia. Association for Computational Linguistics.

Christopher (Petuwaq) Koonooka. 2003. *Ungipaghaghlanga: Let Me Tell You A Story*. Alaska Native Language Center.

G.A. Menovshchikov. 1988. *Materialiy i issledovaniia po iaziku i fol'kloru chaplinskikh eskimosov*. Nauka, Leningrad. Traditional Yupik stories, with stress and length indicated; includes Russian translation.

Sarah Moeller, Ghazaleh Kazeminejad, Andrew Cowell, and Mans Hulden. 2018. A neural morphological analyzer for Arapaho verbs learned from a finite state transducer. In *Proceedings of the Workshop on Computational Modeling of Polysynthetic Languages*, Santa Fe, New Mexico. Association for Computational Linguistics.

Kayo Nagai and Della Waghiyi. 2001. *Mrs. Della Waghiyi's St. Lawrence Island Yupik texts with grammatical analysis*, volume A2-006 of *Endangered Languages of the Pacific Rim Publications Series*. ELPR, Osaka.

Willem J. de Reuse. 1994. *Siberian Yupik Eskimo — The Language and Its Contacts with Chukchi*. Studies in Indigenous Languages of the Americas. University of Utah Press, Salt Lake City, Utah.

Mike Schuster and Kuldip K Paliwal. 1997. Bidirectional recurrent neural networks. *IEEE Transactions on Signal Processing*, 45(11):2673–2681.

Lane Schwartz and Emily Chen. 2017. Liinnaqumalghiit: A web-based tool for addressing orthographic transparency in St. Lawrence Island/Central Siberian Yupik. *Language Documentation and Conservation*, 11:275–288.

Rico Sennrich, Barry Haddow, and Alexandra Birch. 2016. Edinburgh neural machine translation systems for WMT 16. *arXiv preprint arXiv:1606.02891*.

Author Index